项目管理认证考试系列

PMP
解题秘籍

杨 述◎著

人民邮电出版社
北 京

图书在版编目（CIP）数据

PMP 解题秘籍 / 杨述著. -- 北京：人民邮电出版
社，2021.5（2023.4重印）
ISBN 978-7-115-56368-2

Ⅰ．①P… Ⅱ．①杨… Ⅲ．①项目管理－资格考试－
题解 Ⅳ．①F224.5-44

中国版本图书馆CIP数据核字(2021)第066262号

内 容 提 要

项目经济时代充满了创新和机遇，同时也充满了不确定性和挑战。项目管理已成为这个时代的职场必备技能，获得国际通用的项目管理专业人士认证PMP越来越成为职场人士的优先选择。

本书作者围绕项目管理专业认证考试PMP新版考试大纲和PMP知识体系的发展趋势，并结合自己20年项目管理领域的研究、实践和PMP考前辅导的教学经验，精心设计、编写了400道模拟题和详细的解析。在题目的设计上，本书采用中英文对照的形式还原真实的考试场景，并采用与真实考试同等的难度系数和知识点分布比例。在题目的解析上，本书将模拟题中的知识点逐一提炼、解析，使考生通过做题加深对知识点的理解，并掌握解题规律。此外，作者还介绍了新版考试大纲的内容和题型、未来PMP考试的发展趋势，并为考生提供了备考建议和解题原则，帮助考生掌握正确的学习方法，提高学习效率和考试成绩。

本书是参加PMP考试人员的必备参考书，对项目管理人员的实践应用也极具参考价值。

◆ 著　杨　述
　　责任编辑　杨佳凝
　　责任印制　胡　南
◆人民邮电出版社出版发行　　北京市丰台区成寿寺路 11 号
　　邮编 100164　　电子邮件 315@ptpress.com.cn
　　网址 https://www.ptpress.com.cn
北京捷迅佳彩印刷有限公司印刷
◆开本：787×1092　1/16
　　印张：19.25　　　　　　　　　　　2021 年 5 月第 1 版
　　字数：350 千字　　　　　　　　　2023 年 4 月北京第 6 次印刷

定　价：89.80 元

读者服务热线：（010）81055656　印装质量热线：（010）81055316
反盗版热线：（010）81055315
广告经营许可证：京东市监广登字 20170147 号

前 言

无论谷歌、亚马逊、脸书、腾讯、阿里巴巴、字节跳动，还是 SpaceX、特斯拉、华为、科大讯飞等，这些自带创新基因的公司正在推动人类进入一个前所未有的新时代，这个新时代的特征是资源以项目方式组织、产品以项目方式交付、企业以项目方式运营。从这个意义上来说，我们正在进入项目经济时代（PMI《职业脉搏调查》，2020）。这个时代充满了创新和机遇，同时也充满了不确定性和挑战。项目管理已成为这个时代的职场必备技能，同时也是我们抵御风险、把握机遇、引领创新、迎接挑战的核心能力。获得国际通用的项目管理专业人士认证 PMP 越来越成为职场人士的优先选择。

2020 年我所著的《PMP 5A 备考宝典》（以下简称《宝典》）得到很多备考者的认可和喜爱，普遍认为把他们从枯燥而抽象的《PMBOK® 指南》中解救了出来，终于能在实际的项目场景中理解项目管理知识，对备考 PMP 和提升项目管理实战能力非常有帮助。

不过由于篇幅所限，《宝典》中没有办法包含很多 PMP 考题，然而做题是 PMP 备考中最重要的一个环节，只有通过做题才能真正检验你对知识的掌握程度，而且客观地说，相当多的考点知识是通过做题获得的。缺乏必要的做题训练，很容易出现"上课一听就懂，试题一做就错"的尴尬局面。

很多同学向我反映，他们对通过各种渠道获得的 PMP 考题完全没有把握。质量参差不齐的考题对于 PMP 备考非但没有价值，还会给备考者带来许多困惑。比如，题干语无伦次、选项东拼西凑、考点定位不清、考核目的不明，甚至有些题本身就存在逻辑错误，把初学者搞得晕头转向。这些考题的参考答案和解释更是牵强附会、缺乏说服力，甚至完全就是错误的。

PMP 备考之艰辛我也曾亲历，被劣质考题折磨之痛苦我也感同身受。PMP 新版考试大纲有大幅度修改，《PMBOK® 指南》（第 7 版）与以前版本相比可谓脱胎换骨，考试方式和考题形式也出现了前所未有的变化，给备考者带来的是更大的挑战和更多的不确定性。应无数学生的要求，我重新整理了多年来在教学和试题研究过程中积累的大量高质量的考题，并在此基础上，针对新版考试大纲和《PMBOK® 指南》（第 7 版）的知识变化，对 PMP 新的考试进行分析和预测，采用精选、改编和原创相结合的方式，为备考者准备了 400 道 PMP 模拟题，每一道模拟题都与高频考点相对应，有清晰的考核目的和严谨的出题逻辑，同时给出了标准答案和详细的解析。希望备考者通过这些模拟题的训练，精准掌握必考知识点，正确塑造解题思路，扎实养成解题习惯。

无论知识体系、考试大纲、考试方式、考题形式如何变化，万变不离其宗的是 PMP 认证的意义，PMP 考试最终是希望你通过系统的学习和训练，构建起项目管理的认知体系，融入被广泛认可的项目管理理念中，获得在项目管理实战中解决问题的能力。因此，放下包袱、建立信心是成功的第一步。行动起来吧，希望这本书能在你走向成功的路上助你一臂之力！

杨述

2021 年 3 月于清华园

目 录

1

PMP 考试大纲与
知识体系

项目管理大量的知识、方法和工具都是在项目管理实践中被不断总结和提炼出来的，PMP 考试也在不断适应实践的需要，无论是考试的内容还是考试的方式都在与时俱进。新版考试大纲（以下简称新考纲）不再局限于项目管理过程，而是突出人的重要性和项目所处的业务环境。而且，关于敏捷及混合型的项目生命周期的考题将占比50%，因为如今不再是瀑布开发模式一统天下的时代了。新考纲所涉领域及考试内容占比如表 1-1 所示。

表 1-1 新考纲所涉领域及考试内容占比

领域	考试内容占比
一、人员	42%
二、过程	50%
三、业务环境	8%
总计	100%

新考纲中有三个层次：（1）领域；（2）任务；（3）驱动因素。站在项目经理的视角，项目管理涉及的三个领域中共计 35 项任务（如图 1-1 所示），每项任务又包含若干个驱动因素（如图 1-2 所示）。

驱动因素只是完成某项任务时可能采取的几个实例措施，并非穷尽了所有的情况。我们在实践中应该根据项目的业务环境、行业特点和现实需求来决定如何灵活、有效地完成任务。

新考纲从专注于"过程"（事的视角）转变为"任务"（人的视角），可以说是一个进步。而且，新考纲从项目管理者的角度出发，更好地对应人的素质、知识和技能，也使备考者更容易设身处地地理解项目管理者的职责和使命。

领域一　人员（42%）	领域三　业务环境（8%）
任务 1　管理冲突	任务 1　规划和管理项目的合规性
任务 2　领导团队	任务 2　评估并交付项目利益和价值
任务 3　支持团队绩效	任务 3　评估并应对外部业务环境变化对范围的影响
任务 4　向团队成员和相关方授权	任务 4　为组织变更提供支持
任务 5　确保团队成员/相关方完成适当的培训	
任务 6　建设团队	
任务 7　解决和消除团队面临的障碍、妨碍和阻碍	
任务 8　通过谈判确定项目协议	
任务 9　与相关方协作	
任务 10　凝聚共识	
任务 11　让虚拟团队参与进来，并为其提供支持	
任务 12　定义团队的基本规则	
任务 13　指导相关方	
任务 14　运用情商提升团队绩效	
领域二　过程（50%）	
任务 1　执行需要紧急交付商业价值的项目	
任务 2　管理沟通	
任务 3　评估和管理风险	
任务 4　让相关方参与进来	
任务 5　规划并管理预算和资源	
任务 6　规划和管理进度计划	
任务 7　规划和管理产品/可交付成果的质量	
任务 8　规划和管理范围	
任务 9　整合项目规划活动	
任务 10　管理项目变更	
任务 11　规划和管理采购	
任务 12　管理项目工作	
任务 13　确定适当的项目方法论/方法和实践	
任务 14　制定项目治理结构	
任务 15　管理项目问题	
任务 16　确保进行知识交流，使项目得以持续开展	
任务 17　规划和管理项目/阶段的收尾或过渡工作	

图 1-1　新考纲的领域与任务

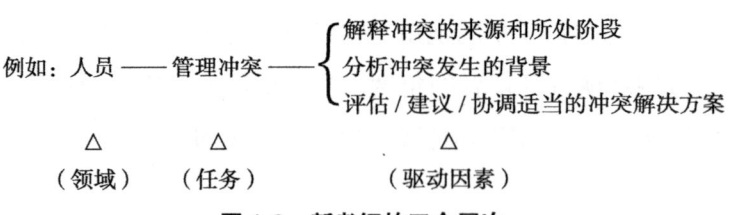

图 1-2　新考纲的三个层次

2

PMP 考试题型及发展趋势

PMP 考试形式的变化

自 2021 年起，除了中国大陆地区，PMP 考试全部采取机考的形式，中国大陆地区暂时仍然采取笔试的形式。机考又可分为两种形式：一是考生在远程控制的电脑上完成考试，二是考生到当地考试中心完成考试。机考的优点是考完当时出成绩。

PMP 考试题型及分数

自 2021 年起，机考形式的考题数量为 180 道，考试时间为 230 分钟，包含两次 10 分钟的休息时间，180 道题全部计分。自 2021 年 9 月起，中国大陆地区笔试考题数量及考试时间与机考一样。新考纲中包含四种题型：单选题、多选题、匹配题和填空题。在这四种题型中，单选题所占比例仍然最大，约占 80%；多选题约占 12%；匹配题约占 7%；填空题约占 1%。不同题型的占比并非完全固定，很可能会不断调整。中国大陆地区笔试的题型暂时只包含单选题和多选题，单选题仍占大部分。下面对多选题、匹配题和填空题进行举例。

多选题举例

项目经理正在带领团队编制项目风险管理计划，以下哪些是可以采用的风险应对方法？（选 3 项）

A. 召回计划

B. 应急计划

C. 遣散计划

D. 弹回计划

E. 权变措施

F. 保险计划

G. 预防措施

H. 纠正措施

（正确答案：BDE）

多选题的难度肯定是高于单选题的，不过目前 PMP 考试中的多选题都会给出正确选项的数量，所以难度有所降低。

匹配题举例

根据塔克曼阶梯理论，项目团队从组建到解散将会经历多个阶段，在不同阶段中，项目经理应该分别采用哪种管理风格？

形成阶段	影响型
震荡阶段	参与型
规范阶段	授权型
表现阶段	指令型

正确答案

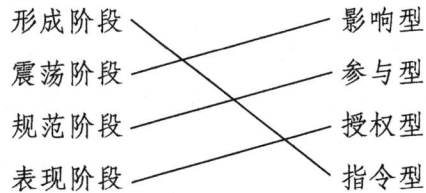

填空题举例

项目团队识别出影响项目进度的四项风险，并且对每项风险的概率和影响都进行了分值评估，如表 2-1 所示：

表 2-1　项目风险的概率和影响

风险	概率	影响
A	0.7	0.3
B	0.5	0.5
C	0.4	0.6
D	0.3	0.8

风险值最高的是风险 _____。

（正确答案：B，风险值是概率分值和影响分值的乘积。）

填空题和单选题非常接近，填空题偏向需要进行简单数字计算或简单分析的考点。

本书包含了新考纲中全部的四种题型，以方便大家适应 PMP 考试的变化。无论哪种题型，其实都是考核考生对项目管理知识的掌握程度和应用能力。

考题按照人员（42%）、过程（50%）和业务环境（8%）三个领域的比例分布，最终的成绩也是按照这三个领域分别统计，成绩的等级由高到低依次用 A\T\B\N 表示，即 Above Target（高于目标）、Target（达到目标）、Below Target（低于目标）、Needs Improvement（有待提高）。最好的成绩为 3A，即三个领域均高于目标（Above Target）。

从项目生命周期的维度出发，传统项目场景（瀑布开发）约占总题量的 50%，而敏捷及混合型场景约占总题量另外的 50%。

PMP 考试的发展趋势

中国大陆地区暂时仍然采取笔试的形式，受电脑读卡阅卷方式的限制，题型暂时没法做到像机考一样丰富，但题型多样化会是 PMP 考试的发展趋势。

3

PMP 备考建议与
解题原则

备考建议

首先，我们不能把 PMP 考场当作被人考核、被人检验的"刑场"，被动地应对考试不但容易使动作变形，而且会使我们萌生各种侥幸心理，比如，"理解不了就背下来""文字多的选项更可能是正确答案""这种题估计不会考"，甚至"选 D 比选 A 更容易蒙对"等，这些想法不但对我们通过 PMP 考试毫无意义，而且背离了我们取得 PMP 认证的初衷。

我们应该把 PMP 备考的过程当作一次认知升级，因为难得有这样的机会让我们系统地了解、接受、吸收一套完整而科学的知识体系。我们不仅可以在工作中应用其中的工具和方法来提升工作能力，而且项目管理的思维方式可以使我们为人处世的境界得到升级。所以，我们应该以积极的心态快乐地吸收这些新的知识，融入项目管理的世界里！

在备考过程中，当你遇到从未接触过的知识时，不必心生恐惧，不要手足无措，应该通过听课、查阅资料、请教老师、与同学交流等方式认真地探索它的真相，你应该庆幸自己又收获了新知识。如果练习题和模拟题答得不理想，不要沮丧，不必遗憾，这正是帮助你高效率地发现自己的短板、找到认知缺口的机会。你需要通过钻研真正理解它，因为这是一次实实在在的提升。

备考可以由"听课""看书""做题""交流""实践"五个过程结合而成。

☐ 听课：通过老师的讲解，可以帮你厘清知识的脉络、构建认知的框架。优秀的老师还会带给你丰富的案例，让你眼界开阔、茅塞顿开。

☐ 看书：加固项目管理知识的框架，弥补认知短板。这里所说的看书，不仅是看《PMBOK® 指南》，而且包括通过互联网获取的可靠的资料以及其他相关书籍。

❑ 做题：检验自己认知水平和学习效果的关键一环。"做题"不应该从备考过程中孤立出来，而应和其他四个过程融合在一起。比如，如果在做题时感觉自己对答案没有把握，就可以回看老师讲课的视频、听上课录音、翻阅书籍资料、和同学交流探讨，并结合自己的工作设身处地去体会。所以，不要纠结是否答对题，而要通过以上的学习过程，让自己彻底领会题目背后的逻辑，这种"通透"的感觉才是让你举一反三、触类旁通的基础。

❑ 交流：与同学探讨、向专家请教。这个过程是对自己知识框架的打磨，有助于对项目管理认知的升华。

❑ 实践：学以致用既是我们学习的目的，又是学习的手段。"百闻不如一见，百见不如一干"，只有"亲测有效"才能把知识内化成自己的能力。积极地实践所学的知识，不仅能够加深对知识的理解，而且能够优化自己的工作环境、提升自己的工作状态。

备考的关键在于点滴积累，贵在坚持。我们首先需要制订合理可行的备考进度计划，每天按计划"日拱一卒"的效果是"周末突击"和"临阵磨枪"完全无法比拟的。本书为大家准备了两套题，但不建议一次做完一套，大家可以把 20 道题作为一组，每天完成一组就好。这里所说的"完成"不是答完题，而是通过钻研和探索彻底理解了考核的知识点和出题人的思路，并且有把握做对同类题。

如果将本书与我所著的《PMP 备考宝典》(《PMP 5A 备考宝典》的升级版)配套使用，效果会更好。

把备考当作一个项目，按计划开始你的项目实践吧！

解题原则

PMP 考题涉及的知识面非常广，场景千变万化，因此解题并无定法。要想取得好成绩，就要放弃所有"旁门左道"和不切实际的幻想，只有扎扎实实地提升自己的认知能力才是王道。

下面是我为备考者总结的六个解题原则。

原则一: 重视做题质量，而不是数量

PMP 备考过程中并不是做题越多越好，因为你从不同渠道获得的题的质量并不都是可靠的，有些题的正确答案不止一个，有些题一个正确答案都没有，甚至有些题完全没有逻辑，这些"脏题"对备考有百害而无一利，你要果断放弃！

如果题的质量足够高，那么你无须做太多。只要每道题都精耕细作，你就会通过一道题掌握一类考点，达到事半功倍的效果。

原则二: 与出题者的思维同频

项目管理的知识来源于全球优秀企业长期实践的总结，但《PMBOK® 指南》的作者以及 PMP 考试的出题者大多来自西方国家，他们的成长经历和接受的教育与中国考生是有差异的。因此，我们在做题时不能完全参照自己的工作经验来做判断，重要的是理解和接受作者、出题者的"项目管理的价值观和方法论"（详见《PMP 备考宝典》），用他们的思维方式去分析问题，这样可以帮助我们更快地找出正确答案。

原则三: 拿出刨根问底的精神

做题切不可选对答案就沾沾自喜，必须问自己"为什么"。你要刨根问底地找到选择这个选项的扎实的依据，也应该知道不能选其他选项的理由。只有这样要求自己，才能训练出"火眼金睛"，在考试时"一击必中"。

原则四: 保持简单，切莫演绎

有的考生喜欢根据题干的信息展开想象，推测出题人的"潜台词"（比如"如果……""万一……"），这种思路是很危险的。其实 PMP 考试的出发点很简单，没有那么多"如果""万一"，出题人的目的很单纯，只有一层意思。所以不要自己臆想出附加的条件和额外的信息。虽然题干中的信息不一定都有用，但题干里没有的就是不存在的！你往简单了想，就会豁然开朗。

原则五: 坚持客观性原则，不要绝对化

选项中如果有"从不""必须""所有""完全"这种不留任何余地的词，那么你就要小心了。"有时""应该""可能""主要"这些谦和、客观的词更有可能是对的。

原则六：相信"仁者无敌"的力量

诚信、公正、尊重、信任、共赢这些满满正能量的价值观放之四海而皆准，它们总能指引你找到正确的答案；而隐瞒、虚假、敌对、投机取巧、目光短浅、损人利己这些包含负能量的选项是一定要排除的。仁者无敌，"善良"才是无坚不摧的力量。

最后，特别提醒：千万不要在题目选项上做任何记号，铅笔也不行！因为这两套题在你备考过程中需要至少做三遍。另外，你需要准备一个本子记录你的答案，隔两周再做一次，只有每次都能准确无误地选出正确答案，才能说明你真正掌握了这个考点。

4

PMP 模拟题
第一套

单选题

1. The company is going to invest in the development of a new product. The project investment review meeting will be held next week. Which document should be prepared before the meeting?

    A. Project charter

    B. Project business demonstration

    C. Project plan

    D. Project scope statement

1. 公司准备投资开发一款新产品，下周要召开项目投资评审会。在会前应准备好哪一份文件？

    A. 项目章程

    B. 项目商业论证

    C. 项目计划

    D. 项目范围说明书

2. According to the digital transformation strategy of the head office, each branch company has started the digital transformation project in combination with its own business. Different from normal business, project teams are generally inexperienced in such projects and their understanding of project objectives varies widely. Which of the following roles is needed by the head office to coordinate and manage such projects?

    A. Portfolio Manager

    B. Program Manager

    C. PMO Leader

D. Change Control Board

2. 根据总公司的数字化转型战略，各分公司结合自己的业务都启动了数字化转型项目。因为此类项目有别于平时的业务，项目团队对这种项目普遍缺乏经验，对项目目标的理解也千差万别，所以总公司最需要以下哪个角色来统筹管理这类项目？

A. 项目组合经理

B. 项目集经理

C. 项目管理办公室（PMO）负责人

D. 变更控制委员会（CCB）

3. During the product design phase, the project team found that upgrading a component to a higher level would increase the cost, but it would effectively improve the stability of the system and greatly reduce the test cost and rework risk. Before applying for a change, which of the following should the team prepare?

A. Supplier selection analysis

B. Alternative analysis

C. Cost-benefit analysis

D. Sensitivity analysis

3. 在产品设计阶段，项目团队发现，如果把某个部件升级到更高级别，虽然会增加一些成本，但是会有效提升系统的稳定性，并大幅降低测试成本和返工风险。在申请变更之前，团队应该准备以下哪一项？

A. 供方选择分析

B. 备选方案分析

C. 成本效益分析

D. 敏感性分析

4. The project manager is responsible for the company's digital transformation project. When reviewing the project charter, the project manager found the definition of scope to be simplistic and vague. What should a project manager do?

A. Interview stakeholders to identify high-level requirements

B. Create a detailed work breakdown structure

C. Brainstorm with the team to redefine scope

D. Refer to the scope of similar projects in the past

4. 项目经理负责公司的数字化转型项目，在审查项目章程时，项目经理发现范围的定义过于简单而且模糊。项目经理应该怎么做？

A. 访谈相关方，以识别高层级的需求

B. 创建详细的工作分解结构（WBS）

C. 和团队一起头脑风暴，重新定义范围

D. 参考历史上其他类似的项目的范围

5. A project stakeholder proposed that adding a feature would be more valuable to future users, but the team evaluated that adding the feature would take a lot of time and would not be able to complete the project by the schedule. Who should decide whether to add this feature?

A. Sponsor

B. Change control board

C. Project manager

D. Technical manager

5. 项目相关方提出增加一个功能会对未来的用户更有价值，但是团队评估增加这个功能需要花很多时间，团队将无法在计划的时间完成项目。是否增加这个功能应该由谁决定？

A. 项目发起人

B. 变更控制委员会

C. 项目经理

D. 技术经理

6. The project manager is analyzing the customer's requirements file and finds that a key requirement cannot be realized because there is no corresponding resource within the company. What should the project manager do?

A. Conduct risk identification

B. Carry out corresponding technical training

C. Communicate with the customer to abandon this requirement

D. Initiate a change request to obtain approval for the procurement

6. 项目经理在分析客户的需求文件时发现一个关键需求。公司内部因没有相应的资源而无法实现，项目经理应该怎么办？

A. 进行风险识别

B. 开展相应的技术培训

C. 与客户沟通，劝说客户放弃这一需求

D. 发起变更，以获得对采购的批准

7. A company is trying to implement agile development on a new project. Where should a company's project management office gather information on continuous improvement?

A. Sprint retrospective meeting

B. Sprint review meeting

C. Sprint plan meeting

D. Daily stand-up meeting

7. 一家公司在一个新项目上尝试实施敏捷开发，其项目管理办公室应该从哪里收集持续改进的信息？

A. 迭代回顾会议

B. 迭代评审会议

C. 迭代计划会议

D. 每日站会

8. Which two process groups provide potentially cyclical inputs to each other?

A. Initiating processes and closing processes

B. Planning processes and executing processes

C. Initiating processes and planning processes

D. Executing processes and closing processes

8. 哪两个过程组彼此提供潜在的循环输入？

A. 启动过程组和收尾过程组

B. 规划过程组和执行过程组

C. 启动过程组和规划过程组

D. 执行过程组和收尾过程组

9. One supplier informed the project manager that their deliverables would be delayed by two weeks. What should a project manager do?

A. Perform earned value analysis

B. Perform integrated change control procedures

C. Review breaches of contract

D. Implement schedule compression technology

9. 一家供应商告知项目经理，他们所负责的可交付成果将延迟两周交付。项目经理应该怎么做？

A. 执行挣值分析

B. 实施整体变更控制程序

C. 审查采购合同中的违约条款

D. 实施进度压缩技术

10. The project manager is required to perform a cost-benefit analysis for the project. Which of the following data can be used to analyze the optimal cost?

A. The cost increased from $150,000 to $200,000, and the benefit increased from $300,000 to $400,000.

B. The cost increased from $300,000 to $400,000, and the benefit increased from $550,000 to $600,000.

C. When the cost is less than $250,000, the BCR is greater than 1. When the cost is greater than $250,000, the BCR is less than 1.

D. When the cost is less than $150,000, the BCR is greater than 1. When the cost is greater than $300,000, the BCR is less than 1.

10. 项目经理被要求为项目执行成本效益分析。以下哪组数据可以分析出最优成本？

A. 成本从 15 万美元增加到 20 万美元，效益从 30 万美元增加到 40 万美元

B. 成本从 30 万美元增加到 40 万美元，效益从 55 万美元增加到 60 万美元

C. 当成本小于 25 万美元时，效益成本比率大于 1；当成本大于 25 万美元时，效益成本比率小于 1

D. 当成本小于 15 万美元时，效益成本比率大于 1；当成本大于 30 万美元时，效益成本比率小于 1

11. During the implementation of the project, the government introduced new regulations to upgrade the environmental impact indicators of such projects. What should a project manager do?

A. Ask for an additional budget in response to regulatory changes

B. Assess the impact and request changes accordingly

C. Ask for and follow the advice of senior management

D. Update the lessons learned register

11. 在项目执行过程中，政府出台了新的法规，对该类项目的环境影响指标进行了升级。项目经理应该怎么办？

A. 申请额外的预算，以应对法规的变化

B. 评估影响并提出相应的变更请求

C. 询问并遵照高级管理层的意见执行

D. 更新经验教训登记册

12. Tailoring objects which can be the following, EXCEPT:

A. Project management process

B. Project life cycle and phases

C. Input, output, technology and tools

D. Project charter

12. 裁剪的对象可以是以下几个选项，除了：

A. 项目管理过程

B. 项目生命周期和阶段

C. 输入、输出及工具技术

D. 项目章程

13. At the project initiation meeting, a stakeholder complained that his request had not been accepted. What should the project manager do?

A. Invite the project sponsor to lead the discussion and make the decision

B. Ignore it, as this party does not represent the majority opinion

C. Add this stakeholder's requirement to the project scope statement

D. Initiate a change request to obtain approval for supplemental requirements

13. 在项目启动会上，一位相关方抱怨自己提的需求没有被采纳，项目经理应该怎么办？

    A. 请项目发起人主持讨论并形成决议

    B. 不用理会，因为这位相关方不能代表大多数相关方的意见

    C. 将这位相关方的需求补充到项目范围说明书中

    D. 发起一项变更请求，获得对补充需求的批准

14. Your company asks you to evaluate whether to approve an energy-saving renovation project. If all the lights in the company are replaced with LED lights, the cost will be $350,000, and the company will save $100,000 in electricity each year. The LED lights will be updated every five years. In 5 years' warranty period, if there is damage to the LED lights, the supplier is responsible for free replacement. The discount rate set by the company is 10% (see Table 4-1). What is the NPV of the project?

Table 4-1　Discount Factor

Year	1	2	3	4	5
Formula	$1/(1+10\%)$	$1/(1+10\%)^2$	$1/(1+10\%)^3$	$1/(1+10\%)^4$	$1/(1+10\%)^5$
Results	0.909	0.826	0.752	0.685	0.621

    A. $29,300

    B. −$150,000

    C. −$29,300

    D. $150,000

14. 公司让你评估是否应该批准一个节能改造项目。如果把公司所有的照明光源都改成 LED 灯，需投入 35 万美元的成本，每年将为公司节约电费 10 万美元。LED 灯每 5 年全部更新一次，5 年质保期内如有损坏，供应商承诺免费更换。如表 4-1 所示，公司设定的折现率为 10%，这个项目的净现值（NPV）是多少？

表 4-1　折现系数

第几年	1	2	3	4	5
公式	$1/(1+10\%)$	$1/(1+10\%)^2$	$1/(1+10\%)^3$	$1/(1+10\%)^4$	$1/(1+10\%)^5$
结果	0.909	0.826	0.752	0.685	0.621

    A. 2.93 万美元

    B. −15 万美元

C. −2.93 万美元

D. 15 万美元

15. The project manager invited all 9 stakeholders of the project to attend the project kick-off meeting, but 2 of them said they could not attend due to the time conflict. What should a project manager do?

A. Postpone the kick-off meeting until everyone is available

B. Meet as scheduled and send minutes to absents

C. Meeting with the two stakeholders separately to gather their opinions and commitments before the kick-off meeting

D. Inviting the absents to sign commitments of waiver of proposal

15. 项目经理邀请项目所有九位相关方参加项目开工会议，但是其中两位相关方表示有时间冲突无法参加。项目经理应该怎么做?

A. 推迟开工会议，直至所有人都能参加

B. 按计划的时间开会，并将会议记录发送给缺席的相关方

C. 在会议召开之前，分别与两位相关方会面，收集他们的意见和承诺

D. 请缺席的两位相关方签署放弃意见的承诺书

16. The following are the enterprise environmental factors for the project, EXCEPT for:

A. The company's financial approval process

B. Relevant laws and industry norms

C. The company's project management information system

D. Lessons learned from similar projects in the past

16. 以下属于项目的事业环境因素，除了:

A. 公司的财务、人事和采购制度

B. 相关的法律和行业规范

C. 公司的项目管理信息系统

D. 以往类似项目中获得的教训

17. The CEO of the company requires the project manager to release the final project report before the end of the fiscal year so that the company can recognize the annual profit.

However, the client refuses to sign the acceptance documents for unaccomplished matters in the project acceptance. What should the project manager do?

A. Promising resolve all unaccomplished matters unconditionally in order to get the client's signature on the acceptance document

B. Release the final project report because sooner or later the client will sign off the acceptance document

C. Release the final project report, and update the risk register client's comments

D. Refuse to release the project final report until the client has signed the project acceptance document

17. 公司首席执行官要求项目经理在财年结算之前发布最终项目报告，以便公司可以确认年度利润。但客户认为项目验收还有未尽事宜，所以拒绝在验收文件上签字。项目经理应该怎么做？

A. 承诺将无条件解决所有未尽事宜，以获得客户在验收文件上的签字

B. 发布最终项目报告，因为客户在验收文件上签字只是时间问题

C. 发布最终项目报告，并将客户意见更新到风险登记册

D. 在客户签署项目验收文件之前，拒绝发布项目最终报告

18. Which of the following is not required to make project charter?

A. Business environment factors

B. Project business demonstration

C. Project schedule

D. Enterprise process assets

18. 下面哪一项不是制定项目章程所需要的依据？

A. 事业环境因素

B. 项目商业论证

C. 项目进度计划

D. 组织过程资产

19. In a weak matrix organization, the project manager finds that one of the project's designers is always working overtime. But the designer's time is spent on other projects, not this one. This has affected the project schedule, what should the project manager do?

A. Report the problem to the project sponsor

B. Apply to the Project Management Office for project priority enhancement

C. Communicate with the head of the design department for a solution

D. Make a change request and update the project schedule baseline

19. 在一个弱矩阵组织中，项目经理发现本项目的一个设计人员总是处于加班状态，但精力都用在其他项目上，没有时间处理本项目的设计任务。这已经影响到了项目进度，项目经理应该怎么办？

A. 将该情况上报给项目发起人

B. 向项目管理办公室申请提升项目的优先级

C. 与设计部门负责人沟通解决方案

D. 提出变更请求，并更新进度基准

20. The project manager leads a project team composed of members from different countries and companies. Which of the following documents should the project manager use to explain to the team members the level of work report, the mechanism of scheme decision-making, and the process of review according to which company?

A. Project charter

B. Project communication management plan

C. Organizational governance framework

D. Project governance framework

20. 项目经理带领一支由不同国家、不同公司成员组成的项目团队，项目经理应该用以下哪个文件向团队成员说明工作汇报的层级、方案决策的机制、评审按哪个公司的流程进行等问题？

A. 项目章程

B. 项目沟通管理计划

C. 组织治理框架

D. 项目治理框架

21. The price of raw materials for the project has gone up. Fortunately, the project manager had identified this risk in the budget and set aside appropriate reserves. What should

the project manager do now?

A. Implement change control procedures and then utilize emergency reserves

B. Implement change control procedures to replace raw materials

C. Direct use of reserves to ensure the supply of materials

D. Report to project sponsor for use of management reserve

21. 项目采购的原材料涨价，还好当时项目经理在做预算时识别到了这个风险，并且预留了相应的储备。项目经理现在应该怎么办？

A. 实施变更控制程序后动用应急储备

B. 实施变更控制程序，以更换原材料

C. 直接动用预留的储备，以保证材料的供应

D. 上报给项目发起人，申请使用管理储备

22. Works of project team members are assigned by their functional managers, but functional managers focus on meeting their department's key performance indicators (KPIs). What is the most likely organizational structure of the company?

A. Matrix organization

B. Project organization

C. Virtual organization

D. Functional organization

22. 项目团队成员的工作都是由各自所在的职能部门经理来指派，但各职能部门经理关注的重点是完成自己部门的关键绩效指标（KPIs）。这家公司的组织结构最可能是?

A. 矩阵型组织

B. 项目型组织

C. 虚拟型组织

D. 职能型组织

23. The following should be incorporated into the configuration management system, EXCEPT:

A. Change control procedures and change log

B. Product versions and features

C. Unit price and quantity of resources

D. Project plans and documents

23. 以下内容应该纳入配置管理系统，除了：

A. 变更控制程序与变更日志

B. 产品的版本与功能

C. 资源的单价与数量

D. 项目计划和项目文件

24. The project manager is busy managing a project but get a new project, the new project is more complicated. The project manager is under a lot of pressure to get help, and he heard that a similar project had been done last year. What should he do now?

A. Consult the members of the project last year to gain experience

B. Apply for more resources from functional managers

C. Obtaining historical records and guiding principles from PMO

D. Recommend other people to be the project manager for the new project

24. 项目经理在忙于管理一个项目的过程中又接到一个新项目，而且这个新项目更为复杂。项目经理感到压力很大，希望得到帮助，他了解到公司去年做过一个和这个新项目很类似的项目，他现在应该怎么办？

A. 请教去年做过那个项目的成员，以获得经验

B. 向职能经理申请更多的资源

C. 从 PMO 处获取历史记录及指导原则

D. 推荐其他人担任这个新项目的项目经理

25. The project manager is responsible for the CRM software upgrade project as part of the company's information systems upgrade. He discovers that a shared module may have a serious defect that affects not only his project, but all other projects that depend on the module, such as financial software, human resource software, procurement software, and so on. Who should the project manager talk to?

A. Information system upgrade program manager

B. Information systems operations manager

C. Technical staff of the project team

D. Project sponsor

25. 项目经理负责公司信息系统升级中的客户关系管理软件的升级项目，他发现有一个共享模块可能存在严重缺陷，这个缺陷不仅影响他的项目，而且影响所有依赖这个模块的其他的项目，比如财务软件、人力资源软件、采购软件等。项目经理应该和谁沟通这个问题？

A. 信息系统升级项目集经理

B. 信息系统运营经理

C. 本项目团队的技术人员

D. 项目发起人

26. The project manager find that works are often delayed by functional managers who are busy with other higher-priority projects. The project manager wants to clarify which priority his project is in. Who is responsible for determining the priority of projects?

A. Program manager of this project

B. Portfolio manager of this project

C. Project management office

D. Supervisors of functional managers

26. 项目经理发现，项目工作经常被职能经理们以忙于其他更高优先级的项目而拖延。项目经理希望明确自己负责的项目处于什么优先级，以下谁对确定项目的优先级负责？

A. 项目隶属的项目集经理

B. 项目隶属的项目组合经理

C. 项目管理办公室

D. 职能经理们的上级领导

27. When the project manager prepared the project plan, he found that a new equipment could greatly shorten the project duration and save cost while ensuring the quality. But the supplier of the equipment is not on the company's list of qualified suppliers. What should the project manager do next?

A. Require the purchasing department of the company to include the supplier in the list of qualified suppliers

B. Comply with the company's purchase management policy and abandon the purchase of new equipment

C. Reporting to the PMO, suggest to organize a special meeting a resolution

D. Initiate procurement directly from the supplier for project performance

27. 项目经理在编制项目计划时发现一种新设备可以大幅缩短项目工期，并且在保证质量的基础上可以有效节省成本。但是该设备的供应商并不在公司的合格供应商清单中，项目经理接下来应该怎么办？

A. 要求公司的采购部门将该供应商列入合格供应商清单

B. 遵守公司的采购管理制度，放弃对新设备的采购

C. 向 PMO 汇报，建议组织一次专项会议，以形成决议

D. 为了项目绩效，直接向该供应商发起采购请求

28. A project manager gets a call from a team member notifying him that there is a variance between the speed of a system on the project and the desired speed in the project plan. The project manager is surprised because that performance measurement was not identified in planning. If the project manager then evaluates whether the variance wants a response, he is in which part of the project management process?

A. Planning

B. Executing

C. Monitoring and controlling

D. Closing

28. 项目经理刚得到团队成员的通报，项目系统的速度和最初计划的速度有偏差。项目经理很惊讶，因为这个绩效衡量没有在规划中被识别。如果项目经理稍后评估是否需要对这个偏差做出反应，那么项目经理是在哪个管理过程中？

A. 规划

B. 执行

C. 监控

D. 收尾

29. A project stakeholder believes that the monthly project status report does not meet their needs to understand the project status. The project manager is required to report weekly

on the status of the project in person. What should a project manager do first?

A. Modify the form and frequency of project status reports to meet stakeholder needs

B. Explain to stakeholders that the monthly project status report conforms to the communication management plan

C. Review stakeholder participation plan to reassess the stakeholder needs

D. Review the communication management plan to confirm the effectiveness of the monthly project status report

29. 一个项目相关方提出，因为月度项目状态报告不能满足他们了解项目状态的需要，所以要求项目经理每周亲自来汇报项目状态。项目经理首先应该怎么做？

A. 修改项目状态报告的形式和频率，以满足相关方的需求

B. 向项目相关方解释月度项目状态报告符合沟通管理计划

C. 审查相关方参与计划，以重新评审该相关方的需求

D. 审查沟通管理计划，以确认月度项目状态报告的有效性

30. A team member underestimated the difficulty of the activity, resulting in an apparently insufficient duration estimate of activity. It took him two days to complete the work on weekends. Fortunately, the project schedule and activities of other team members were not affected. Which document should he record in this matter?

A. Lessons learned register

B. Risk register

C. Issue log

D. Change log

30. 一名团队成员因为低估了活动的难度，导致估算的活动时间明显不足。他周末连续加了两天班才把工作完成，好在没有影响其他人员的工作和项目进度。他应该把这件事记录到哪里？

A. 经验教训登记册

B. 风险登记册

C. 问题日志

D. 变更日志

31. In an Agile team, where team members want to keep abreast of each other's progress

and difficulties, which of the following meetings should be used?

A. Daily stand-up meeting

B. Sprint Planning Meeting

C. Sprint Review Meeting

D. Sprint Retrospective Meeting

31. 在敏捷团队中，团队成员希望及时了解彼此的进展和困难，应召开以下哪种会议？

A. 每日站会

B. 冲刺计划会

C. 冲刺评审会

D. 冲刺回顾会

32. All the following must be performed during project initiating, EXCEPT:

A. Identify and document business needs

B. Create a project scope statement

C. Divide a large project into phases

D. Accumulate and evaluate historical information

32. 以下各项均应在启动过程中完成，除了：

A. 识别并归档业务需求

B. 创建项目范围说明书

C. 把项目分成不同的阶段

D. 搜集并评估历史信息

33. The project performance report shows that the project cost exceeds the budget and the quality fails to meet the expectation, which makes the sponsor very dissatisfied. The conflict between the cost manager and the quality manager breaks out, blaming each other for the current situation. What should a project manager do?

A. Ask two managers to stay away from project meetings to avoid escalation

B. Negotiate with quality manager to relax quality standards to avoid cost overruns

C. Negotiate additional budget with cost manager to meet quality requirements

D. Discuss options for improving project performance openly with both managers

33. 项目绩效报告显示，项目成本超出预算且质量无法达到预期。项目发起人对此非常不满意，成本经理和质量经理发生冲突，互相指责是对方的原因造成了现在的局面。项目经理应该怎么做？

    A. 当召开项目会议时请两位经理回避，以避免冲突升级

    B. 与质量经理协商放宽质量标准，以避免成本超支

    C. 与成本经理协商追加预算，以满足质量要求

    D. 与两位经理开诚布公地讨论改进项目绩效的措施

34. When it comes to changes, the project manager's attention is BEST focused on:

    A. Promoting changes

    B. Tracking and recording changes

    C. Informing project sponsor

    D. Preventing unnecessary associated changes

34. 当变更即将发生时，项目经理的注意力最好集中在：

    A. 促进变更发生

    B. 跟踪和记录变更

    C. 通知项目发起人

    D. 避免不必要的关联变更

35. The project technical team strongly recommends the use of a new technology to improve the performance of the product, but this new technology has never been used by the team, which may bring risks in terms of duration and cost, so it is opposed by the market, cost and other departments. The project manager rejected the technical team's suggestion and asked the technical team to develop using mature technologies. What conflict resolution approach is the project manager using?

    A. Compromise/reconcile

    B. Withdraw/avoid

    C. Smooth/accommodate

    D. Force/direct

35. 项目技术团队强烈建议使用一种新技术来提升产品的性能，但团队从未使用过这种新技术，可能会带来工期及成本上的风险，因此遭到市场部、成本部等部门的

反对。项目经理拒绝了技术团队的建议并要求他们使用成熟的技术进行开发。项目经理采用的是哪种冲突解决方法？

A. 妥协 / 调解

B. 撤退 / 回避

C. 缓和 / 包容

D. 强迫 / 命令

36. A functional manager wants to change an activity duration estimate. The project manager analyzes the change and determines that it will cause a delay to the entire project. Who should authorize the change?

A. Senior management

B. Project sponsor

C. Project manager

D. Change control board

36. 一位职能经理想修改某活动的估算时间。项目经理经过分析后认为，这会导致整个项目的延期。谁有权批准该变更？

A. 高级管理层

B. 发起人

C. 项目经理

D. 变更控制委员会

37. A project is short of time, involves many professionals, and has great technical difficulties. Whether the project can be delivered on schedule directly affects the survival of the company. Which of the following technologies should the project manager adopt to improve the team performance?

A. War room

B. Technical training

C. Virtual team

D. Incentive plan

37. 一个时间紧迫、涉及专业多、技术难度大的项目，能否按期交付直接影响公司的生存。项目经理应该采取以下哪种技术来提升团队绩效？

A. 集中办公

B. 技术培训

C. 虚拟团队

D. 激励计划

38. When the scope of a product development project is confirmed with the client before the end of the first stage. A key deliverable is rejected by the client. The project manager realizes that the rework will lead to the cost increase and the failure to deliver the final product on time. The client insists that this is not the responsibility of the buyer, therefore refuses to change the baselines of cost and schedule. What should the project manager do?

A. Apply to senior management for extra resources

B. Report the overall risk of the project to senior management

C. Negotiate with the client to reduce project scope appropriately

D. Assess the impact of rework with the team and make a change request to CCB

38. 产品开发项目在第一阶段结束前与客户进行范围确认时，一项关键的可交付成果被客户拒绝了。项目经理意识到如果返工，将导致成本增加且无法按期交付最终产品，客户坚持认为这不属于买方责任，并因此拒绝变更成本基准和进度基准。项目经理应该怎么办？

A. 向高级管理层申请额外的资源

B. 向高级管理层上报这个项目的整体风险

C. 与客户协商适当缩减项目范围

D. 与团队评估返工的影响，并向变更控制委员会提出变更请求

39. The client complained about the poor quality of the product. The project manager found that most of the quality problems were caused by a small number of reasons. What kind of tools did the project manager use?

A. Histogram

B. Pareto chart

C. Scatter diagram

D. Hierarchy

39. 客户抱怨产品质量很差。项目经理通过分析发现大部分的质量问题都是由某几个原因造成的。项目经理使用的是哪种工具？

A. 直方图

B. 帕累托图

C. 散点图

D. 层级图

40. A key project stakeholder requests that a team member make a modification to a feature. The team member decides that the modification could be implemented in a short time. The team member implements the modification without informing the project manager. During confirm scope, the project manager finds out about the modification. After conducting a detailed analysis, the project manager finds that the team member's initial analysis was incomplete. The modification affects multiple functions and underlying logic, needs additional effort and time, and affects the project schedule directly. What should the project manager do next?

A. Revoke the modification and proceed to the next stage by the original plan, then inform the stakeholder

B. Discuss the change impact assessment report with the stakeholder to verify the necessity of the modification and emphasize the impact on cost and schedule. If the stakeholder insists that the modification must be included, the project manager should initiate a change request to CCB for approval

C. Explain to the stakeholder the impact of modification on cost and schedule. Inform that the modification could not be included in current phase of the project

D. Escalate to the sponsor about the stakeholder directly interacting with the team member

40. 一名关键的项目相关方要求团队成员对某项功能进行修改，团队成员认为修改需要的时间很短。因此，在没有通知项目经理的情况下，就进行了修改。在确认范围期间，项目经理发现了这个变动。在进行详细的分析之后，项目经理发现团队成员考虑得很不全面。这项修改影响多个功能和底层逻辑，需要投入额外的人工量和时间并直接影响项目总工期。项目经理下一步应该怎么做？

A. 撤销团队成员所做的修改，继续按原计划执行下一个阶段的工作，同时通知

项目相关方

B. 就变更影响评估报告与项目相关方展开讨论，确认该变更的必要性，强调对成本和进度的影响。如果该相关方坚持要将这项变更包含在内，项目经理要向变更控制委员会发起变更请求，以获得批准

C. 向项目相关方说明变更对成本和进度的影响。告知在目前项目所处的阶段，不能将变更包含在内

D. 将项目相关方直接与团队成员交流的事上报给项目发起人

41. The project manager learned that a team member was leaving. The project manager reviewed the responsibility allocation matrix and schedule network diagram and found that the work the member was responsible for was not on the critical path and had a total floating time of 3 days. Which of the following conclusions can the project manager draw?

A. The member's departure will have no impact on the overall project schedule

B. As long as replacement members are found within three days, there will be no impact on the project schedule

C. If other team members can work overtime for three days of floating, the influence of the member's leave can be offset

D. If the member's work is delayed by more than three days, the critical path of the project will change

41. 项目经理得知一位团队成员即将离职，于是查阅了责任分配矩阵和进度网络图，发现该成员负责的工作并不在关键路径上，而且有 3 天的总浮动时间。项目经理可以得到以下哪个结论？

A. 该成员的离职不会对项目整体进度产生影响

B. 只要 3 天内找到替补的成员，就不会对项目进度计划产生任何影响

C. 如果其他团队成员加班争取出 3 天的浮动时间，就可以抵消该成员离职的影响

D. 如果该成员负责的工作延误 3 天以上，那么项目的关键路径将发生改变

42. The client requests a scope change after accepting the design. This change will have potential impacts on several project components. What is the project manager's most appropriate response?

A. Convince client to delay the change

B. Update project plan based on this change

C. If this change is critical, then implement it and inform the CCB

D. Estimate the cost and schedule affected by the change, get approval before implement

42. 客户在接受设计之后提出了一项范围变更，这项变更可能对许多项目组成部分产生影响。项目经理最适当的回应是什么？

A. 说服客户推迟变更

B. 基于变更修改项目计划

C. 如果该变更十分关键，则进行变更，并通知变更控制委员会

D. 评估变更对成本和进度的影响，在实施变更之前获得批准

43. The project manager finds that a stakeholder with a high level of power has less interest in participating in the project. How is that stakeholder treated in the stakeholder participation plan?

A. Focus on management and strengthen communication with this stakeholder to enhance his/her participation in the project

B. Ensure that the stakeholder is kept informed of the important progress and results of the project

C. Regularly monitor and observe the change of the stakeholder's attitude towards the project in order to cope with it in advance

D. Ensure that the stakeholder is satisfied, try to meet his/her needs and maintain his/her current participation status

43. 项目经理发现一位权力等级很高的相关方参与项目的兴趣较低。在相关方参与计划中，这位相关方应该如何被对待？

A. 重点管理并加强与该相关方的沟通，以提升他对项目的参与度

B. 将项目的重要进展和成果及时告知该相关方，以确保其知晓

C. 定期监督、观察该相关方对项目的态度变化，以提前应对

D. 令其满意，尽力满足该相关方的需求，并保持他当前的参与状态

44. A change request has been approved by CCB, and the team has updated the plan.

Before implementing the new plan, which of the following must the team do?

A. Summarize lessons learned

B. Update the organizational process assets

C. Assess the risk of the change

D. Inform project stakeholders

44. 一项变更请求已经获得变更控制委员会批准，而且团队已经更新了计划。在执行新计划之前，团队必须做下列哪一项？

A. 总结经验教训

B. 更新组织过程资产

C. 评估变更的风险

D. 通知项目相关方

45. During the iteration review, the quality manager did not agree to release a new feature that had not passed the full test, while the marketing manager stressed that the new feature was critical to the product's competitive advantage and required that it be released in this round. The project manager evaluated that if the new function is defective, it will have a very bad impact on all users. The project manager has decided to cancel this new feature in this round of releases. Which conflict resolution approach is this?

A. Force/direct

B. Withdraw/avoid

C. Compromise/mediate

D. Cooperation/solve

45. 在迭代评审会上，质量经理认为，一项新功能尚未通过完整的测试，所以不能发布；而市场经理强调这项新功能对产品获得竞争优势至关重要，要求本轮必须发布。项目经理经过评估，发现一旦新功能存在缺陷，将对所有用户造成非常恶劣的影响，于是决定取消这项新功能在本轮的发布。这属于冲突解决方法中的哪一种？

A. 强迫 / 命令

B. 撤退 / 回避

C. 妥协 / 调解

D. 合作 / 解决

46. The project manager is responsible for a product development project. Product development completed and passed the test. Before the final release, the client found a key issue that had to be fixed and agreed to pay for the costs associated with the product change. What should the project manager do first?

A. Reject the client's request and suggest to fix the problem in the subsequent release

B. Immediately fix the problem according to the client's requirement and postpone the release date

C. With the team to evaluate the cost and duration of the change, and sign a supplementary agreement with the client

D. Assess the impact of the change with the team and prepare a written change request to CCB

46. 项目经理负责一个产品开发项目。产品开发完成并通过了测试。在最终版本发布之前，客户发现了一个必须修复的关键问题，并同意支付由于产品变更而产生的相关费用。项目经理首先应该怎么做？

A. 拒绝客户的请求，并建议在后续版本中修复这个问题

B. 按照客户的要求立即修复问题，并延后发布时间

C. 与团队评估因变更产生的成本和工期，与客户签署补充协议

D. 与团队评估变更的影响，准备书面变更请求并交给变更控制委员会

47. During the project implementation, the project manager found that the sponsor directly communicated with the team members about task priorities and guided the team members to implement methods, etc. What should a project manager do?

A. Through interpersonal skills make the sponsor comply with the project communication management plan

B. According to the team charter, team members are required to ignore the opinions of the sponsors

C. Update stakeholder participation plan and encourage sponsors to communicate directly with team members

D. Collect sponsors' comments from team members in a timely manner and update the requirements traceability matrix

47. 在项目实施过程中，项目经理发现发起人直接与团队成员沟通任务优先级，并指导团队成员实施方法等。项目经理应该怎么做？

A. 使用人际关系技能让发起人遵守项目沟通管理计划

B. 按照团队章程要求团队成员不要理会发起人的意见

C. 更新相关方参与计划，鼓励发起人直接与团队成员沟通

D. 及时向团队成员收集发起人的意见，并更新需求跟踪矩阵

48. As the project drew to a close, the sponsor proposed that a new feature be added. The project team evaluated that if meet the customer's requirements would violate the delivery time in the contract. What should the project manager do?

A. Initiate a change request

B. Require the team to work overtime to meet customer requirements and deliver on schedule

C. Reject customer requests to ensure delivery on schedule

D. Ignore contractual delivery times to meet customer requirements

48. 项目已接近尾声，发起人提出必须增加一项新功能。项目团队经过评估发现，如果满足客户的这个要求，就会违反合同中规定的交付时间，项目经理应该怎么办？

A. 发起一个变更请求

B. 让团队加班，满足客户要求并按期交付

C. 拒绝客户的要求，以确保按期交付

D. 忽略合同中的交付时间，以满足客户的要求

49. The project performance report shows that the project is one week behind schedule. What should the project manager do to recover progress?

A. Fast-tracking activities on the non-critical paths

B. Request additional resources for activities with free float time

C. Adjust some resources on the non-critical path to the critical path through resource optimization

D. Crashing the total float time of the activities on the non-critical paths

49. 项目绩效报告显示项目进度比计划落后一周。若要赶上进度，项目经理应该怎么做？

    A. 快速跟进非关键路径上的活动

    B. 为有自由浮动时间的活动申请额外的资源

    C. 通过资源优化，将非关键路径上的部分资源调整到关键路径上

    D. 压缩非关键路径上的活动的总浮动时间

50. All the following are parts of the scope baseline, EXCEPT:

    A. Scope management plan

    B. Project scope statement

    C. Work breakdown structure

    D. WBS dictionary

50. 下面是范围基准的组成部分，除了：

    A. 范围管理计划

    B. 项目范围说明书

    C. 工作分解结构（WBS）

    D. WBS 词典

51. The project manager finds that team members are interested in developing features that they consider valuable, but that are not in the project scope statement. The project manager is very worried so project schedule and cost will be out of plan. How should, the project manager do?

    A. Update the project scope statement in time to include team members' development efforts

    B. Encourage team members to innovate and communicate with the Change Control Board for approval

    C. Assess the impact of scope creep on the project and report to the project sponsor

    D. Emphasize to team members that any activity out of scope must go through the change control procedures beforehand

51. 项目经理发现团队成员正在饶有兴趣地开发他们认为很有价值的功能，但这些功能并不在项目范围说明书中。项目经理非常担心这样下去项目的工期和成本都会

脱离计划。项目经理应该怎么做？

A. 及时更新项目范围说明书，将团队成员的开发工作纳入其中

B. 鼓励团队成员创新，并与变更控制委员会沟通，以获得批准

C. 评估范围蔓延对项目的影响，并汇报给项目发起人

D. 向团队成员强调任何超出范围的活动都必须事先经过变更控制程序

52. During the project planning process, team members disagreed on the level of planning detail. Some people believed that it was not necessary to plan in detail because there would always be changes. Some people think that the plan must be detailed enough, otherwise it cannot be implemented. What should a project manager do?

A. Ask team members to plan the duration, resources and risks of each activity in detail

B. Do only sketchy planning and execute as quickly as possible to retain flexibility for change

C. Allow team members to determine the level of detail of the plan as they wish, without having to force unanimity

D. Adopt a rolling plan, in which the level of detail of the work is determined by the time of the work, and the further the work is from the present, the more sketchy the plan

52. 在项目规划过程中，团队成员对规划的详细程度产生了分歧，有人认为规划没必要太详细，因为总会有变化；有人认为规划必须足够详细，否则没法落实。项目经理应该怎么办？

A. 要求团队成员对每项活动的历时、资源、风险等做出详细规划

B. 只做粗略的规划并尽快执行，以保持应对变化的灵活性

C. 允许团队成员根据自己的意愿决定规划的详细程度，不必强求一致

D. 采取滚动式规划，根据时间远近决定规划的详细程度，即时间越近，规划越详细；时间越远，规划越粗略

53. Halfway through the project, the team discovered a new way to effectively save resources, which would be released. What should the project manager do if the project sponsor proposes to implement a new feature using these resources?

A. Implement the new function with the resources saved according to the initiator's opinion

B. Refuse to implement the new feature because it is not included in the project scope

C. Initiate change requests for new functions in accordance with the integrated change control procedures

D. Release the saved resources to reduce the project cost

53. 项目中途，团队发现了一种可以有效节约资源的新方法，省出来的资源将被释放。项目发起人提出，可以利用这些资源实施一项新功能。项目经理应该怎么办？

A. 按照发起人的意见，利用省出来的资源实施新功能

B. 拒绝实施新功能，因为它不包含在项目范围内

C. 按照整体变更控制程序发起新功能的变更请求

D. 释放节省的资源，以降低项目成本

54. To control the schedule, a project manager is analyzing the sequence of activities with the least amount of scheduling flexibility to predict the project duration. What technique is she using?

A. Critical path method

B. Flow chart

C. Precedence Diagramming Method (PDM)

D. Milestone chart

54. 为了控制进度，项目经理采取了最小浮动时间来分析活动之间的顺序，以此来预测项目持续时间。她使用的是哪种技术？

A. 关键路径法（CPM）

B. 流程图

C. 紧前关系绘图法（前导图）

D. 里程碑图

55. The project manager wants each team member to think independently and express their own opinions. Which of the following techniques should be used?

A. Brain storming

B. Focus group

C. Facilitated workshop

D. Nominal groups

55. 项目经理希望每一位团队成员都能独立思考，并发表各自独立的见解。项目经理应该采用下列哪一项技术？

A. 头脑风暴

B. 焦点小组

C. 引导式研讨会

D. 名义小组

56. The product had been tested and was ready to be released the next day as planned, when the developers discovered a serious defect and began to fix it without notifying anyone. What should the project manager do when he learns this?

A. Ignore the defect and release the product as planned

B. Initiate a change request and follow the change control procedures

C. Delay the release until the defect is resolved

D. Release the product as planned and continue to resolve the defect

56. 产品测试已经完成，团队准备按计划在第二天发布该产品。这时，开发人员发现了一个严重的缺陷，于是在没有通知任何人的情况下开始解决这个缺陷。项目经理了解到这个情况后应该怎么办？

A. 忽略该缺陷，按既定计划发布产品

B. 发起一项变更请求，并遵循变更控制程序

C. 推迟产品发布，直至缺陷被解决

D. 按既定计划发布产品，并继续解决这个缺陷

57. As the project is being closed, the company asks the project team to start a new project with tight deadlines. What should the project manager do?

A. Stop everything and work on the new project

B. Complete project closure to ensure that all project documents are complete and accurate

C. Refer to previous similar projects to complete the project closing documents

D. Delegate the remainder of the closing to the replacement

57. 项目正在收尾过程中，公司要求项目团队开始一个工期很紧的新项目，项目经理应该怎么做？

A. 停止所有工作，并投入新项目中

B. 完成项目收尾，确保所有项目文件完整、准确

C. 参考之前类似项目的资料，补齐项目收尾文件

D. 将剩余的收尾工作委托给接替的人员

58. The data of the old system is migrated to the new system. The optimistic estimate is 4 days. It is most likely to estimate 7 days. Pessimistic estimate is 16 days, and the beta distribution is adopted to calculate the expected value and standard deviation. Which of the following is true?

A. Expected value is 9 days, standard deviation is 2 days

B. Expected value is 8 days, standard deviation is 1 day

C. Expected value is 7 days, standard deviation is 2 days

D. Expected value is 8 days, standard deviation is 2 days

58. 将旧系统的数据迁移至新系统，乐观估计是 4 天，最可能估计是 7 天，悲观估计是 16 天。团队采用贝塔（β）分布计算期望值和标准差。以下结果正确的是？

A. 期望值是 9 天，标准差是 2 天

B. 期望值是 8 天，标准差是 1 天

C. 期望值是 7 天，标准差是 2 天

D. 期望值是 8 天，标准差是 2 天

59. During the execution of the project, the project team decided that the current number of quality checks was excessive, unnecessary, and seriously affected the project schedule. What should a project manager do?

A. Ask project team follow the quality management plan strictly

B. Reduce the number of quality checks to meet schedule requirements

C. Initiate a change to update the project schedule baseline

D. Work with QA department to analyze the feasibility of reducing the number of inspections

59. 项目执行期间，项目团队认为目前的质量检查次数过多，不仅没有必要，而且严

重影响了项目进度。项目经理应该怎么做?

A. 要求项目团队严格遵循质量管理计划

B. 减少质量检查次数,以满足进度要求

C. 发起一项变更,更新项目进度基准

D. 与质量保证部门一起分析减少检查次数的可行性

60. One project team member reported that because the technical staff who had been cooperating with her had left, they needed to re-recruit the replacement one, so the original start time of the activity had to be delayed by 2 weeks. Because the project is very important to the company, this unexpected situation has caused the management to be very nervous. As the project manager, when you report the progress of the project, you insist that the project can be completed on schedule without worrying about it. Why can you say that?

A. The activity is on the critical path and you will focus on it

B. The activity is on the non-critical path, and the total floating time is greater than 2 weeks

C. The activity is on a non-critical path, regardless of how the total project duration is not affected

D. The activity is on the critical path and the team can work overtime

60. 一名项目团队成员报告说,因为和她配合的技术人员离职了,需要重新招募替代人员,因此活动原定的开始时间需要顺延两周。因为该项目对公司非常重要,所以这个突发情况导致管理层很紧张。你作为项目经理在汇报项目进展时却坚持说,项目可以按期完成,不必担心。你这样说的依据是什么?

A. 活动处于关键路径上,你会重点关注

B. 活动处于非关键路径上,且总浮动时间大于两周

C. 活动处于非关键路径上,无论如何都不会影响总工期

D. 活动处于关键路径上,团队可以加班赶回来

61. After the project performance evaluation, the team found that the project schedule had fallen significantly behind the baseline, and the project manager suggested using fast-tracking to ensure that the project could be delivered to the customer in accordance with the contract. Which of the following conforms to the project manager's suggestion?

A. Reduce testing and simplify documentation

B. Sets lead time for activities on critical paths

C. Add resources to activities on critical paths

D. Add resources to activities on non-critical paths

61. 经过项目绩效评估，团队发现项目进度已明显落后于计划。项目经理建议接下来采取快速跟进的措施，以保证能够按照合同约定的时间向客户交付项目。以下哪个选项符合项目经理的建议？

A. 减少测试和简化文档工作

B. 为关键路径上的活动设置提前量

C. 为关键路径上的活动增加资源

D. 为非关键路径上的活动增加资源

62. Which of the following is not true?

A. The critical path can help to derive the project's total project duration

B. On the critical path, the duration of the activity cannot be compressed

C. The critical path is the path with the least float time

D. The floating time may be negative

62. 下面哪一个选项是不正确的?

A. 关键路径可以帮助推导项目总工期

B. 在关键路径上，活动的工期无法压缩

C. 关键路径是浮动时间最少的路径

D. 浮动时间可能出现负值

63. Multiple core functions in a project can only be developed by the same key developer, and if developing these functions simultaneously causes that developer to become seriously overworked, what should the project manager do?

A. Implementation of resource leveling

B. Implementation of resource smoothing

C. Crashing the project

D. Fast-tracking the project

63. 项目中多个核心功能只能由同一位关键的开发人员负责。如果同时开发这些功能，就会导致这位开发人员严重超负荷工作。项目经理应该怎么办？

   A. 实施资源平衡

   B. 实施资源平滑

   C. 实施赶工

   D. 实施快速跟进

64. After the preparation of the project schedule, the project manager found that the resource manager could not provide enough development engineers, but promised to provide more test engineers by then. The development and testing were on the critical path of the project, and the delivery date agreed in the project contract could not be delayed. What should the project manager do?

   A. Assign development tasks to the test engineer

   B. Make the development engineer work overtime to ensure delivery on time

   C. Level development resources and work quickly during the test phase

   D. Fast-tracking and test simultaneously during development

64. 在编制完项目进度计划后，项目经理发现资源经理无法提供足够数量的开发工程师，但承诺届时可以提供更多的测试工程师。开发和测试都在项目的关键路径上，并且项目合同约定交付日期不可延误。项目经理应该怎么办？

   A. 让测试工程师承担开发任务

   B. 让开发工程师加班，确保按期交付

   C. 对开发阶段进行资源平衡，在测试阶段赶工

   D. 进行快速跟进，边开发边测试

65. Due to the global epidemic, some team members cannot arrive on time, which may affect the delivery time of the project. What should the project manager do first?

   A. Conduct risk identification

   B. Assess risk impact

   C. Perform quantitative risk analysis

   D. Implement risk response

65. 受全球新冠肺炎疫情的影响，部分团队成员无法按时到位，这将可能影响项目的

交付时间。项目经理首先应该怎么办?

A. 进行风险识别

B. 评估风险影响

C. 执行风险定量分析

D. 实施风险应对

66. According to the information provided in Table 4-2, if you need to compress the project duration for one-week, which activity should you compress first?

Table 4-2   List of Activities

Activity	Preceding Activity	Duration (weeks)
A	–	5
B	–	4
C	A	3
D	A, B	5
E	C, D	1

A. Activity A

B. Activity B

C. Activity D

D. Activity E

66. 根据表 4-2 提供的信息,如果你需要将项目工期压缩 1 周,你首先应该压缩哪个活动?

表 4-2   活动列表

活动	紧前活动	活动历时(周)
A	–	5
B	–	4
C	A	3
D	A、B	5
E	C、D	1

A. 活动 A

B. 活动 B

C. 活动 D

D. 活动 E

67. The company intends to invest in a hotel in an earthquake zone, what should the project manager do?

A. Subcontract the project to transfer the risk

B. Conduct quantitative risk analysis and plan risk response

C. Perform reserve analysis to mitigate risk

D. The company is advised to relocate the hotel to avoid the earthquake zone

67. 公司拟在一个地震多发地带投资一家酒店，项目经理应该如何做？

A. 将项目外包，以转移风险

B. 进行风险定量分析，并规划风险应对办法

C. 进行储备分析，以减轻风险

D. 建议公司重新选址，以避开地震带

68. For emergency and managed reserves, which of the following statements is correct:

A. Emergency reserves are used to deal with known risks, and management reserves are used to deal with unknown risks

B. Emergency reserves are included in the cost baseline, and management reserves are not included in the cost baseline

C. The emergency reserves shall not be managed by the project manager, and the management reserves shall be managed by the project manager

D. Emergency reserves are included in the project budget and management reserves are not

68. 对于应急储备和管理储备，以下表述哪一项是正确的？

A. 应急储备用于应对已知风险，管理储备用于应对未知风险

B. 应急储备包含在成本基准中，管理储备不包含在成本基准中

C. 应急储备不归项目经理管理，管理储备归项目经理管理

D. 应急储备包含在项目预算中，管理储备不包含在项目预算中

69. The project manager and sponsors are regularly reviewing the benefit management plan. The procurement manager says that the impact of recent tax rate changes on purchasing costs is unknown. What should the project manager do?

A. Assess the impact of tax rate changes and revise the benefit management plan

B. Recommend that sponsors increase management reserves in response to changes in tax rates

C. Update the risk register and plan the risk response

D. Update procurement management plan and implement procurement

69. 项目经理与发起人正在定期评审效益管理计划。采购经理说近期税率的变化对采购成本的影响还不可知。项目经理应该怎么做？

A. 评估税率变化的影响，并重新修订效益管理计划

B. 建议发起人增加管理储备，以应对税率的变化

C. 更新风险登记册并规划风险应对

D. 更新采购管理计划并实施采购

70. Estimate at completion (EAC) is a periodic evaluation of:

A. The cost of the completed work

B. The value of the work performed

C. Total cost estimates when the project is completed

D. Estimates of the costs that are still required from now to the completion of the project

70. 完工估算（EAC）是下面哪一选项的定期评估？

A. 已完成工作的成本

B. 已完成工作的价值

C. 预测项目完成时的总成本

D. 预测完成项目还将需要的成本

71. A project of 12 months, with $ 12 million cost. In the past 8 months, only 50% of the work has been completed, and $ 7.5 millions have already been used. What is the current state of the project?

A. Ahead of schedule and cost overrun

B. Ahead of schedule and cost saving

C. Behind schedule and cost saving

D. Behind schedule and cost overruns

71. 一个项目计划工期为 12 个月，预算为 1 200 万美元，现在已经过去 8 个月，完成了 50% 的工作，花掉了 750 万美元的预算，项目当前的状态是什么？

A. 进度超前，成本超支

B. 进度超前，成本节约

C. 进度落后，成本节约

D. 进度落后，成本超支

72. If earned value (EV) = 350, actual cost (AC) = 400, and planned value (PV) = 300, what is cost variance (CV) and schedule variance (SV)?

A. 100, 50

B. −100, −50

C. 50, −50

D. −50, 50

72. 如果挣值（EV）= 350，实际成本（AC）= 400，计划值（PV）= 300，那么成本偏差（CV）和进度偏差（SV）分别是多少？

A. 100，50

B. −100，−50

C. 50，−50

D. −50，50

73. For a project with a budget of $2 million, 40% of the work has been completed, but 50% of the cost has been used up. The reason for the deviation is that the tariff increase caused the material cost to increase by 15% after the project just signed the agreement. If the tariff remains at the current high level, how much will it cost to complete the project?

A. $1 million

B. $1.2 million

C. $1.5 million

D. $1.8 million

73. 一个预算为 200 万美元的项目，当前已经完成了 40% 的工作，但已经用掉了 50% 的成本，引起偏差的原因是项目刚刚签署协议后，关税增长导致材料成本增加了 15%。如果关税维持现在的高水平，那么完成该项目还需要多少成本？

A. 100 万美元

B. 120 万美元

C. 150 万美元

D. 180 万美元

74. A project with a total budget of $1 million is scheduled for completion in six months. The budget for the first three months was $500,000, the actual cost was $600,000 and 40% of all the work was done. Based on the current project cost performance level, how much will it cost to complete the project?

A. $1.3 million

B. $1.5 million

C. $1.8 million

D. $2 million

74. 某项目总预算为 100 万美元，计划六个月完成。前三个月的预算是 50 万美元，实际成本为 60 万美元，完成了所有工作的 40%。根据当前项目成本绩效水平预测，完成项目总共需要花费多少成本？

A. 130 万美元

B. 150 万美元

C. 180 万美元

D. 200 万美元

75. The project manager is going to take on a new project. In the project resource library, there are four alternative projects that match the team's ability. The basic information of the project is as Table 4-3. Which project should the project manager choose?

Table 4-3 The Basic Information of The Project

Project ID	Business Value ($ million)	Development Period (month)
10045	8	6
12107	6	4
20124	10	6
21116	12	8

A. 10045

B. 12107

C. 20124

D. 21116

75. 项目经理准备接一个新项目，在项目资源库中与团队能力匹配的有四个备选项目，项目基本信息如表 4-3 所示。项目经理应该选择哪个项目呢？

表 4-3　项目基本信息

项目编号	商业价值（百万美元）	开发周期（月）
10045	8	6
12107	6	4
20124	10	6
21116	12	8

A. 10045

B. 12107

C. 20124

D. 21116

76. The project earned value analysis report shows that the schedule performance index (SPI) is 0.85 and the cost performance index (CPI) is 0.92. Which of the following is the most reasonable explanation for this situation?

A. Underestimating the workload of key activities and investing more resources

B. Project team members are transferred to other projects and project resources are reduced

C. More expensive but more advanced tools were procured, and productivity increased

D. New requirements were added, but no additional budget was made

76. 项目挣值分析报告显示，进度绩效指数（SPI）为 0.85，成本绩效指数（CPI）为 0.92。下面哪一选项是出现这种情况的最合理的解释？

A. 低估了关键活动的工作量，投入了更多的资源

B. 项目团队成员被抽调到其他项目上，项目资源减少了

C. 购买了更贵、更先进的工具，工作效率提升了

D. 增加了新的需求，但没有追加预算

77. The project manager is supervising a serious risk which cannot be avoided, controlled or transferred. It needs additional funds to deal with this risk. What should the project manager do?

A. Mitigate the risk

B. Use emergency reserve

C. Perform qualitative analysis

D. Report to senior management

77. 项目经理正在监督一个无法避免、无法控制、也无法转移的严重风险，应对这个风险需要额外的资金。项目经理应该怎么做？

A. 减轻风险

B. 使用应急储备

C. 执行定性分析

D. 上报给高级管理层

78. In which process group does process improvement occur?

A. Planning process group

B. Executing process group

C. Monitoring process group

D. Closing process group

78. 过程改进发生在哪个过程组中？

A. 规划过程组

B. 执行过程组

C. 监控过程组

D. 收尾过程组

79. Because of the sudden and extreme tariff changes, the cost of imported equipment has increased by 25%. How should the project manager deal with the cost overrun?

A. Coping with increase of cost through change control procedures

B. Use management reserve to cope with the increase of cost

C. Modify cost baseline to increase cost

D. Use emergency reserve to cope with the increase of cost

79. 因为突然和极端的关税变化，进口设备的成本增加了 25%。项目经理应该如何应对成本超支问题？

    A. 通过变更控制程序应对成本的增加

    B. 使用管理储备应对成本的增加

    C. 修改成本基准应对成本的增加

    D. 使用应急储备应对成本的增加

80. If seven consecutive data points appear on the same side of the average line in the control chart, what should be done?

    A. Delete this set of data

    B. Adjust the control chart to draw a new average line

    C. Find the root cause and correct it

    D. Nothing needs to be done because it's normal

80. 如果控制图中出现连续七个数据点在平均线同一侧，应该怎么办？

    A. 删除这组数据

    B. 调整控制图，画出新的平均线

    C. 找到根本原因并纠正

    D. 什么也不用做，因为这属于正常现象

81. The project manager realizes that product quality may be affected by many variables. If he wants to know the correlation between quality and these variables, which of the following tools should he choose?

    A. Pareto chart

    B. Fishbone diagram

    C. Histogram

    D. Scatter diagram

81. 项目经理意识到产品质量可能受到很多变量的影响。如果想知道质量和这些变量的相关性，项目经理应该选择下面哪一个工具？

    A. 帕累托图

    B. 鱼骨图

    C. 直方图

D. 散点图

82. The standard deviation is the measurement:

A. Deviation between the estimated value and the maximum estimation value

B. Measure the dispersion degree of relative mean of data

C. The distance between maximum and minimum values

D. Deviation between measurement values and standards

82. 标准差是衡量：

A. 估算值与最高估算值的偏差

B. 测量数据相对均值的离散程度

C. 最大值和最小值之间的距离

D. 测量值与标准之间的偏差

83. The specification line of canned coffee is set as 492g ~ 508g, and the control line is 494g ~ 506g. When the quality controller finds that a can of coffee weighs 493g, what should he do?

A. It's in the qualified range. Don't worry about it

B. Stop production, find and eliminate the cause of deviation

C. Sort out this can of coffee and refill it

D. Warn senior management of potential quality hazards

83. 罐装咖啡的规格线设定为 492 克 ~ 508 克，控制线为 494 克 ~ 506 克。质量控制人员发现一罐咖啡重 493 克，应该如何处理？

A. 属于合格范围，不用理会

B. 停止生产，找到并消除产生偏差的原因

C. 将这一罐咖啡分拣出来重新罐装

D. 向高级管理层预警存在质量隐患

84. Which of the following is the core method of continuous quality improvement?

A. Root cause analysis

B. Plan-do-check-action cycle

C. Benchmarking

D. Assumptions analysis

84. 下列哪一项是持续质量改进的核心方法？

A. 根本原因分析

B. "计划—实施—检查—行动"循环

C. 标杆对照

D. 假设分析

85. The project manager observed that the team conflict was decreasing during this period, and the team members began to accept each other and actively cooperate with each other. At this time, which leadership style should the project manager adopt?

A. Directive type

B. Influence type

C. Participative type

D. Authorized type

85. 项目经理观察到这段时间团队冲突在减少，团队成员开始彼此接受并主动配合对方。这时项目经理应该采取以下哪种领导风格？

A. 指令型

B. 影响型

C. 参与型

D. 授权型

86. A new member of the project team is difficult to communicate with the project manager and other team members because he can't know the network diagram, the critical path and the floating time. How should the problem be solved?

A. The functional department manager of the new member is responsible for providing targeted training

B. Project manager is responsible for providing targeted training to the new member

C. The human resources department of the company is responsible for providing targeted training to the new member

D. The new member should be required to self-study project management to meet the needs of work

86. 项目团队的一位新成员因为看不懂网络图，也不知道关键路径、浮动时间这些术语，所以他很难与项目经理和其他团队成员交流。这个问题应该如何解决？

    A. 新成员所在的职能部门经理有责任提供针对性培训

    B. 项目经理有责任为新成员提供针对性培训

    C. 公司人力资源部有责任为新成员提供针对性培训

    D. 要求新成员自学项目管理，以满足工作需要

87. There are only 10 days left from the scheduled product release time, and there are still five functions in the plan that have not been realized. Although these functions do not affect the basic use of users, the product manager insists that these functions should be completed according to the plan before the product release. The development team emphasizes that the resources are occupied due to the continuous changes in the development process. In order to ensure the smooth release of the developed functions, they should be released abandon these five functions, or more resources should be added. As the project manager, what should you do?

    A. Ask the development team to work overtime to complete these five functions

    B. Update the scope specification and delete the five functions

    C. Report conflict to project sponsor

    D. Evaluate impact and implement integrated change control procedures

87. 离预定的产品发布时间只剩下 10 天，计划中还有 5 个功能没有实现。这些功能虽然不影响用户的基本使用，但产品经理坚持这些功能应该在产品发布前按计划完成。开发团队强调因为开发过程中需求不断变更导致资源被占用，为了保证已开发功能顺利发布，应该放弃这 5 个功能，否则只有补充更多的资源才可能实现。作为项目经理，你应该怎么办？

    A. 要求开发团队加班完成这 5 个功能

    B. 更新范围说明书，删除这 5 个功能

    C. 将冲突上报给项目发起人

    D. 评估影响并实施整体变更控制程序

88. Team performance appraisals are different from project performance assessment. Team performance appraisals focus on, EXCEPT:

A. Team member skill improvement

B. Improvement of project team capability

C. Enhance team cohesion

D. Increased user satisfaction

88. 团队绩效评估和项目绩效评估不同，团队绩效评估关注以下内容，除了：

A. 团队成员技能的改进

B. 项目团队能力的改进

C. 团队凝聚力的增强

D. 用户满意度的提升

89. The project manager is delivering a new project for a client in a country. The client can only speak the local language and cannot communicate with the project team normally. Moreover, the cultural differences between the two sides are also very significant. What should the project manager do to avoid the negative impact of communication barriers on the project?

A. Adhere to the principle of written communication

B. Organize project team to learn local language

C. Subcontract work to local suppliers whenever possible

D. Employ professionals proficient in both languages and cultures of the two countries

89. 项目经理正在为某国客户交付一个新项目，客户只会讲当地语言，无法与项目团队正常交流，而且双方文化差异也非常显著。项目经理应该如何避免沟通障碍给项目造成的负面影响呢？

A. 坚持书面沟通的原则

B. 组织项目团队学习当地语言

C. 尽可能地将工作分包给当地供应商

D. 聘请精通两国语言和文化的专业人士

90. The project manager finds that his project team members lack trust, conflict, and morale is low. What stage might the team be in? What type of leadership style should the project manager adopt?

A. Storming phase, Instructional

B. Norming phase, Participative

C. Norming phase, Authorized

D. Storming phase, Influential

90. 项目经理发现项目团队成员之间缺乏信任、冲突不断、士气低落。团队可能进入了什么阶段？此时项目经理应该采取哪种类型的领导风格？

A. 震荡阶段，指导型

B. 规范阶段，参与型

C. 规范阶段，授权型

D. 震荡阶段，影响型

91. In the commercial demonstration stage of the project, the sponsor entrusts the project manager to prepare a high-level cost estimate. The project manager can only obtain similar projects that have been completed before. What kind of cost estimate method should the project manager adopt?

A. Analogous Estimating

B. Expert Judgment

C. Parametric Estimating

D. Bottom-Up Estimating

91. 在项目商业论证阶段，发起人委托项目经理编制一份高层级的成本估算。项目经理能够获得的只有以前完成过的类似项目的成本估算。项目经理应该采用哪种成本估算方法？

A. 类比估算

B. 专家判断

C. 参数估算

D. 自下而上估算

92. The project scope is well defined and the project team has performed this type of work before. The schedule performance index is 0.7. After investigating the deviation, the project manager realizes that one of the team members, working onsite is being asked by the project sponsor to perform extra activities believed important to the project. Which action should the project manager take to avoid situations?

A. Improve project communications, making sure all needs are being satisfied

B. Make changes to the project's scope based on the new demands

C. Give a clear statement to the coworker do discontinue the scope creep

D. Communicate that changes must be done through the change control board

92. 项目范围已有明确定义，且项目团队之前做过此类工作。进度绩效指数为 0.7。在调查完差异之后，项目经理了解到，项目发起人要求在现场工作的一名团队成员去执行他认为对项目很重要的额外的活动。若要避免这种情况发生，项目经理应该如何做？

A. 改进项目沟通，确保所有需求都得到满足

B. 根据新的需求对项目范围进行变更

C. 跟这位同事明确说明停止范围蔓延

D. 对于必须完成的变更，与变更控制委员会进行沟通

93. The project manager found that a team member was interested in what he thought was very meaningful work. The project manager judged that the work was not within the scope of the project and was not necessary for the project. At the same time, other work assigned to the team member had been seriously delayed. What should the project manager do?

A. Add work within project scope to the team member

B. Encourage the team member to work creatively

C. Clarify the scope of the project with the team member and stop the scope spreading

D. Get approval from the change control board for what the team member is doing

93. 项目经理发现一位团队成员兴趣盎然地沉浸在他自己认为很有意义的工作中。项目经理判断这项工作不在项目范围内，而且也不是项目所必需的，同时，分配给该成员的其他工作已经被严重拖延。项目经理应该怎么办？

A. 给这位团队成员增加项目范围内的工作

B. 鼓励这位团队成员创造性地开展工作

C. 与这位团队成员明确项目范围，并停止范围蔓延

D. 就这位团队成员正在做的工作获得变更控制委员会的批准

94. Which of the following ways to improve the efficiency of the team communication and promote the adaptation of the team is the most effective?

A. War Room

B. Virtual Team

C. Distributed Team

D. Specialized Subcontracting Team

94. 下列哪一种方式对提升团队沟通效率和促进团队磨合最有效?

A. 集中办公

B. 虚拟团队

C. 分布式团队

D. 专业分包团队

95. The following are the principles that agile development should follow, EXCEPT:

A. Face to face

B. Short cycle

C. Embrace change

D. Document norm

95. 下面是敏捷开发过程中应该遵守的原则,除了:

A. 面对面

B. 短周期

C. 拥抱变化

D. 文档规范

96. When monitoring and controlling risks, the project manager has seen the monthly project performance report and found that the contingency plan needs to be implemented. What should the project manager do next?

A. Update the project schedule and budget to coincide with the implementation of the contingency plan

B. Make a change request and get approval before the implementation of the contingency plan

C. Record the lessons learned from the implementation of the contingency plan

D. Inform all stakeholders about the implementation of the contingency plan

96. 在监督和控制风险时，项目经理在看过月度项目绩效报告后发现，需要实施应急计划。项目经理接下来应该怎么做？

A. 更新项目进度计划和预算，以配合应急计划的实施

B. 提出变更请求，在应急计划实施前获得批准

C. 记录因实施应急计划而获得的经验教训

D. 将实施应急计划的信息通知所有相关方

97. A highly infectious virus is spreading around the world. The project manager organized the team members to analyze the potential impact of the epidemic on the project and make a response plan. When a large number of infected people suddenly appear in the city where the project is located, the project manager informs all team members to start the home online working mode from now on to ensure the smooth progress of the project. The project manager adopts the following methods:

A. Contingency plan

B. Fallback plan

C. Workaround response

D. Risk mitigation

97. 一种传染性极强的病毒正在全球范围内蔓延，项目经理组织团队成员分析了疫情对项目的潜在影响并做出了应对计划。项目所在城市突然出现大量感染者，项目经理通知所有团队成员即日起启用居家在线的工作方式，以保证项目顺利开展。项目经理采用的是什么方法？

A. 应急计划

B. 弹回计划

C. 权变措施

D. 风险减轻

98. During the implementation of the project, due to the endless changing requirements of the clients, the cost increased significantly, and the time limit was seriously delayed. After the earning value analysis, the project manager found that the actual cost could not be covered by the project budget and the project could not be delivered in accordance with the contract. Two change requests were made: one was that the project

would not accept new functionality after entering the integration test phase, and the other was that the additional budget would be used to introduce more test resources. What risk response strategies did the project manager adopt?

A. Avoid and transfer

B. Transfer and mitigation

C. Transfer and avoid

D. Avoid and mitigation

98. 项目实施过程中由于客户无休止的变更需求，导致成本大幅上升，而且工期严重滞后。项目经理在进行挣值分析之后发现，如果按照现在的趋势发展下去，项目预算无法覆盖实际成本，且无法按照合同规定的时间交付项目。于是项目经理提出两项变更请求：一是项目进入集成测试阶段，不再接受新增功能的需求；二是追加预算，用于引进更多的测试资源。项目经理分别采取的是哪种风险应对策略？

A. 规避和转移

B. 转移和减轻

C. 转移和规避

D. 规避和减轻

99. A project team identifies 4 risks and assesses probability of occurrence and potential impact on cost and schedule for each risk. This information is presented in Table 4-4 shown. If the importance of schedule objectives is 3 times to project cost. Which is the most critical risk for the project?

Table 4-4　Risk Probability And Impact

Risk	Probability	Impact on schedule	Impact on cost
A	75%	0.3	0.2
B	50%	0.4	0.5
C	30%	0.7	0.6
D	25%	0.8	0.9

A. Risk A

B. Risk B

C. Risk C

D. Risk D

99. 如表 4-4 所示，项目团队识别出了若干风险发生的概率和每个风险对成本、进度的潜在影响。对项目而言，进度和成本的权重比为 3∶1。那么评级最高的风险是哪一个？

表 4-4 风险发生的概率和影响

风险	概率	对进度的影响	对成本的影响
A	75%	0.3	0.2
B	50%	0.4	0.5
C	30%	0.7	0.6
D	25%	0.8	0.9

A. 风险 A

B. 风险 B

C. 风险 C

D. 风险 D

100. The project manager is comparing two solutions for the project. The probability of success is 80% for solution 1. If it works, it could save $1 million for the project, but if it doesn't work, it's going to increase the cost of $1 million on the project. Solution 2 has 50% probability of success. If it works, it could save $2 million, but if it doesn't work, it's going to increase the cost of $1 million. Which solution should the project manager recommend? What is the reason?

A. Solution 1, because the EMV of solution1 is $100,000 more than the EMV of solution 2

B. Solution 2, because it can save $1 million more than the solution 1

C. Solution 1, because its probability of success is 30% higher than that of solution 2

D. Solution 2, because the EMV of solution2 is $200,000 more than the EMV of solution 1

100. 项目经理正在为项目准备两个备选方案。方案一成功的概率是 80%，如果成功，可以为项目节省 100 万美元；但是如果失败，就要增加 100 万美元的成本。方案二成功的概率是 50%，如果成功，可以节省 200 万美元；如果失败，就会增加 100 万美元的成本。那么项目经理应该推荐哪个方案？理由是什么？

A. 方案一，因为预期货币价值（EMV）比方案二多 10 万美元

B. 方案二，因为项目如果成功，方案二可以比方案一多节省 100 万美元

C. 方案一，因为方案一成功的概率比方案二高 30%

D. 方案二，因为预期货币价值（EMV）比方案一多 20 万美元

101. During the implementation of the project, a supplier asked to increase the supply price by 15% due to the sharp rise in the price of raw materials, otherwise they would rather bear the penalty than continue to supply. The project manager judges that if the supplier's requirements are met, the project cost will exceed the budget. What should the project manager do?

A. Terminate the contract with this supplier and look for alternative one

B. Update risk register and carry out risk quantitative analysis

C. Initiate a change and evaluate the impact of the price increase on the project

D. Agree to the supplier's request and change the cost base accordingly

101. 项目实施过程中，一家供应商告知因为原材料价格大幅上涨，所以要提价 15%，否则宁可承担违约金也拒绝继续供货。项目经理判断，如果答应供应商的要求，项目成本会突破预算。项目经理应该怎么做？

A. 终止和这家供应商的合同并寻找替代的供应商

B. 更新风险登记册，并实施风险定量分析

C. 发起一项变更请求，并评估涨价对项目的影响

D. 答应该供应商的要求，并相应地更改成本基准

102. When the project team did the requirement analysis, they found that the development of a function module required new technologies that had never been encountered by the team, and they had no experience in the development of this function module. After discussion, the team decided to outsource the module. What kind of purchase contract should be adopted to control the risk?

A. Cost plus fixed fee contract

B. Firm fixed price contract

C. Fixed price plus economic price adjustment contract

D. T&M contract

102. 项目团队在做项目需求分析时，发现一个功能模块的开发需要用到团队从未接触过的新技术，而且团队对这个功能模块的开发完全没有经验，团队讨论后决定将该模块外包。为了控制风险，应该采用哪种采购合同？

A. 成本加固定费用合同

B. 固定总价合同

C. 总价加经济价格调整合同

D. 工料合同

103. During the execution of the contract, Party A and Party B have different understanding of the terms of the contract, which leads to the failure of the execution of the contract. If both sides do not want to escalate the conflict and resolve the dispute as soon as possible, which of the following ways should be preferred?

A. Negotiation

B. Alternative dispute resolution

C. Arbitration

D. Litigation

103. 合同执行过程中甲乙双方对合同条款的理解产生了分歧，导致合同无法执行下去。如果双方都不想让冲突升级，并尽快解决这个争议，那么应该优先选择以下哪种方式？

A. 谈判

B. 替代争议解决

C. 仲裁

D. 诉讼

104. The contract stipulates that the cost allowed in the list shall be borne by the buyer. And the contract stipulates that the seller can share 20% of the cost savings compared with the project budget. What type of contract is signed between the buyer and the seller?

A. Fixed price plus incentive fee contract (FPIF)

B. Cost plus incentive fee contract (CPIF)

C. Cost plus award fee contract (CPAF)

D. Cost plus percentage of cost fee (CPPC)

104. 合同规定，清单中允许的成本都由买方承担，并且，相比项目预算节约的成本，卖方可以分享其中的 20%。买卖双方签订的合同属于什么类型？

A. 总价加激励费用合同

B. 成本加激励费用合同

C. 成本加奖励费用合同

D. 成本加成本百分比合同

105. The buyer and seller bargain on a cost plus incentive fee contract, the aim cost of the contract is $5 million, the aim fee is $1 million, the sharing ratio is 80/20, if the seller accomplished the fact cost is $4.5 million, how much should the buyer pay for the seller totally?

A. $ 5.5 million

B. $ 5.6 million

C. $ 5.9 million

D. $ 6 million

105. 买方和卖方签订了成本加激励费用合同，合同的目标成本是 500 万美元，目标费用是 100 万美元，分享比例为 80/20。卖方完成工作的实际成本为 450 万美元，那么最终买方要向卖方支付多少合同款？

A. 550 万美元

B. 560 万美元

C. 590 万美元

D. 600 万美元

106. The current project schedule performance index of SPI was 0.7. In order to meet the schedule requirements, the team assessed and decided to outsource part of the remaining of the project to the subcontractor through tendering. Which of the following tasks does the project manager need to complete before signing a contract with the subcontractor?

A. Change procedures, bidder conferences, independent cost estimates and procurement negotiations

B. Make or buy decision, independent cost estimates, bidder conferences and procurement negotiations

C. Earned value analysis, independent cost estimates, procurement audits and procurement negotiations

D. Make or buy decision, claims management, request for proposal (RFP) and procurement audits

106. 当前项目的进度绩效指数（SPI）为 0.7。为了满足进度要求，团队经过评估决定将项目剩余的一部分工作通过招标的方式外包给分包商。在与分包商签订合同之前，项目经理需要完成以下哪些工作？

A. 变更程序、投标人会议、独立估算和采购谈判

B. 自制外购分析、独立估算、投标人会议和采购谈判

C. 挣值分析、独立估算、采购审计和采购谈判

D. 自制外购分析、索赔管理、建议邀请书（RFP）、采购审计

107. A subcontractor of the project proposed to the project manager that one of the functional requirements in the contract has fallen behind, and the requirement should be updated to ensure the commercial value of the product. The project manager and the subcontractor signed a cost plus fixed fee contract, and the updated requirement will lead to the project cost exceeding the budget. The contract signed by the project manager and the client is a fixed price plus incentive fee contract, which means that if the requirement is updated, the expected profit of the project will be greatly reduced. What should the project manager do?

A. Accept the loss of profit and inform the subcontractor to update the requirement

B. Inform subcontractor to develop according to original requirement to avoid change

C. Ask the client to compensate the subcontractor for the increased cost due to the update requirement

D. Initiate a change process to update the requirement and obtain approval from the change control board

107. 项目的一家分包商向项目经理提出，合同中有一项功能需求已经落后，应该更新需求以保证产品的商业价值。项目经理和分包商签署的是成本加固定费用合同，更新需求将导致项目成本超出预算。项目经理与客户签署的是总价加激励费用合同，这意味着如果更新需求，项目预期利润将大幅减少。项目经理应该怎么做？

A. 接受利润损失，通知分包商更新需求

B. 通知分包商按照原需求开发，以避免变更

C. 要求客户向分包商补偿因更新需求而增加的成本

D. 启动更新需求的变更流程，并获得变更控制委员会的批准

108. A project stakeholder requires an important change to the scope of the project, which is critical to the stakeholder. Project manager carries out necessary analysis to the change requirement. Due to the change, project cost and schedule will have significant impacts. This change needs to be approved by the change control board (CCB), but the change is refused by CCB. What should the project manager do next?

A. Implement the change despite the decision made by the CCB, because the change is critical to the stakeholder and the satisfaction of stakeholders' is standard for success of the project

B. Record the decision of CCB to the change log and feedback the results to the stakeholder and project team truthfully

C. Recommends stop the project immediately for new requirements gathering and risk assessment

D. Meeting with members of CCB individually to influence their decision to change

108. 一位项目相关方要求对项目范围进行重大变更，该变更对于相关方来说至关重要。项目经理对变更开展了必要分析，由于变更对项目成本和进度均会产生显著影响，所以变更需要得到变更控制委员会（CCB）的批准，但 CCB 拒绝了这个变更。项目经理接下来应该怎么做？

A. 不理会 CCB 的决定，实施变更，因为这个变更对这位相关方来说至关重要，并且把相关方满意看成是项目成功的标准

B. 将 CCB 的决定记录到变更日志中，并向相关方和项目团队反馈这个情况

C. 建议立即停止该项目，进行新的需求收集和风险评估

D. 与 CCB 的成员分别单独会面，以此来影响他们改变决定

109. Several scrum teams jointly develop a large and complex product. Each team sends representatives to attend the scrum of scrums (SOS) meeting. The following contents should be exchanged at the meeting, EXCEPT:

A. What has the team accomplished since the last meeting

B. Resources left by the team since the last meeting

C. What difficulties does the team have and need the assistance of other teams

D. What tasks does the team plan to complete by the next meeting

109. 多个 Scrum 团队联合开发一个大型复杂的产品。每个团队派代表参加 "Scrum of Scrums" 会议，会上应该交流以下内容，除了：

A. 从上次会议到现在团队完成了哪些任务

B. 从上次会议到现在团队所剩的资源

C. 团队有哪些困难需要其他团队协助

D. 到下次会议召开前团队计划完成哪些任务

110. The project manager is responsible for a project of client's internal management information system. Contract with the client has been signed and the project charter has been confirmed. However, in the process of carrying out the project, project manager repeatedly encountered various kinds of incoordination and even obstructions from different levels of different departments within the client company. Which of the following analysis can be used to avoid this?

A. Stakeholder analysis

B. Requirements analysis

C. Assumption and constraint analysis

D. File analysis

110. 项目经理正在负责一个为客户打造内部管理信息系统的项目，已与客户签署合同并确定了项目章程。但是在开展项目工作的过程中，不断遇到客户公司内部不同部门、不同层级的各种不配合，甚至阻挠。深入应用以下哪个分析可以避免这种情况的发生？

A. 相关方分析

B. 需求分析

C. 假设条件和制约因素分析

D. 文件分析

111. The team received a project to develop a new product. Based on the lack of understanding

of the real needs of potential users, the team decided to follow the development principle of minimum viable product. Which of the following is not true about the statement of the develoment principle of minimum viable product?

A. It allows product to get in touch with users earlier and get feedback from users

B. It gives the highest priority to essential functions

C. Do the work right the first time and avoid a lot of rework

D. It can get market validation quickly and reduce the cost of trial and error

111. 团队接到一个开发新产品的项目，基于对潜在用户的真实需求缺乏了解，团队决定遵循最小可行产品的开发原则。关于最小可行产品的开发原则的表述，以下哪一个不正确？

A. 可以让产品更早接触到用户并获得用户反馈

B. 可以让必不可少的功能获得最高的优先级

C. 可以一次就把工作做对，避免大量的返工

D. 可以快速获得市场验证并减少试错的成本

112. The project manager has identified many stakeholders in a new project, but the power, urgency, and legitimacy of each stakeholder is different. Which of the following tools should the project manager use to determine the priority to which stakeholders should be concerned to determine appropriate stakeholder management strategies?

A. Stakeholder engagement assessment matrix

B. Power/interest grid

C. Stakeholder cube

D. Salience model

112. 项目经理已经识别出一个新项目的许多相关方，但每个相关方的权力大小、需要被关注的紧迫性和参与项目的合法性都不同。项目经理应该使用以下哪个工具来确定相关方应该被关注的优先级，以便确定合适的相关方管理策略？

A. 相关方参与度评估矩阵

B. 权力 / 利益方格

C. 相关方立方体

D. 凸显模型

113. Which of the following should the scrum team focus on in the sprint review meeting?

A. Review priorities for the next sprint

B. Review the team's communication and collaboration efficiency in the current sprint

C. Confirm whether everyone needs help from others in the current sprint

D. Demonstrate the results of the current sprint to confirm availability

113. Scrum 团队在冲刺评审会上，应该聚焦在以下哪个方面？

A. 评审下一个冲刺应该优先开展的工作

B. 评审团队在当前冲刺中沟通和协作的效率

C. 确定每个人在当前冲刺中是否需要别人的协助

D. 演示当前冲刺的成果，以确认是否可用

114. A project manager has put in place rules covering who will have access to controlled documents, how changes to these items will be recorded and approved, and how everyone will know what the current version is. The project manager is therefore creating a:

A. Work authorization system

B. Change control system

C. Configuration management system

D. Project management information system

114. 项目经理制定了一系列规定，包括谁有权使用受控文件、这些文件的变更如何被记录和批准，以及所有人如何了解当前文件的版本信息等。项目经理正在创建：

A. 工作授权系统

B. 变更控制系统

C. 配置管理系统

D. 项目管理信息系统

115. The project manager finds that a team member is dissatisfied with his current status and cannot be recognized by others. The project manager hopes to effectively motivate the team member. Which of the following schemes has better incentive effect?

A. Promise to give high reward to him after completing the project

B. Provide reasonable salary and reliable guarantee

C. Provide comfortable working environment and suitable tools and equipment

D. Provide challenging opportunities and timely encouragement

115. 项目经理发现一名团队成员不仅自己对现状不满，而且得不到其他人的认可。项目经理希望有效激励这名团队成员，以下哪种方案具有更好的激励效果？

A. 承诺完成项目后兑现高额奖励

B. 提供合理的薪酬和可靠的保障

C. 提供舒适的工作环境和合适的工具、设备

D. 提供富有挑战的机会和适时的鼓励

116. What is correct for the project team and project management team?

A. Project team is the project management team

B. Project management team includes project team

C. Project management team includes project team members who are involved in project management activities

D. The project management team members do not need to participate in the implementation of the activities

116. 以下对项目团队和项目管理团队的表述哪一个是正确的？

A. 项目团队就是项目管理团队

B. 项目管理团队包含项目团队

C. 项目管理团队包括参与项目管理活动的项目团队成员

D. 项目管理团队成员不需要参与活动的执行

117. An agile team is in the middle of a sprint when the sponsor asks the project manager to stop work on several user stories in the current sprint. With a recent news announcement of new technology soon to hit the market, the sponsor is inclined to think that these user stories would be of little value. What should the project manager do?

A. Remove the user stories indicated by the sponsor from the sprint backlog

B. Ignore the sponsor's input and instruct the team to proceed as originally planned

C. Contact the product owner and ask if the user stories are still having priority

D. Conduct market research to confirm the announcement of the new technology

117. 一个敏捷团队正在进行冲刺，这时发起人要求项目经理停止当前冲刺中几个用户故事的开发。由于最近一则新技术即将上市的消息，所以发起人认为这些用户故事没有什么价值。项目经理应该怎么做？

A. 从冲刺待办事项列表中移除发起人提到的用户故事

B. 忽略发起人的意见，并指示团队按原计划进行

C. 联系产品负责人，询问这些用户故事是否仍然是优先待办事项

D. 进行市场调查，以确认新技术的发布

118. Electric bus R&D project, project manager starts collecting needs from customers, then objectively analysis these needs, and translate these needs into design, development and production indicators. What is he using?

A. Joint application design and development (JAD)

B. Quality function deployment (QFD)

C. User story

D. Backlog

118. 在某个电动大客车的研发项目中，项目经理从收集客户需求开始，然后客观地对这些需求进行分析，并一步步地将这些需求转化为设计、开发和生产指标。他用的是下列哪种技术？

A. 联合应用设计和开发（JAD）

B. 质量功能展开（QFD）

C. 用户故事

D. 待办事项列表

119. In the process of requirement identification of a product R & D project, the client rejects the proposal from the project manager over and over again. The project manager feels that the client may not really know what he wants. Which of the following is the best way for a project manager to identify requirements?

A. Brain storming

B. Observation method

C. Delphi method

D. Prototype method

119. 在一个产品研发项目需求识别的过程中，客户总是一遍一遍地否决项目经理提出的方案，项目经理感觉到客户可能并不真正清楚自己想要什么。那么项目经理最好采用以下哪种方法来识别客户的需求？

A. 头脑风暴法

B. 观察法

C. 德尔菲法

D. 原型法

120. The project team identified a number of risks, and the project manager said that at the following risk review meeting, the stakeholders must be reported on which changes in risks had the greatest impact on the project's final performance and should be prioritized from high to low. Which of the following techniques does the project team need to use?

A. Sensitivity analysis

B. Decision tree analysis

C. Earned value analysis

D. Monte Carlo analysis

120. 项目团队识别出很多个风险。项目经理说在接下来的风险评审会上，必须向项目相关方汇报哪些风险的变化对项目最终绩效的影响最大，而且应该由高到低排出顺序。项目团队需要用到下面哪一种技术？

A. 敏感性分析

B. 决策树分析

C. 挣值分析

D. 蒙特卡洛分析

121. In a sprint, team members realize that the new communication mechanism adopted in the sprint does not work. On the contrary, it increases the misunderstanding among team members and causes more rework. What should scrum master do?

A. Discuss the issue during the retrospective meeting

B. Discuss the issue during the review meeting

C. Discuss the issue during the next planning meeting

D. Discuss the issue in the next daily stand-up meeting

121. 在一个冲刺中，团队成员意识到这个冲刺采用的新的沟通机制并没有起到良好的作用，反而增加了团队成员之间的误解，造成更多返工。敏捷专家应该怎么做？

A. 在冲刺回顾会上讨论该问题

B. 在冲刺评审会上讨论该问题

C. 在下一次冲刺计划会上讨论该问题

D. 在下一次每日站会上讨论该问题

122. After speaking with the product owner, a project team developer added a critical feature to the current sprint that will secure a new sale. The team has already started developing this feature. What should the Scrum Master do next?

A. Instruct the project team to stop developing the feature until change control procedures are followed

B. Commend that developer for taking the initiative to add this feature and communicate to the owner that the feature will available after the current sprint

C. Direct the team to finish development the feature if will not impact the deliverables of any other features currently in progress

D. Escalate the issue to the human resources department to ensure that the owner does not bypass the chain of command in the future

122. 在与产品负责人交谈后，一位项目团队开发人员为当前冲刺添加了一项关键功能，以确保获得一笔新业务。团队已经开始开发该功能。敏捷专家下一步应该怎么做？

A. 指示团队停止开发该功能，直到遵循完变更控制程序

B. 建议开发人员主动添加该功能，并告知产品负责人该功能在当前冲刺后可用

C. 如果不影响当前正在进行的任何其他功能的交付，就可以指导团队完成该功能的开发

D. 将该问题上报给人力资源部门，以确保产品负责人将来不会绕过命令链

123. The team formed two different opinions on the technical scheme, the conflict became more and more intense, and the work could not be carried out normally. The project manager leads the team members to focus on the part that can reach a consensus rather than the difference. What conflict resolution strategy does the project manager adopt?

A. Force/direct

B. Withdraw/avoid

C. Smooth/accommodate

D. Compromise/reconcile

123. 团队内部就技术方案形成两种不同的意见，冲突愈演愈烈，工作无法正常开展。项目经理引导大家着眼于能够达成共识的部分，而不是存在分歧的部分。项目经理采取的是哪种冲突解决策略？

A. 强迫 / 命令

B. 撤退 / 回避

C. 缓和 / 包容

D. 妥协 / 调解

124. During the iteration to deliver a product's features, a stakeholder asks for a new feature that was not included in the planned scope of work, the stakeholder threatens to escalate the issue to senior management if this new features is not included in the current iteration, what should the agile practitioner do?

A. Meet with the stakeholder to discuss implementation only part of the new feature now

B. Collaborate with the team and product owner to reprioritize the new features

C. Ask the stakeholder to obtain approval from senior management

D. Request guidance from senior management

124. 在交付某个产品功能的迭代过程中，相关方要求提供不包含在计划工作范围内的一项新功能。该相关方威胁说，如果这项新功能未包含在当前迭代中，将会把问题升级上报给高级管理层。若要解决这个问题，敏捷管理专业人士应该怎么做？

A. 与该项目相关方开会，就现在仅实施的部分新功能进行讨论

B. 与团队和产品负责人合作，重新确定这项新功能的优先级

C. 要求该项目相关方获得高级管理层的批准

D. 向高级管理层请求指导

125. The team has just completed the sprint planning meeting and received the news that due to the typhoon, the equipment needed for the main work in the sprint cannot be in place. What should the team do?

A. Pay attention to the weather forecast, wait for the typhoon to pass, and start the sprint when the equipment is in place

B. Report the problem to the scrum master and ask the scrum master to remove the obstacle

C. Immediately re-plan the sprint and replace other tasks that do not depend on this equipment

D. Start the sprint and believe there will be a solution before the end of the sprint

125. 团队刚刚完成冲刺计划会，收到消息称，受台风影响，冲刺中主要工作需要的设备无法到位。团队应该怎么办？

A. 关注天气预报，等待台风过去、设备到位再启动冲刺

B. 将问题报告给敏捷专家，请敏捷专家排除这个障碍

C. 立即重新规划本冲刺，置换不依赖这个设备的其他工作

D. 启动冲刺，相信冲刺结束前会有解决办法

126. One project team has 11 team members who work together. They implement the work stably. In the ninth iteration, some team members quit the job and are taken over by the members in different geographical locations. What expectations should the project manager place on the new team?

A. The team will experience the stage of formation and implement work at the speed the same with that of the previous project team

B. Before the team implements work stably, the team will experience the stage of fluctuations and become standardized in the more frequent communication

C. The team will continue to handle and solve any possible team conflicts

D. Team members will focus on their deliverable results and progress

126. 一个项目团队拥有 11 名集中办公的团队成员，他们稳定地开展工作。在第 9 次迭代中，有些团队成员离职，并由分布在不同地理位置的成员代替。项目经理应对新团队有何预期？

A. 团队将经历形成阶段，并将以之前项目团队相同的速度水平开展工作

B. 在稳定地开展工作之前，团队将经历震荡阶段，并在更频繁的沟通中变得规

范化

C. 团队将持续处理和解决所发生的任何团队冲突

D. 团队成员将专注于他们的可交付成果和进展

127. A team is just starting to use agile methods. The product owner hopes that the user story in the to-do list can be accurately understood by the team. The followings are what he should do, EXCEPT:

A. User stories should be fully defined, and the more specific the user stories at the top of the list are

B. The granularity of user stories must be small enough to be completed by a team member independently

C. User stories should be dynamic, adding, deleting and reordering as the project progresses

D. The workload of user stories should be estimated and priorities should be maintained continuously

127. 一个团队刚刚开始使用敏捷方法。产品负责人希望待办事项列表中的用户故事能够被团队准确理解。以下是他应该做到的，除了：

A. 用户故事应该被充分定义，越是排在列表顶层的应该越具体

B. 用户故事的颗粒度必须足够小，能够由一名团队成员独立完成

C. 用户故事应该是动态的，根据项目进展不断添加、删除和重新排序

D. 用户故事的工作量应该是经过估算的，其优先级应该被持续维护

128. What can agile team use to assure customer that they are moving towards achieving goals of a product release?

A. Burnup or burndown chart

B. General progress status report

C. Requirement analysis report

D. Retrospective chart

128. 敏捷团队可以使用什么向客户保证，他们正朝着实现产品发布的目标前进？

A. 燃起图或燃尽图

B. 总体进展情况报告

C. 需求分析报告

D. 回顾图表

129. When discussing the development plan of a user story, there are differences within the team. How to solve this problem?

A. It's up to the product owner

B. It's up to the Scrum Master

C. It's up to the technical experts

D. It is decided by team members through full discussion and voting

129. 在讨论一个用户故事的开发方案时，团队内部产生了分歧，这个问题应该怎么解决？

A. 由产品负责人决定

B. 由敏捷专家决定

C. 由技术专家决定

D. 由团队成员充分讨论并通过表决方式决定

130. A project sponsor requests a brief overview of agile. What should the agile team explain about agile project execution?

A. The project will follow the plan at all times

B. The project will focus on technical excellence and delivering value

C. The project will focus on predictability over adaptability

D. The project will have well-defined processes and less reliance on individuals

130. 项目发起人要求提供敏捷的简要概述。敏捷团队应该如何解释敏捷项目执行？

A. 项目将始终遵循计划

B. 项目将关注技术卓越和交付价值

C. 项目将关注可预测性胜过适应性

D. 项目将具有定义良好的过程并减少对个人的依赖

131. The company is promoting agile transformation. Agile methods emphasize self-organizing teams. These are the characteristics of self-organizing teams, EXCEPT:

A. Team leaders are recommended by team members themselves, not appointed by the organization

B. Teams have clear and unified goals for which all members work

C. Team members have the right to manage themselves and decide how best to do their work

D. Team members understand and respect each other and resolve their differences in a democratic way

131. 公司正在推动敏捷转型。敏捷方法强调自组织团队。以下都是自组织团队的特征，除了：

A. 由团队成员自己推举团队领导者，而不是组织任命

B. 团队有清晰、明确而且统一的目标，所有人都为这个目标而努力

C. 团队成员有权自我管理并自己决定如何最好地完成工作

D. 团队成员相互了解、彼此尊重，通过民主的方式解决分歧

132. When preparing a business case with a financial analyst, what key document is needed?

A. Cost-benefit analysis

B. Statement of work

C. Contract

D. Project charter

132. 在与财务分析师准备商业论证时，需要以下哪一份关键文件？

A. 成本效益分析

B. 工作说明书

C. 合同

D. 项目章程

133. The project manager takes over a project with poor performance in the middle of the project. The project manager observes that the team morale is low, and the team members generally have no confidence in completing the project. Moreover, the project has been replaced by three project managers successively, and the team members do not believe that the new project manager can bring substantial change. The project manager helps the team members to find the root cause of poor performance, and optimizes the schedule, cost and resources with the team members. The rigorous attitude and scientific method win the respect and trust of the team. Which of the following powers does the project manager use?

A. Expert power

B. Referential power

C. Situational power

D. Formal power

133. 项目经理中途接手一个绩效很差的项目。项目经理观察到团队士气低落，团队成员对完成项目普遍没有信心，而且该项目已经先后换过三任项目经理，团队成员并不相信新的项目经理能够带来实质性改变。项目经理帮助团队成员找到绩效不佳的根本原因，并和团队成员一起优化进度、成本和资源，凭借严谨的态度和科学的方法赢得了团队的尊重和信任。项目经理主要使用的是下列哪种权力？

A. 专家权力

B. 参照权力

C. 情境权力

D. 正式权力

134. For a project manager on a new project team, the following behaviors should be developed, EXCEPT:

A. Describe the vision and inspire the team to work together

B. Encourage team innovation and breakthrough

C. Match words with deeds, set an example for others

D. Take responsibility to make up for the shortcomings of others

134. 对于一个新项目团队的项目经理来说，应该养成以下行为习惯，除了：

A. 描绘愿景，感召团队共同奋斗

B. 鼓励团队勇于创新、突破现状

C. 言行一致，为他人树立榜样

D. 主动担当，弥补他人的不足

135. The project manager gets the support of the vast majority of stakeholders, but one stakeholder opposes the project plan, which is difficult to implement. The project manager repeatedly communicates with the stakeholder, but it still has no effect. What

should the project manager do?

A. Ignore the stakeholder's comments and remove him from the stakeholders register

B. Unconditionally meet the requirements of the stakeholder to obtain his support

C. Assume that the stakeholder is supportive and implement the project plan

D. Mobilize other influential stakeholders to influence him

135. 项目经理得到了绝大多数相关方的支持，只有一位相关方反对项目计划。如果得不到这位相关方的认可，项目计划就很难实施。项目经理反复与这位相关方沟通，但仍然没有效果。项目经理应该怎么办？

A. 忽略该相关方的意见并将其从相关方登记册中删除

B. 无条件满足该相关方的要求，以获得他的支持

C. 假定这位相关方是支持自己的，并实施项目计划

D. 动员其他影响力大且支持项目的相关方去影响该相关方

136. Daily stand-up meeting should follow these principles, EXCEPT?

A. As the beginning of a day

B. Keep it under 15 minutes

C. Make sure all team members attend

D. Keep the same place at the same time every day

136. 每日站会应该遵循以下原则，除了：

A. 把每日站会作为一天的开始

B. 控制在 15 分钟之内

C. 确保所有团队成员都参加

D. 保持每天在同一时间、同一地点召开

137. When the project team encounters technical difficulties, the project manager judges that it has been unable to deliver the product according to the schedule, but delivery on time is very important to the client. Fortunately, this risk has been identified and contingency plan has been made when developing the project plan. Using the contingency plan can deliver the product on time and meet the basic needs of users, but the lower performance indicators must be accepted. What should the project manager do?

A. Inform team to adopt contingency plan

B. Report to the client truthfully and ask for more development time

C. Ask the team to work overtime to overcome technical difficulties and deliver the product on time

D. Application of contingency plan through change control procedures

137. 项目团队遇到了技术困难，项目经理判断已经无法按规定的时间交付产品，然而交付时间对客户至关重要。幸好团队当初在做项目计划时就已经识别出这个风险，并做了应急计划。团队采取应急计划可以按时交付产品，也能满足基本的产品使用需求，但客户必须接受较低的性能指标。项目经理应该怎么办？

A. 通知团队采用应急计划

B. 如实向客户汇报，并争取更多的开发时间

C. 要求团队加班克服技术困难，并按期交付产品

D. 通过变更控制程序申请启用应急计划

138. A project incident has been found and registered by a project team member, and corrective actions are defined and implemented. One month later, another project team member detects a similar incident with the same characteristics. What should the project manager review to gain understanding of these incidents and communicate that information to the team?

A. Issue log

B. Performance report

C. Risk register

D. Change log

138. 一名项目团队成员发现并登记了一个项目事故，同时制定、实施了纠正措施。一个月后，另一名项目团队成员发现了具有相同特征的类似的事故。项目经理应查阅哪一份文件了解这些事故并与团队沟通该信息？

A. 问题日志

B. 绩效报告

C. 风险登记册

D. 变更日志

139. The two project teams need to use a high performance workstation, which is not compatible with each other, and the contradictions are constantly escalating. The project manager sought a solution by understanding the real needs of the other party and communicating openly. Later, it was found that the two project teams could share the workstation by staggering the use time. Which of the following conflict resolution methods is used by the project manager?

A. Compromise/reconcile

B. Collaborate/problem-solve

C. Withdraw/avoid

D. Smooth/accommodate

139. 两个项目团队都要使用一台高性能的工作站，互不相让，矛盾不断升级。项目经理通过了解对方的真实需求并开诚布公地沟通以寻求解决办法，后来发现两个项目团队完全可以错开使用时间共享这台工作站。项目经理采用的是下列哪个冲突解决办法？

A. 妥协 / 调解

B. 合作 / 解决

C. 撤退 / 回避

D. 缓和 / 包容

140. Project stakeholders are concerned about a project's progress. To address the concern, the project manager creates a report showing which work packages are not yet started, are in-process, or are finished. What report did the project manager create?

A. Risk report

B. Quality report

C. Work performance report

D. Feasibility study report

140. 项目相关方对项目进展感到担忧。为了解决这个问题，项目经理创建了一份报告，显示哪些工作包还未开始，哪些工作包正在进行当中，以及哪些工作包已经完成。项目经理创建的是哪一份报告？

A. 风险报告

B. 质量报告

C. 工作绩效报告

D. 可行性研究报告

141. The R & D of new energy vehicles includes three project teams: motor, battery and electronic control, which are respectively in charge by three project managers. The three teams need to cooperate closely in terms of technical solutions and development progress, because any team can't deliver on time, and new energy vehicles can't be launched on time. In order to ensure the success of the project, which of the following roles is essential?

A. Program manager

B. Portfolio manager

C. Project expediter

D. Project coordinator

141. 新能源汽车研发包含电机、电池、电控三个项目团队，分别由三位项目经理负责。这三个团队需要在技术方案和开发进度方面密切配合，因为如果任何一个团队不能按期交付，新能源汽车都无法如期上市。为了确保项目成功，以下哪个角色是必不可少的?

A. 项目集经理

B. 项目组合经理

C. 项目联络员

D. 项目协调员

142. At the initiating meeting, the sales director proposed new requirements. Meeting these new requirements is expected to increase costs and extend schedules. What should a project manager do?

A. Persuade the sales director to withdraw these requirements

B. Allocate resources for new requirements and incorporate them into the project plan

C. Perform the integrated change control procedures

D. Waiting for the formal confirmation of these new requirements from the project sponsor

142. 在项目启动会上，销售总监提出新的需求，如果要满足这些新需求，预计要增加成本并延长工期。项目经理应该怎么做?

A. 劝说销售总监收回这些需求

B. 为新需求配置资源并纳入项目计划

C. 实施整体变更控制程序

D. 等待项目发起人对这些新需求进行正式确认

143. During the final acceptance of the project, the client thought that a number of deliverables could not meet the use requirements, so refused to sign on the project acceptance report. If this situation is to be avoided, what should the project manager do in advance?

A. Identify requirements in advance to ensure that client's requirements are accurately understood

B. Check the deliverables with the project scope statement in advance

C. Test in advance to confirm the availability of the deliverables

D. Confirm the scope with client in stages in advance

143. 在项目最终的验收过程中,客户认为多项可交付成果无法满足使用要求,因此拒绝在项目验收报告上签字。如果要避免这种局面发生,项目经理事先应该做什么?

A. 提前进行需求识别,确保客户需求被准确理解

B. 提前将可交付成果与项目范围说明书进行核对

C. 提前进行测试,确认可交付成果可用

D. 提前分阶段与客户进行范围确认

144. A project was completed one year ago, and the project manager and resources are assigned to another project. The client emails the chief operation officer claiming that a deliverable is not within the expected quality level and requests a change to this deliverable, before responding to the client, what document should the chief operation officer review first?

A. Requirements management plan

B. Client acceptance documents

C. Quality inspection report

D. Statement of work

144. 项目已在一年前完成，项目经理和资源已分配到另一个项目。客户向首席运营官发送电子邮件，声称一个可交付成果不符合预期的质量级别，请求对该可交付成果进行变更。在答复客户之前，首席运营官应该首先审查什么文件？

A. 需求管理计划

B. 客户验收文件

C. 质量检查报告

D. 工作说明书

145. All the project's deliverables have passed the quality inspection, but the client does not clear about the process of quality management and still lack confidence in the quality. What should the project manager do?

A. Retrospect quality management plan with the client

B. Check the quality again with the client

C. Show the client the after-sales service terms in the contract

D. Through quality audit to prove that the quality assurance process is rigorous

145. 项目的可交付成果全部通过了质量检查，但客户不了解质量管理过程，仍然对质量缺乏信心。项目经理应该怎么做？

A. 与客户一起回顾质量管理计划

B. 与客户一起再次检查质量

C. 向客户展示合同中的售后服务条款

D. 通过质量审计证明质量保证过程是严谨的

146. A project manager collects requirements for a new project. Stakeholders are from different departments and have various requirements. In order to confirm all requirements can be collected from stakeholders, which of the following techniques should be used by the project manager?

A. Focus group

B. Facilitated workshop

C. Nominal group

D. Delphi technology

146. 项目经理为一个新项目收集需求，相关方来自不同的专业部门，并且需求也各不相同。为了确保相关方的需求都能够被收集，项目经理应该使用下列哪一项技术？

A. 焦点小组

B. 引导式研讨会

C. 名义小组

D. 德尔菲技术

147. The stakeholders of the project are numerous and distributed around the world. Complaints from some stakeholders are always unable to get project information in time, and some other stakeholders complain that the video conferences are too many and too long. What should the project manager do?

A. Change video conference mode to email communication

B. All information of the project shall be sent to all stakeholders in time

C. Prepare stakeholder engagement plan according to stakeholder register

D. According to the power/interest matrix, only meeting the requirements of important stakeholders

147. 项目的相关方众多而且分布在世界各地，有的相关方投诉总是不能及时得到项目的相关信息，也有的相关方抱怨视频会议太多、时间太长。项目经理应该怎么办？

A. 将视频会议变更为邮件沟通

B. 将项目的所有信息及时群发给所有相关方

C. 根据相关方登记册编制相关方参与计划

D. 根据权力 / 利益矩阵，只关注重要相关方的需求

148. Team members ask the project manager about acceptance criteria for deliverables. Which document should the project manager advise the team members to refer to?

A. Quality management plan

B. Project scope statement

C. Requirements management plan

D. Work breakdown structure (WBS)

148. 团队成员向项目经理询问可交付成果的验收标准。项目经理应该建议团队成员查阅哪份文件?

A. 质量管理计划

B. 项目范围说明书

C. 需求管理计划

D. 工作分解结构

149. The project manager takes over a project with many stakeholders in the middle of the project. He finds that some stakeholders are very active, while others are just the opposite. The project manager wants to know which stakeholders should be guided to actively participate in the project. Which document should he refer to?

A. Power/interest matrix

B. Responsibility allocation matrix

C. RACI matrix

D. Stakeholder engagement assessment matrix

149. 项目经理中途接手一个拥有众多相关方的项目,他发现一部分相关方表现得非常积极主动,而另外一部分相关方却正好相反。项目经理想知道应该引导哪些相关方积极参与项目工作,他应该查阅以下哪一份文件?

A. 权力 / 利益矩阵

B. 责任分配矩阵

C. RACI 矩阵

D. 相关方参与程度评估矩阵

150. During the project acceptance, a deliverable does not meet the client's requirements. The project manager checks the records to confirm that the deliverable meets the quality requirements. Then, which process is the most likely cause of this situation?

A. Define scope

B. Confirm scope

C. Collect requirements

D. Scope control

150. 在项目验收阶段,一个可交付成果不符合客户的需求,于是项目经理查阅了记录并确认这个可交付成果满足质量要求，那么这种情况最可能是哪个过程出了问题导致的？

A. 定义范围

B. 确认范围

C. 收集需求

D. 控制范围

151. Several functional department managers of the company have different understanding of the project. They had serious differences at the project plan review meeting. The meeting was held several times, and each time they broke up in a bad mood. What should the project manager do?

A. Discuss the project plan separately with each functional manager for their approval

B. Invite senior leaders of the company to attend the meeting and approve the project plan

C. Ask them to approve what they can agree on and start implementing the plan

D. Develop stakeholder engagement plan and manage their expectations

151. 公司的几位职能部门经理对项目有着不同的理解，他们在项目计划评审会上分歧严重，开了好几次会议，每次都不欢而散。项目经理应该怎么办？

A. 分别与每位职能部门经理单独讨论项目计划，以获得他们的批准

B. 邀请公司高层领导出席会议并批准项目计划

C. 请他们先批准可以达成共识的部分并开始实施计划

D. 制订相关方参与计划并管理他们的期望

152. When the project team prepared the schedule plan, it estimated that an activity would take three days, but even if the activity actually took five days, it would not affect the total duration of the project. Which of the following conclusions can be drawn?

A. This activity is on a critical path and has a free float of 2 days

B. This activity is on a non-critical path and has a free float of 2 days

C. This activity is on the critical path and has a total floating time of 2 days

D. This activity is on a non-critical path and has a total floating time of 2 days

152. 项目团队在编制进度计划时估算出一项活动的历时为 3 天，不过即便这项活动实

际用时 5 天也不影响项目的总工期。我们可以得到以下哪个结论？

A. 这项活动在关键路径上，而且有 2 天的自由浮动时间

B. 这项活动在非关键路径上，而且有 2 天的自由浮动时间

C. 这项活动在关键路径上，而且有 2 天的总浮动时间

D. 这项活动在非关键路径上，而且有 2 天的总浮动时间

153. The earned value analysis report shows that the CV of the project is +\$200,000 and the SV is -\$300,000. Which of the following is a reasonable explanation?

A. Work worth \$100,000 has not been completed

B. Compared with the plan, \$500,000 have not been spent

C. Cost savings of \$200,000

D. Project progress ahead of schedule but cost overrun

153. 挣值分析报告显示，项目的成本偏差为 +20 万美元，进度偏差为 -30 万美元。以下哪一个是合理解释？

A. 有价值 10 万美元应该完成的工作没有完成

B. 与计划相比，有 50 万美元的预算还没有花出去

C. 成本节约了 20 万美元

D. 项目进度超前，同时成本超支

154. An organization is launching a project in an emerging market. The legal, economic, raw material, and labor markets of emerging markets are all subject to various uncertainties. What tools or techniques should the project manager use when asked by the project sponsor to provide cost estimates with different probabilities?

A. Cost-benefit analysis

B. Sensitivity analysis

C. Probability and impact matrices

D. Monte Carlo technology

154. 一家组织正在一个新兴市场启动一个项目。新兴市场的法律、经济、原材料和劳务市场都存在着各种不确定性。项目发起人要求项目经理提供不同概率下的成本估算，项目经理应使用什么工具或技术？

A. 成本效益分析

B. 敏感性分析

C. 概率和影响矩阵

D. 蒙特卡洛技术

155. The project has to pay a high rental fee for large equipment every day. The Financial Officer suggests increasing the number of shift workers, which can effectively improve the efficiency of the equipment and save the rental fee. Which of the following should the project manager take?

A. Cost-benefit analysis

B. Lease-purchase analysis

C. Trend analysis

D. Earned value analysis

155. 因为项目每天都有大型设备高昂的租赁费用支出，所以财务主管建议增加人员施行倒班制，以有效提升设备的使用效率，进而节省租赁费。项目经理应该采用下面哪一项分析技术？

A. 成本效益分析

B. 租赁购买分析

C. 趋势分析

D. 挣值分析

156. While generating the status report for a budget-constrained project, the project manager identifies that the project is one week behind schedule. What should the project manager do to bring the project back on track?

A. Draw people from non-critical paths to critical paths

B. Request additional time from the project sponsor

C. Ask the project management office (PMO) for additional team members

D. Give up part of the work in the project plan

156. 在为一个有预算限制的项目生成状态报告时，项目经理发现该项目比进度计划落后一周。若要将项目拉回正轨，项目经理应该怎么做？

A. 从非关键路径上抽调人手到关键路径上来

B. 向项目发起人要求额外的时间

C. 请求项目管理办公室（PMO）增加团队成员

D. 放弃计划中的一部分工作

157. The sponsor is worried that the cost of completing the project according to the current situation will exceed the budget. Which of the following should the project manager do to dispel the concerns of the sponsor?

A. Reserve analysis

B. Deviation analysis

B. Trend analysis

D. Cost-benefit analysis

157. 发起人担心按照现在的状况发展，完成项目的成本会突破预算。项目经理应该做以下哪种分析来打消发起人的顾虑？

A. 储备分析

B. 偏差分析

C. 趋势分析

D. 成本效益分析

158. A project sponsor offers a bonus if a project can be completed one month ahead of schedule. The project team is motivated by this offer and accelerates the schedule. The quality director is concerned about process compliance. Which of the following measures should be taken to remove the quality director's doubt?

A. Risk audit

B. Configuration item verification and audit

C. Quality audit

D. Quality inspection

158. 项目发起人设置了一笔奖金，如果项目能够比进度计划提前一个月完成，项目团队就能得到这笔奖金。项目团队受到这笔奖金的激励，加快了速度。公司质量总监表示，很担心过程合规的问题。项目经理应该采取下列哪项措施来消除质量总监的疑虑？

A. 风险审计

B. 配置项核实与审计

C. 质量审计

D. 质量检查

159. The agile team was informed that the software would go online one week in advance. Which of the following is the most reasonable solution?

A. Change sprint cycle from two weeks to one week

B. Increase development team members

C. Arrange the development team to work overtime

D. Return low priority requirements

159. 敏捷团队接到通知，软件要提前一周上线。以下哪一项是最合理的方案？

A. 冲刺周期由两周改为一周

B. 补充开发团队成员

C. 安排开发团队加班

D. 退回优先级低的需求

160. A functional manager needs to know when certain resources allocated to a project will become available for other assignments. What should the project manager provide to the functional manager?

A. Staff release plan

B. Resource calendar

C. Responsibility assignment matrix (RAM)

D. Pre-assignment plan

160. 职能经理需要知道分配给某个项目的某些资源何时可以分配到其他任务上。项目经理应该向职能经理提供什么文件？

A. 人员遣散计划

B. 资源日历

C. 责任分配矩阵（RAM）

D. 预分派计划

161. There is a lot of pressure on the project schedule. A development engineer suggests adopting a new development tool can significantly improve the development efficiency.

The project manager thinks that the team switching new tool needs learning cost, and there may be greater uncertainty in the schedule control. What should the project manager do?

A. On the safe side, stick to the original development tool

B. Adopt the new tool and organize team training on it

C. Implement risk quantitative analysis to provide data support for decision-making

D. Evaluate impact with team, update project management plan and get approval

161. 项目进度压力很大，一位开发工程师建议采用一种新的开发工具，可以显著提升开发效率。项目经理认为团队切换新工具需要学习成本，而且进度管控可能存在更大的不确定性。项目经理应该怎么办？

A. 稳妥起见，坚持使用原来的开发工具

B. 采用新工具，并组织团队参加新工具的培训

C. 进行风险定量分析，为决策提供数据支持

D. 与团队评估影响，更新项目管理计划并获得批准

162. In the meeting with the client, the client proposed a modification to a function. The project manager thought the modification was unnecessary, but the client insisted on the modification so much that the meeting could not continue. The project manager assessed that the modification function had little impact on the project and chose to accept the client's request. What conflict management techniques do project managers use?

A. Smooth/accommodate

B. Collaborate/problem-solve

C. Compromise/reconcile

D. Withdraw/avoid

162. 在和客户的会议中，客户提出对一项功能进行修改，项目经理认为这项修改并无必要，但是客户非常坚持这个要求，导致会议无法继续下去。项目经理评估修改这项功能对项目影响很小，于是选择接受客户的要求。项目经理使用的是哪种冲突管理技术？

A. 缓和 / 包容

B. 合作 / 解决

C. 妥协 / 调解

D. 撤退 / 回避

163. One of the many stakeholders in the project is very picky. He always puts forward different opinions on the project plan, and often complains that the project report can't be understood at all. What kind of communication mode should the project manager adopt for such stakeholders?

A. Push communication

B. Pull communication

C. Interactive communication

D. Vertical communication

163. 在众多项目相关方中，有一位相关方非常挑剔，对项目计划总是提出不同意见，还经常抱怨根本无法看懂项目报告。针对这样的相关方，项目经理采取以下哪种沟通方式才是最有效的?

A. 推式沟通

B. 拉式沟通

C. 交互式沟通

D. 垂直式沟通

164. The development manager tells the project manager of project A that the company's other project B with higher priority is entering the critical delivery phase. If the delivery of Project B is difficult, 3 technical backbones from Project A will be transferred. Which document should the project manager of project A first update?

A. Responsibility assignment matrix (RAM)

B. Risk register

C. Resource management plan

D. Issues log

164. 开发部经理告诉项目 A 的项目经理，公司另一个优先级更高的项目 B 正在进入关键交付阶段。如果项目 B 交付困难，将抽调项目 A 中的 3 位技术骨干进行支援。项目 A 的项目经理应该首先更新哪一份文件?

A. 责任分配矩阵（RAM）

B. 风险登记册

C. 资源管理计划

D. 问题日志

165. In the quality report provided by the third party, a large amount of data shows that there are many kinds of defects in the product. Which tool should the project manager use to decide which defects should be solved first?

A. Affinity diagram

B. Scatter diagram

C. Fishbone diagram

D. Pareto diagram

165. 在第三方提供的质量报告中，大量数据表明产品存在很多种缺陷。项目经理应该利用下面哪个工具来决定应该优先解决哪些缺陷？

A. 亲和图

B. 散点图

C. 鱼骨图

D. 帕累托图

166. Company A has entrusted company B to develop A software. Company B believes that all the work stipulated in the contract has been delivered, but company A believes that the software fails to meet the requirements for use and refuses to pay the fee to company B. After several rounds of negotiations, the two sides still haven't reached an agreement, and both companies don't want the situation to be completely public, preferring to settle the dispute as easily as possible. Faced with this situation, which dispute resolution method should be chosen?

A. Alternative dispute resolution (ADR)

B. Arbitration

C. Litigation

D. Negotiations

166. A 公司委托 B 公司开发一款软件。B 公司认为合同规定的工作都已交付，但是 A 公司认为软件未能满足使用要求，所以拒绝向 B 公司支付费用。虽然双方经过多轮谈判仍未达成共识，但并不希望这个局面完全公开，都倾向于通过尽可能简便的方式解决这个争议。面对这种情况，双方应该选择哪种争议解决方法？

A. 替代争议解决（ADR）

B. 仲裁

C. 诉讼

D. 谈判

167. During the selection of suppliers for a complex project, the project manager wants to ensure that potential suppliers have an accurate grasp of all tender requirements. The project manager lists five potential suppliers that have passed the prequalification. What's the next step?

A. Review the suppliers' proposals

B. Conduct contract negotiations with potential suppliers

C. Conduct 1v1 meetings with each supplier

D. Invite the suppliers to a bidder conference

167. 在为一个复杂项目选择供应商期间，项目经理希望确保潜在供应商都能准确把握全部招标内容。项目经理列出了通过资格预审的五家潜在供应商，下一步应该怎么做？

A. 审查供应商的建议书

B. 与潜在供应商进行合同谈判

C. 分别与每家供应商进行一对一会议

D. 邀请潜在供应商参加投标人会议

168. The project manager takes over a complex project halfway through. There are many stakeholders involved in the project, but the project manager's energy is limited, so he hopes to evaluate which stakeholders should be taken care of in the first place and which stakeholders can be contacted later. In addition, the current participation status of stakeholders can be controlled to avoid unnecessary engagement escalation. Which of the following tools is best used by the project manager?

A. Salience model

B. Stakeholders management plan

C. Power/interest grid

D. Stakeholder engagement assessment matrix

168. 项目经理中途接手一个复杂的项目。项目相关方众多，而项目经理精力有限，希望给相关方评级，评估哪些相关方应该第一时间关照，哪些相关方可以稍后联系，并且可以控制相关方现在的参与状态，避免不必要的参与度升级。项目经理最好使用下面哪个工具？

A. 凸显模型

B. 相关方管理计划

C. 权力／利益方格

D. 相关方参与度评估矩阵

169. While reviewing the project management plan during the planning phase, the sponsor indicates that they want to decrease the budget by removing some requirements. What should the project manager do?

A. Discuss with stakeholders to determine if this scope change is feasible

B. Issue a change request to decrease the project's scope

C. Update the plan to include only the new set of requirements

D. Perform a cost-benefit analysis to determine what requirement can actually be remove

169. 在规划阶段审查项目管理计划时，发起人表示他们希望通过删除一些需求来减少预算。项目经理应该做什么？

A. 与相关方讨论，以确定此范围变更是否可行

B. 签发变更请求，以减少项目范围

C. 更新计划，仅包含新的需求集

D. 执行成本效益分析，以确定实际可以删除哪些需求

170. During the project milestone review, the project manager discusses with the project team the lessons learned from the previous phase. Because of the many technical challenges that need to be addressed and the high schedule pressures, team members expect the project manager to defer the lessons learned discussion until all project milestones have been completed. What should a project manager do?

A. Gather lessons individually with each team member after the meeting

B. Take the advice of team members and concentrate to solve technical problems and catch up with the schedule

C. Let the team focus on solving technical problems and the project manager himself update the lessons learned register

D. Creating a climate of trust and explaining lessons learned must be discussed and collected in a timely manner

170. 在项目里程碑评审期间，项目经理与项目团队讨论从上一阶段获得的经验教训。由于许多技术难题亟待解决，而且进度压力很大，所以团队成员希望项目经理将经验教训的讨论推迟到所有项目里程碑都完成之后。项目经理应该怎么做？

A. 会后向每一位团队成员单独收集经验教训

B. 采纳团队成员的建议，集中精力解决技术难题并赶上进度

C. 让团队专注解决技术难题，项目经理自己更新经验教训登记册

D. 营造信任氛围，和大家解释经验教训必须及时讨论和收集

171. The project manager needs to confirm the project requirements with several key stakeholders separately. What is the most appropriate communication method?

A. Push communication

B. Pull communication

C. Interactive communication

D. Virtual communication

171. 项目经理需要分别与多位关键相关方确认项目需求，最适合采用哪种沟通方式？

A. 推式沟通

B. 拉式沟通

C. 交互式沟通

D. 虚拟式沟通

172. The project manager is in charge of a big data project that is supported by most stakeholders but strongly opposed by a key stakeholder. What should the project manager do?

A. Ignore the opposing stakeholder and start the project

B. Ask the project sponsor to limit the objector's participation

C. Conduct stakeholder analysis to identify the main reasons for objections

D. Modify project objectives according to requirements of the opposing stakeholder

172. 项目经理在负责一个大数据项目,这个项目获得了大部分相关方的支持,只有一位关键相关方强烈反对。项目经理应该怎么做?

A. 忽略这位反对的相关方,并开始实施项目

B. 请求项目发起人限制这位反对者的参与

C. 执行相关方分析,找到其反对的主要原因

D. 根据反对的相关方的要求修改项目目标

173. As the project is about to be delivered, the project sponsor proposes to add a new feature that requires additional cost and time and affects many existing features. What should the project manager do?

A. Develop the new feature and update the requirements tracking matrix as soon as possible

B. Work with the team to assess the impact and request approval from the change control board

C. Feedback to sponsors that adding the new feature is too costly and reject the requirement

D. Ignore this requirement and continue to complete the project as planned. Perhaps the sponsor will change his mind

173. 项目即将交付,项目发起人提出增加一个新功能,这需要额外的成本和时间,并且会影响到已有的很多功能。项目经理应该怎么办?

A. 尽快开发新功能并更新需求跟踪矩阵

B. 和团队一起评估影响并请求变更控制委员会的批准

C. 向发起人反馈增加新功能代价太大并拒绝这个需求

D. 先不理会这个需求,继续按原计划完成项目,或许发起人会改变主意

174. The project manager implemented the project for a large enterprise with branches all over the country. Distributed teams often don't focus on summarizing and documenting lessons learned. What should a project manager do?

A. After the project, organize a face-to-face retrospective meeting to summarize the lessons learned

B. Arrange special members to travel to branch offices to collect lessons learned

C. Hold regular video conferences to gather information and update the lessons learned register

D. Don't worry about lessons learned as long as the project goes well

174. 项目经理为一家在全国各地都有分公司的大型企业实施项目。分布式的团队普遍不重视经验教训的总结和记录。项目经理应该怎么做？

A. 项目结束后，组织大家召开一次面对面的回顾会议，总结经验教训

B. 安排专人去各地巡回调研，收集经验教训

C. 定期召开视频会议，收集信息并更新经验教训登记册

D. 只要项目进展顺利，就不必在意经验教训

175. The project manager is in charge of a leading technology development project. The marketing department wants to work with the media to warm up the market by reporting the progress of the project in advance, but the knowledge management department stresses the need for strict protection of technical secrets and is prepared to apply for patents. What should a project manager do?

A. Cooperate with the marketing department to publicize in advance. After all, business value is the most important

B. Strictly confidential as required by the knowledge management department

C. Discuss with stakeholders to form a resolution and update the communication management plan

D. Decide which department to cooperate with according to their position in the company

175. 项目经理正在负责一个技术领先的开发项目。市场部门希望能与媒体合作，提前报道项目进展以预热市场，但是知识管理部门强调必须严格保护技术机密，并准备申请专利。项目经理应该怎么做？

A. 配合市场部门提前宣传，毕竟商业价值是最重要的

B. 按照知识管理部门的要求进行严格保密

C. 召集相关方开会讨论形成决议，并更新沟通管理计划

D. 根据这两个部门在公司里的地位决定如何与他们配合

176. The project manager is leading the team to deploy the security system for the client's servers around the world. The work is half done, and based on the trend analysis, the project should be completed within the contracted time. The manufacturer of security system released a new version at this moment, claiming it can defend against the latest deadly hacker attacks. Deploying the new version requires a rigorous testing process, and means the deployment has to start all over again. What should the project manager do?

A. Pause the deployment and start testing the new version

B. Test the new version and deploy it on the remaining unfinished servers

C. Ignore the new release and complete the deployment as planned

D. Evaluate the impact of the updated version and submit the change request

176. 项目经理正在带领团队为客户遍布全球的服务器部署安全系统，已经完成了一半的工作。根据趋势分析，团队应该可以在合同规定的时间完成项目。这时安全系统的制造商发布了新版本，声称可以防御刚刚发现的致命的黑客攻击。如果要部署新版本，团队需要经过一项一项严格的测试流程，而且意味着部署工作得全部重来。项目经理应该怎么办？

A. 暂停部署，马上开始测试新版本

B. 测试新版本并将其部署在剩下未完成的服务器上

C. 忽略新版本并按原计划完成部署

D. 评估更新版本的影响并提交变更请求

177. The project manager is responsible for a new project. The project charter and project plan have been approved. What should the project manager do next if he wants to start the project implementation?

A. Hold the project initiating meeting

B. Hold the project kick-off meeting

C. Hold the project requirements workshop

D. Hold the project planning meeting

177. 项目经理负责一个新项目，项目章程和项目计划已经获得批准。如果要开始实施项目，项目经理下一步应该做什么？

A. 召开项目启动会议

B. 召开项目开工会议

C. 召开需求研讨会

D. 召开项目规划会

178. The project manager took over a project halfway through. With only half time to the delivery date, the project performance is poor and team morale is low. The project manager organized an anonymous evaluation among team members. The results showed that many of them scored very low on each other. What should the project manager do?

A. Ask functional managers to replace a group of team members and rebuild the team

B. Conflicts between team members should be resolved by the team members themselves and the project manager should not be involved

C. Carry out team building activities and lead the team through the run-in period as soon as possible

D. Record the situation truthfully in the issue log and report to the sponsor

178. 项目经理中途接手一个项目，项目离交付日期只剩下一半的时间，项目绩效却很糟糕，团队士气低落。项目经理组织了一次团队成员之间的匿名评价，结果显示很多成员彼此之间打了非常低的分数。项目经理应该怎么办？

A. 要求各职能经理更换一批团队成员，重新组建团队

B. 团队成员之间的矛盾应该由团队成员自己解决，项目经理不应该介入

C. 开展团队建设活动，带领团队尽快度过磨合期

D. 把现状如实记录在问题日志中，并上报给发起人

179. The project budget is $1 million, the current time is more than half, the actual cost is $600,000, but only 40% of the work has been completed. The analysis found that the rework was caused by the wrong understanding of the requirements, which has been corrected. The sponsor asks what the final cost of the project will be. How should the project manager respond?

A. Calculate the estimate at completion using EAC = BAC/CPI and report to the sponsor that the final cost will exceed the budget

B. Calculate the estimate at completion using EAC = AC + (BAC–EV) and report to the sponsor that the final cost will exceed the budget

C. Improve the cost performance, correct the cost variety, report to the sponsor the final cost will not exceed the budget

D. According to the trend analysis, report to the sponsor the project will be completed ahead of schedule and within budget

179. 项目预算是 100 万美元，目前时间已经过半，实际成本是 60 万美元，但只完成了 40% 的工作。经过分析发现，对需求理解错误造成了返工，现已纠正。发起人询问项目的最终成本将会是多少，项目经理应该如何回复？

   A. 利用公式 EAC = BAC / CPI 计算出完工估算，报告给发起人，最终成本将超出预算

   B. 利用公式 EAC = AC+（BAC–EV）计算出完工估算，报告给发起人，最终成本将超出预算

   C. 改进成本绩效，纠正成本偏差，报告给发起人，最终成本不会超出预算

   D. 根据趋势分析，报告给发起人，项目将提前完工，而且成本不会超出预算

180. The project manager took over a project in the middle of the project, and he observed that the performance of the stakeholders involved in the project was very different from his own vision. He argues that those who should be active are passive and those who should be limited are active. Which of the following helps the project manager verify that his or her judgment is correct?

   A. Stakeholders register

   B. Power/interest grid

   C. Salience model

   D. Stakeholders engagement assessment matrix

180. 项目经理中途接手一个项目，他观察发现项目相关方的表现和自己的设想有很大出入，他认为应该主动参与的相关方却很消极，应该有限参与的相关方却很积极。下列哪一项有助于项目经理验证自己的判断是否正确？

   A. 相关方登记册

   B. 权力 / 利益方格

C. 凸显模型

D. 相关方参与度评估矩阵

181. The project manager is responsible for a new project and the team members are from different departments. Designers believe that discussion within the team should be face-to-face to ensure effective communication, but engineers insist that discussion should be more time-efficient and clearly documented by email. What should a project manager do?

A. Support designer's opinion, the advantage of face to face communication cannot be replaced

B. Support engineer's opinion, communication records are necessary

C. Organize team to conduct communication style assessment and determine communication rules

D. Encourage team members to communicate in the way they are used to

181. 项目经理负责一个新项目，团队成员来自不同的部门，设计师认为团队内部只有面对面讨论问题才能保障沟通效果，但是工程师坚持认为讨论问题应该通过电子邮件，这样更能节省时间，而且有沟通记录、责任清晰。项目经理应该怎么办？

A. 支持设计师的意见，当面沟通的优势无法被替代

B. 支持工程师的意见，沟通记录十分必要

C. 组织团队开展沟通风格评估并确定沟通规则

D. 鼓励团队成员按照自己习惯的方式开展沟通

182. When the project manager prepares the project schedule, he first needs to obtain all activity duration estimates. What should the project manager do?

A. Determine activity duration by referring to estimates from similar projects in the past

B. Determine the duration of each activity based on the project manager's own experience

C. Invite an external consulting team to provide a duration estimate

D. Evaluate appropriate estimation methods with the team and estimate activity duration together

182. 项目经理在编制项目进度计划时，首先要获得所有活动历时估算，项目经理应该怎么做？

A. 参考过去类似的项目估算活动历时

B. 根据自己的经验估算每项活动的历时

C. 邀请外部咨询团队给出活动历时估算

D. 与团队评估合适的估算方法并一起估算活动历时

183. The project manager is in charge of a garbage disposal project. The project was forced to suspend after a massive boycott by residents of the local community. What should a project manager do?

A. Request local police to maintain order by presenting project approval documents

B. Proactively communicate with representatives of community residents and involve them in stakeholder's participation plan

C. Project sponsors to eliminate obstacles

D. Suspend the project and collect evidence to sue the local community residents

183. 项目经理负责一个垃圾无害化处理项目，但因为遭到当地社区大批居民的抵制，项目已被迫暂停。项目经理应该怎么办？

A. 出示项目立项审批文件，请求当地警方维持秩序

B. 与社区居民代表主动沟通，并将他们纳入相关方参与计划

C. 要求项目发起人消除项目障碍

D. 中止项目，并收集证据向法院起诉当地社区居民

多选题

184. At the project planning review meeting, a number of stakeholders indicated that the schedule was too aggressive and the risk of scheduled delivery was high. They want the project manager to take measures to reduce the risk of delay. Which of the following measures can the project manager take? (Choose 3)

A. Outsource the main part of the project to a professional team

B. Adding buffers to the schedule

C. Transfer the project to a more experienced project team

D. Increase resources on critical path

E. Prioritizing projects in the company

F. Get more experienced project resources

G. Increase the reserve for delay damages

H. Purchase corresponding insurance

184. 在项目计划评审会上，多位相关方表示，进度计划过于激进，能够按期交付的风险较大。他们希望项目经理采取措施降低项目延期的风险。以下哪些是项目经理可以采取的措施？（选 3 项）

A. 将项目的主体部分外包给专业团队

B. 在进度计划中增加安全时间

C. 将项目移交给更有经验的项目团队

D. 在关键路径上增加资源

E. 提高项目在公司的优先级

F. 获取经验更加丰富的项目资源

G. 增加延期赔偿的准备金

H. 购买相应的保险

185. When a stakeholder proposed to add a new feature to the product, what steps can the project manager take if he is following the integrated change control porcedures? (Choose 4)

A. Carry out project business demonstration

B. Evaluate the impact of the change on the project

C. Update project charter

D. Determine whether the change affects baselines

E. Amendment of contract terms

F. Claim for damages

G. Obtain approval for change

H. Update project files

185. 相关方提出要在产品中增加一个新功能，项目经理如果按照整体变更控制程序，可能涉及以下哪些步骤？（选 4 项）

A. 进行项目商业论证

B. 评估变更对项目的影响

C. 更新项目章程

D. 判断变更是否影响基准

E. 修订合同条款

F. 根据损失提出索赔

G. 获得对变更的批准

H. 更新项目文件

186. After the start of the project, the change continues. What are the possible countermeasures that the project manager may adopt? (Choose 3)

A. Reserve analysis

B. Monte Carlo analysis

C. Delphi method

D. Corrective measures

E. Root cause analysis

F. Preventive measures

G. Hypothesis analysis

H. Defects remedy

186. 项目启动之后，变更持续不断。项目经理可能采用的应对措施有哪些？（选 3 项）

A. 储备分析

B. 蒙特卡洛分析

C. 德尔菲法

D. 纠正措施

E. 根本原因分析

F. 预防措施

G. 假设分析

H. 缺陷补救

187. It is clear in the project charter that integrated management is the responsibility of the project manager. What does the project manager need to integrate? (Choose 5)

A. Study various alternative options

B. Tailoring processes for achieving project objectives

C. Managing interest relations among sponsors

D. Managing the relationship between knowledge domains

E. Managing competitive relationship between suppliers

F. Resource allocation

G. Balancing competitive requirements

H. Dealing with contradictions among functional departments

187. 项目章程中明确了整合管理是项目经理的职责。项目经理主要需要整合什么？

（选 5 项）

A. 研究各种备选方法

B. 为实现项目目标裁剪过程

C. 管理发起人之间的利益关系

D. 管理知识领域之间的关系

E. 管理供应商之间的竞争关系

F. 资源分配

G. 平衡竞争性需求

H. 解决各职能部门之间的矛盾

188. The project manager is working out a configuration management plan for a software development project. What should be included? (Choose 4)

A. Version management

B. Change management

C. Resource management

D. Conflict management

E. Risk management

F. Document management

G. Processes management

H. Man hour management

188. 项目经理正在编制一个软件开发项目的配置管理计划，该计划应该包括以下哪些选项？（选 4 项）

A. 版本管理

B. 变更管理

C. 资源管理

D. 冲突管理

E. 风险管理

F. 文档管理

G. 过程管理

H. 工时管理

189. In the middle of the project, the project manager received a notice from the sponsor that the project had to be cancelled due to policy reasons. Which of the following tasks should the project manager complete? (Choose 4)

A. Complete the functions under development

B. Acceptance of final deliverables

C. Execution of project closure

D. Collate and archive experience and lessons

E. Disband the team

F. Close the procurement contracts

G. Finish the budget according to the plan

H. Complete quality inspection

189. 项目经理在项目中途接到发起人的通知，因为政策原因，项目被迫取消。项目经理应该完成以下哪几项工作？（选 4 项）

A. 正在开发中的功能

B. 使最终可交付成果获得验收

C. 执行项目收尾

D. 整理并归档经验教训

E. 解散团队

F. 关闭采购合同

G. 按计划完成预算

H. 完成质量检查

190. The company encourages all product teams to adopt the method of minimum viable product to confirm user requirements as soon as possible. Which of the following is the method of minimum viable product? (Choose 5)

A. Guarantee

B. Simulation

C. Product introduction video

D. Crowd-funding

E. Endorsement

F. Advertisement

G. Prototype

H. Open to booking

190. 公司鼓励各产品团队用最小可行产品来尽早确认用户需求。以下哪些是最小可行产品的做法？（选 5 项）

A. 担保

B. 仿真

C. 产品介绍视频

D. 众筹

E. 代言

F. 广告

G. 原型

H. 预售

191. What is the correct statement about contract closure and administrative closure? (Choose 3)

A. Start with contract closure and then start administrative closure

B. Finish the contract closure first, then finish the administration closure

C. Procurement audit is used for contract closure and review summary is used for administrative closure

D. Contract closure is external handover, and administrative closure is internal handover

E. Contract closure is the responsibility of procurement department, and administrative closure is the responsibility of project manager

 F. Both contract closure and administrative closure occur at the end of the project

 G. The contract closure shall be signed by the buyer and the administrative closure shall be signed by the project manager

 H. Settlement of contract payment belongs to contract closure, and acceptance of deliverable belongs to administrative closure

191. 关于合同收尾和行政收尾，以下说法哪些是正确的？（选 3 项）

 A. 先开始合同收尾，再开始行政收尾

 B. 先完成合同收尾，再完成行政收尾

 C. 可采用采购审计完成合同收尾，可采用回顾总结完成行政收尾

 D. 合同收尾是对公司外部的交接，行政收尾是对公司内部的交接

 E. 合同收尾是采购部门的责任，行政收尾是项目经理的责任

 F. 合同收尾和行政收尾都是在项目结束时发生的

 G. 合同收尾由买方签字确认，行政收尾由项目经理签字确认

 H. 结清合同款项属于合同收尾，验收可交付成果属于行政收尾

匹配题

192. The team has completed all the deliverable, and the project manager is preparing the closing process. Please match the correct order.

Step 1	Collection and filing of lessons learned
Step 2	Complete financial settlement and final accounts
Step 3	Final acceptance and handover of the deliverables
Step 4	Disband the team
Step 5	Satisfaction survey of stakeholders
Step 6	Closing the procurement contracts
Step 7	Archiving workflows, data, templates
Step 8	Hold a celebration

192. 团队已经完成了所有可交付成果，项目经理正在准备收尾流程。正确的匹配顺序是什么?

第 1 步	经验教训的收集和归档
第 2 步	完成项目财务结算与决算
第 3 步	可交付成果的最终验收和移交
第 4 步	解散团队
第 5 步	相关方满意度调查
第 6 步	关闭采购合同
第 7 步	归档工作流程、数据、模板
第 8 步	举行庆祝会

193. There are five common meetings in agile development process. Please match these meetings and their roles.

Backlog grooming meeting	Show the results of the sprint
Sprint planning meeting	Communicate everyone's progress
Daily stand-up meeting	Summarize the advantages and disadvantages of the work and improvement measures
Sprint review meeting	Analyze the user stories in the next sprint
Sprint retrospective meeting	Assess to-do workload and claim tasks in this sprint

193. 敏捷开发过程中有五种常见的会议，请将这五种常见的会议与它们的作用进行匹配。

待办事项整理会议	展示冲刺的工作结果
冲刺计划会议	沟通每个人的工作进度
每日站会	总结工作优缺点和改进措施
冲刺评审会议	分析下一个冲刺中的用户故事
冲刺回顾会议	评估本冲刺中待办事项的工作量并认领任务

194. In different stages of team development, project manager should adopt different leadership styles, please make the right match.

Forming stage	Participative
Storming stage	Authorized
Norming stage	Directive
Performing stage	Affective

194. 在团队发展的不同阶段，项目经理应该采取不同的领导风格，请做出正确的匹配。

形成阶段	参与型
震荡阶段	授权型
规范阶段	指令型
表现阶段	影响型

195. The project manager needs to choose the appropriate response strategy according to the specific situation of the risk. Please match the project manager's practice with the corresponding response strategy.

Avoid	The project manager added team members to ensure that the project was delivered on time
Transfer	The project manager prepares to use the contingency reserve when the risk arises
Mitigate	The project manager reported to the PMO the policy risks affecting the company's strategy
Accept	The project manager subcontracts the work that the team is not good at to a third-party professional company
Report	The project manager gave up the uncertain innovative scheme and chose the conservative one

195. 项目经理需要根据风险的具体情况选择合适的应对策略，请将项目经理的做法和对应的应对策略进行匹配。

规避	项目经理为确保项目按时交付补充了团队成员
转移	项目经理准备当风险发生时动用预留的应急储备
减轻	项目经理向 PMO 汇报了影响公司战略的政策风险
接受	项目经理把团队不擅长的工作分包给第三方专业公司
上报	项目经理放弃了没有把握的创新方案，而选择了保守方案

196. Choosing the right contract type is the key to procurement management. Which contract type should be selected in the following situations?

FP-EPA	The scale of the project is small and the scope is clear. The buyer hopes that the contract is simple and the risk is low
FPIF	The cost cannot be determined in advance, what can be determined is the fee promised by the buyer to the seller
T&M	The contract period is long, and the influence of price fluctuation on contract payment must be considered
CPFF	The cost overrun shall be shared by the buyer and the seller, and the fee shall be separately agreed
CPIF	The cost overrun shall be shared by the buyer and the seller. The fee shall be separately agreed and the maximum price shall be set
FFP	The cost is reimbursed, and the buyer promises to give award according to the seller's performance
CPAF	Workload cannot be accurately evaluated, only according to the actual use of time and materials

196. 选择合适的合同类型是采购管理的关键。针对以下情况，应该分别选择哪种合同类型？

总价加经济价格调整合同	项目规模小且范围清晰，买方希望合同简单且风险低
总价加激励费用合同	成本无法事先确定，能确定的是买方承诺给卖方的费用
工料合同	合同周期长，必须考虑物价波动对合同支付的影响
成本加固定费用合同	成本超支的部分应由买卖双方分担，费用另行约定
成本加激励费用合同	成本超支的部分应由买卖双方分担，费用另行约定，并且设置最高限价
固定总价合同	成本实报实销，买方承诺根据卖方表现给予奖励
成本加奖励费用合同	工作量无法准确评估，只能根据实际使用的人工和材料结算

填空题

197. The time of a project with a budget of 1 million US dollars is more than half, but only 40% of the task has been completed. The schedule performance index (SPI) concerned by the sponsor is _____.

197. 一个 100 万美元预算的项目，时间已经过半，但任务只完成了 40%，发起人关心的进度绩效指数（SPI）为 _____。

198. The tuition fee of the new online course is $10 per person, the cost of course development is $50,000, and each set of paper teaching materials (including freight) is $5 per person. The course can recover the cost with _____ paid learning users.

198. 新的在线课程的学费是 10 美元 / 人，课程开发成本是 5 万美元，每套纸质教材（含运费）是 5 美元 / 人，该课程要有 _____ 名付费学习用户才可以收回成本。

199. A test equipment is needed in the test phase of the project. There are two schemes, scheme A is to buy an equipment, which will cost US $55,000, and the cost of maintaining the equipment is US $500 / day; scheme B is to rent an equipment, the rent is US $3,000 / day. The expected test period is 20 days, so scheme _____ should be chosen.

199. 项目在测试阶段需要一台测试设备，有两种方案：A 方案为购买一台设备，将花费 5.5 万美元，维护设备的成本为 500 美元 / 天；B 方案为租一台设备，租金是 3 000 美元 / 天，预计测试期为 20 天，那么应该选择 _____ 方案。

200. The project manager analyzes the four main risks in the project, and their probability and impact on the project cost are shown in Table 4-5. The risk _____ has the greatest impact on the project cost.

Table 4-5 Risk Probability And Impact

Risk	A	B	C	D
Probability	30%	50%	70%	90%
Impact	0.6	0.4	0.3	0.2

200. 项目经理分析了项目中的四项主要风险，它们发生的概率和对项目成本的影响分值如表 4-5 所示，其中，对项目成本影响最大的是 _____ 风险。

表 4-5 风险发生的概率和影响

风险	A	B	C	D
概率	30%	50%	70%	90%
影响	0.6	0.4	0.3	0.2

5

PMP 模拟题
第一套答案及解析

单选题

1 B

题干中提示公司要召开的是投资评审会，说明项目还未确定是否投资，属于项目前期的准备阶段，所以公司需要的文件是项目商业论证。其他三个选项都是项目确定启动后才会产生的文件。

2 A

题干中强调了各分公司做的都是数字化转型项目，都是为了同一个战略目标。各个分公司的业务可能不一样，相互之间也不一定有关联，但是大战略下相同类型的项目所具有的很多共性问题，其处理经验可以被共享。为了更好地实现战略目标，应该有一个项目组合经理来统筹管理这些项目。

项目集经理应该管理的是相互关联、可以实现"1+1 > 2"效果的多个项目。PMO负责人通常支持和服务一个公司或一个事业部的所有项目。题干提示的信息和变更管理不吻合。因此，选项 B、C、D 都不合适。

3 C

增加成本能否带来足够的效益增加，这属于成本效益分析，是变更决策的依据。

4 A

章程中包含项目的高层级需求，如果无法准确理解，就必须与相关方反复沟通，以确认对项目需求的理解准确、完整，所以选项 A 正确。章程是编制计划的依据，对章程理解得不到位，WBS 被创建得再详细也没有用，所以选项 B 不正确。需求来自相关方，项目经理和团队闭门造车更不对。每个项目都有其独特性，不能完全参考以往其他项目的需求，所以选项D不正确。

5 B

这属于典型的需求变更，题干中也提示了如果增加这个功能将影响进度基准，所以必须由变更控制委员会做出决策。

6 D

当公司的内部资源无法满足项目需求时，应该通过采购的方式获取外部资源，但是要将原本自己开发的工作改为外包，就必须经过变更控制程序。

7 A

迭代回顾会议主要讨论本迭代中获得的经验、存在的问题、改进的思路等，这属于持续改进的过程。

8 B

虽然五大过程组之间都可能存在相互的影响，但规划和执行彼此互为输入、输出的关系最为密切。执行过程中产生的绩效数据是计划调整的依据，而新版的计划又是执行过程的输入。

9 B

供应商无法按时交付成果，这意味着项目执行和计划将出现偏差，必须经过变更控制程序来解决。

10 C

成本效益分析的指标是BCR（Benefit Cost Ratio），是效益增量和成本增量的比值。选项C中，当成本小于25万美元时，BCR大于1；当成本大于25万美元时，BCR小于1，说明25万美元是分界点，此时的成本是最优成本，其他选项都无法直接找出这个分界点。因此，选项C正确。

11 B

法规的变化属于事业环境因素的改变，会对项目产生一定的影响，团队应遵守整体变更控制程序。

12 D

裁剪是项目经理主导的工作，其根据项目的特点和需要来决定适合的裁剪对象，包括 A、B、C 三个选项。项目章程是由发起人批准发布的，一般不能轻易修改，即便必须修改，也得由发起人做出决策。

13 A

注意题干中指明是在项目启动会上，启动会通常是由发起人召集和主持并宣布项目启动。此时还没有项目计划，甚至还没有任命项目经理，所以还没有项目范围说明书，更不存在变更。此时，相关方的需求和建议应由会议主持人（项目发起人）主持讨论并决策，或者等项目启动后，在收集需求时再做记录。

14 A

净现值（NPV）是指将每年折现到项目投资时刻的收益累加之后减去投资额剩下的部分。

NPV=（10×0.909 + 10×0.826 + 10×0.752 + 10×0.685 + 10×0.621）- 35 = 2.93（万美元）

15 C

项目开工会议需要所有相关方对项目计划的理解达成一致，因此，要尽可能地让所有相关方都参加。如果相关方因特殊情况而无法参加，项目经理也应该单独与其沟通，收集他们的意见和承诺，而不能忽略任何一方。

16 D

以往类似项目中获得的教训属于组织过程资产，而事业环境因素强调项目必须遵守的法律、规章、制度、公司通用的管理流程等。

17 D

客户签署项目验收文件是项目收尾最关键的里程碑，只有客户签署了项目验收文件才意味着项目可以真正结束了。在此之前，发布项目最终报告都是不可靠的，也是不严肃的。选项 A 会造成对客户过度承诺，给自己和公司带来巨大风险。

18　C

项目进度计划需要依据章程来制定。项目商业论证、组织过程资产和事业环境因素都是制定章程的依据。

19　C

在弱矩阵组织中，项目团队成员的工作是由职能经理分配和考核的。想要改变现状，项目经理只能与该成员所在的职能部门经理沟通。不能选择选项 B 的原因是，项目经理应先积极主动地与职能经理沟通，这种方法比提升项目优先级更直接，并且项目优先级也不是谁想升级就能做到的。

20　D

项目治理框架为项目相关方提供管理项目的结构、过程、角色、职责、终责和决策模型。

21　A

原材料涨价的风险属于已知—未知风险，团队只能使用应急储备。不过启用应急储备也需要经过变更控制程序。选项 B 更换原材料往往风险更大、流程更复杂，不能轻易这样做。

22　D

资源掌握在职能经理手里、工作由职能经理分派是典型的职能型组织的特征。选项 C 虚拟型组织是指通过互联网协作的项目团队。

23　C

配置管理计划主要管理产品功能组件、过程资料文档、知识经验教训等。资源的单价和数量属于成本管理的范畴，不应纳入配置管理计划中。

24　C

项目经理获取以往做过的其他项目的资料（组织过程资产）的正规途径是通过项

目管理办公室（PMO），因为组织过程资产需要经过 PMO 的筛选、整理、评估、裁剪及保密设定。请教以前项目的成员应获得 PMO 的许可，且只能作为补充手段。

25　A

信息系统升级是一个项目集，客户关系管理软件是该项目集中的一个项目，共享模块也会影响项目集中的其他项目。按照整合式风险管理的原则，共性的风险应该上报给项目集经理。

26　C

项目管理办公室（PMO）通常是确定公司项目优先级的部门，而项目组合经理负责已经确定了优先级的同一组合里的项目。

27　C

新设备对项目绩效非常有利，但供应商不在合格供应商清单中，所以该问题不是简单变更供应商就可以解决的，需要上报给高层管理者，比如 PMO，由其进行专项讨论并做出决策。

28　C

题干中只要有"偏差""绩效衡量"这样的关键词，我们就可以确定项目是在监控过程组。

29　C

"某个相关方对报告不满意"属于相关方参与计划管理的范畴，如果是相关方普遍不满意，而且是共性问题，那么需要审查和优化沟通管理计划。

30　A

团队成员先发现了问题，又经过努力解决了问题，虽然没有造成更大的影响，但是低估了活动的难度，所以可以将其作为一个教训记录下来，避免以后再次发生。团队成员可以直接记录经验教训。

31 A

每日站会的目的就是为了团队成员了解彼此的进展和困难。这道题考核的是对敏捷常见会议的概念的理解。

32 B

选项 B 项目范围说明书是用来定义范围的输出，属于规划过程组中的工作，其余选项都属于启动过程组中的工作。

33 D

就事论事的冲突属于良性冲突，不用限制和回避，应该积极主动地面对。与发生冲突的双方开诚布公地讨论解决问题的措施就是正确的选择。

34 D

注意题干强调的是变更即将发生，也就意味着还没发生。此时，项目经理必须关注变更的影响范围，因为一个变更往往会引发其他的连锁变更反应。为了避免项目失控，项目经理的重点工作就是避免不必要的变更。

35 D

项目经理从大局出发，强迫技术团队收回使用新技术的提议。虽然技术团队的感受可能不好，但项目经理采用该方法迅速解决了这个冲突。这是强迫/命令的冲突解决方法。

36 D

题干中提示修改活动的估算时间会导致整个项目延期，说明会影响进度基准。影响基准的变更都需要经过 CCB 批准。

37 A

提升团队绩效最直接、有效的方法就是集中办公（War Room）。团队成员在一起工作，除了可以提升氛围、方便沟通，也能加速磨合，快速度过塔克曼阶梯理论中的"形成—磨合—规范"阶段，到达绩效水平最高的表现阶段。

38 D

返工不在计划内，就需要走变更控制程序。不管是谁的责任，都要先评估影响，走变更控制程序。

39 B

帕累托原理告诉我们，20% 的原因导致了 80% 的问题，所以，只要我们找到并解决了少数原因导致的问题，就能解决大部分问题。

40 B

主动与相关方沟通变更的影响，确定变更必要性并履行变更控制程序是处理这类问题的标准做法。

41 D

虽然离职人员负责的工作有 3 天的总浮动时间，但不能说只要 3 天内找到替补的成员就不会对进度计划产生任何影响。这样做会使进度计划中原路径的浮动时间减少，这就是影响，所以选项 B 不正确。再争取出 3 天的浮动时间，也只是浮动时间变多了，没有接替的人，还是会影响项目进度计划的，所以选项 C 不正确。离职人员负责的工作延误 3 天以上，路径上的总浮动时间被耗尽，该路径就成为关键路径，同时总工期也延长了。所以，只有选项 D 是正确的。

42 D

与变更相关的考题，"评估影响—获得批准"是标准选项。如果没有更具针对性且把握更大的选项的话，这个选项往往就是正确的。

43 D

题干表明，该相关方权力大但兴趣低，属于权力 / 利益矩阵中第二象限的相关方。因为项目和他的利益关系不密切，所以通常他的要求也不会太多。在相关方参与计划中，要尽量满足他的要求，以确保其满意。而且，最好不要改变他的参与状态，避免因其过度参与项目而给项目经理带来更多的沟通压力。

44　D

按照变更控制程序，执行更新的计划前必须先通知相关方，请相关方做出相应的调整。

45　A

项目经理在冲突中利用自己的职位和权力强制取消新功能在本轮的发布。虽然市场经理可能不满意，但这么做是为了避免造成更加恶劣的影响，这属于冲突解决方法中的强迫/命令。

46　D

通过测试不能代表验收全部完成，有必须修复的问题仍然在变更控制范围内，所以要按变更控制程序执行。

47　A

项目沟通管理计划中定义了沟通的路径和原则。按照常规，发起人不应该直接去影响和指挥团队成员的工作，所以，项目经理应该利用沟通管理计划去纠正发起人的这种不适当的做法。但与发起人沟通需要注意方式方法，使用人际关系技能是指尽量采用发起人容易接受的方式来达到沟通的目的。

48　A

只要是在计划发布之后、项目验收之前，增加新功能都属于变更。无论CCB最终接受还是拒绝，项目经理都应该发起变更请求，按照变更控制程序来进行决策。

49　C

这道题可采用排除法做答。A、B、D三个选项都无法赶上进度。只有选项C正确，通过资源优化中的资源平滑法调动非关键路径上的活动资源，并用其支援关键路径上的活动，以实现工期压缩。

50′　A

范围管理计划是指如何管理范围的规则文件。范围基准是对项目包含的工作内容的具体描述，包括项目范围说明书、WBS和WBS词典。

51 D

不在项目范围说明书中的功能都不应该去开发。如果团队认为特别有必要，也必须事先经过变更控制程序才能将其补充到范围说明书中。这个规则必须向团队成员说明。

52 D

项目计划既不能太粗略，也不能过于细致，同时详细程度不应该因人而异。滚动式规划指的是对近期工作详细描述、对远期工作粗略描述，并且随着项目的进展，获取的信息越来越丰富，进而一次次逐渐细化的规划方法。

53 C

节约出来的资源不能被直接用于范围之外的工作。如果确实有必要开发新功能，也必须走变更控制程序。

54 A

关键路径就是浮动时间最少的路径，所以题干里的信息提示，这种方法就是关键路径法。

55 D

名义小组的特点就是参会者互不干扰、独立思考、独立发表见解，并投票表决出最优方案。

56 B

当发生影响项目计划的问题时，应该通过变更控制程序来决定应对方案。

57 B

因为项目收尾的优先级高于新项目，所以项目经理应该善始善终，先做好上一个项目的收尾工作。

58 D

期望值 $T_e = (O + 4M + P)/6 = (4 + 4 \times 7 + 16)/6 = 8$；标准差 $\sigma = (P - O)/6 =$

（16 - 4）/6 = 2

59 D

项目经理应该首先尊重团队的意见。检查次数是否过多，需要与质量保证部门一起分析质量管理计划是否需要调整。

60 B

首先，能够有把握说活动顺延两周而不影响总工期，我们从中可以判断出，这项活动肯定在非关键路径上，因为关键路径上的活动一旦顺延，总工期一定相应顺延；其次，这项活动的浮动时间如果大于两周，就可以包容两周的顺延时间而不改变路径的长度，所以总工期暂时不会受到影响。

61 B

项目经理可以建议团队为后序工作设置提前量。比如，把FS的逻辑改为"FS-3"，也就是说，后序工作提前3天开始，与前序工作并行3天，这样可以有效压缩项目进度。

62 B

虽然关键路径上的活动的浮动时间最少，但不代表其不可以被压缩。而且，只有优先对关键路径上的活动下手，压缩工期才会有效。

63 A

如果同时进行由相同资源负责的活动，就会导致资源过载，也就是超出这个开发人员的承受范围。这时需要考虑将同时进行的活动的时间错开，变成按先后顺序进行，这样就可以解决资源过载的问题，这个方法就是资源平衡。但需要注意的是，将活动并行改为按顺序进行，很可能会导致项目总工期延长。

64 C

题干指出，开发工程师数量不足，而测试工程师有富余。项目经理应该优先考虑增加测试资源，通过赶工压缩测试时间，为开发争取更多的时间，这样就可以对开发阶段进行资源平衡，解决开发资源不足的问题。

65　B

疫情影响是风险，需要先评估风险对项目的影响。下一步应该走变更控制程序，以获得 CCB 对应对措施的批准。

66　A

根据图 5-1 我们可以看出，A—D—E 是关键路径。压缩工期首先要从关键路径下手，关键路径上有 A、D、E 三项活动，应该压缩哪个呢？

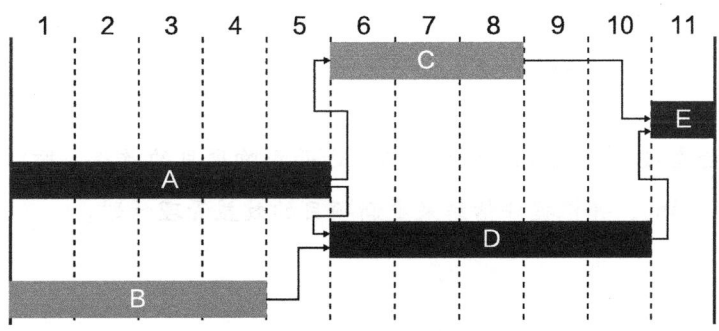

图 5-1　甘特图（压缩工期前）

活动 E 只有 1 周，再压缩 1 周是不可能的。活动 A 和活动 D，不管压缩哪个，都可以实现工期缩短 1 周。这种情况下，应该压缩先发生的活动，那就是活动 A，如图 5-2 所示。

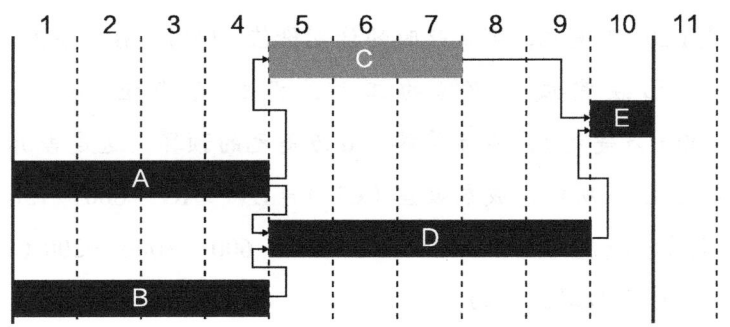

图 5-2　甘特图（压缩工期后）

这样安排，活动 D 还有机会留在以后有需要的时候再压缩，否则先压缩活动 D 的话，错过了活动 A，就再没有机会压缩活动 A 了。需要注意的是，压缩活动 A 后，活动 B 也在关键路径上了。

67 B

针对地震这种风险，它的概率和影响都有历史经验和数据可以参考。采取定量分析可以更科学地做出投资决策。

68 B

应急储备包含在成本基准中，由项目经理掌握，并面向已知—未知风险；而管理储备专门用于应对未知—未知风险，不归项目经理掌握，也不包含在成本基准中。因此，只有选项 B 正确。

69 A

税率变化会直接影响项目的采购成本，进而影响项目的效益，所以项目经理应该评估税率变化的影响，并根据评估结果更新项目的效益管理计划。

70 C

选项 A，已完成工作的成本是实际成本（AC）；选项 B，已完成工作的价值是挣值（EV）；选项 D，预测完成项目还将需要的成本是完工尚需估算（ETC）。

71 D

计划工期是 12 个月，已经过去 8 个月，按计划，项目应该进展三分之二，完工预算（BAC）是 1 200 万美元，那么此时的计划价值（PV）= BAC × 2/3 = 1 200 × 2/3 = 800（万美元）；已经完成了 50% 的工作，意味着挣值（EV）= BAC × 50% = 1 200 × 50% = 600（万美元）；实际花掉 750 万美元的预算，这是告诉我们实际成本（AC）= 750（万美元）。所以，成本偏差（CV）= EV − AC = 600 − 750 = −150（万美元），代表成本超支；进度偏差（SV）= EV − PV = 600 − 800 = −200（万美元），代表进度落后。所以，选项 D 是正确的。

72 D

CV = EV − AC = 350 − 400 = − 50

SV = EV − PV = 350 − 300 = 50

73 C

偏差是由于关税上涨引起的，而且题干中强调关税维持高水平，也就是说，这属于典型偏差，后期无法纠正。还需多少成本指的是完工尚需估算（ETC）。完工预算（BAC）= 200（万美元），完成了 40% 的工作，那么 EV = BAC × 40% = 200 × 40% = 80（万美元）；用掉了 50% 的成本，那么 AC = BAC × 50% = 200 × 50% = 100（万美元）。由此得出成本绩效指数（CPI）= EV/AC = 80/100 = 0.8，完工估算（EAC）= BAC/CPI = 200/0.8 = 250 万美元，ETC = EAC − AC = 250 − 100 = 150（万美元）。所以，选项 C 是正确的。

74 B

BAC = 100，前三个月 PV = 50（万美元），AC = 60（万美元），EV = 100 × 40% = 40 万美元。预测完成项目的总成本是计算完工估算（EAC），按照当前的绩效水平预测，也就是说，在未来的工作中，不需要修正成本绩效水平。所以先计算 CPI，CPI = EV/AC = 40/60 = 2/3，那么 EAC = BAC/CPI = 100/（2/3）= 150（万美元）。

75 C

题干给出了不同项目的商业价值和开发周期，我们应该综合考虑这两个因素。从原则上来讲，商业价值越高越好，开发周期越短越好，所以，项目的优先级分数与商业价值成正比，与开发周期成反比。用每个项目的商业价值除以开发周期，所得的分数就可以作为优先级的判断依据。通过计算得出，编号为 20124 的项目的优先级分数 = 商业价值 / 开发周期 = 10/6 = 1.67（百万美元 / 月），其余项目的比值均小于这个数值。因此，选项 C 是正确的。

76 A

SPI 和 CPI 都小于 1，说明进度延误，同时成本超支。只有关键路径上的工作延误了，必须投入更多的资源赶工，才能解释这个状况，所以选项 A 是符合的。选项 B，项目资源减少可能导致进度变慢，但是成本并不一定增加，反而可能减少；选项 C，购买了更贵、更先进的工具，虽然成本增加了，但效率也提升了，进度应该更快；选项 D，需求发生了改变，意味着工作量可能增加也可能减少，没有追加预算意味着也可能并不需要对预算进行增加。

77 D

本题考核的是负面风险（威胁）的应对策略（规避、转移、减轻、接受和上报），可采用排除法。题干中明确提示风险无法避免，所以规避可排除；风险无法控制，所以减轻可排除；风险无法转移，所以转移可排除。那么只剩下接受和上报两种策略。题干中提示该项目存在严重风险而且需要额外的资金，所以项目经理不能自作主张选择接受，应及时上报给高级管理层，正确选项为D。选项B使用应急储备似乎也是合理的，但题干中没有给出风险影响的量化评估，我们无从知晓应急储备是否足够应对风险。也就是说，该项目缺乏动用应急储备的条件。而且，我们从题干表述的内容可以分析出本题考核的是风险应对策略，选项B使用应急储备和选项C执行定性分析，都不属于风险应对策略。

78 B

管理质量又称质量保证（QA）。针对质量管理过程的有效性，我们在执行过程中可能发现优化的机会，这就是过程改进的含义。

79 A

关税通常相对稳定，突然发生变化说明是未知—未知风险，极端变化表明关税对项目的影响很大。应对这种风险，要么动用管理储备，要么修改成本基准增加预算，这取决于对变更影响的评估，而且变更应对措施需要通过变更控制程序得到批准。

80 C

控制图的规则是只要出现以下几种情况，就需要找到根本原因并排除：（1）连续七点在均值一侧；（2）连续七点呈单调上升或下降趋势；（3）数据点出现在控制线之外。

81 D

分析产品质量与不同变量之间的相关性，需要用到散点图，其他选项中的工具都没有这个用途。

82 B

标准差 σ 是衡量概率分布曲线的"胖瘦"，也就是概率分布数据与均值（期望值）

的离散程度。

83　B

如果有检测数据出现在控制线之外，即便它还在规格线以内，它也符合质量标准，不影响出厂。但因为它已经触发了控制图中的控制门槛，所以必须停下来找到原因并消除掉才可以继续生产。控制门槛还包括连续七点在均值一侧，或连续七点持续上升或下降。

84　B

戴明的 PDCA 循环就是持续质量改进的核心。

85　C

注意题干中提示团队冲突在减少，成员之间开始彼此接受并互动配合对方，说明目前团队处于塔克曼阶梯理论的规范阶段。项目经理在规范阶段应该采取参与型的领导风格，逐步放权给团队成员，必要时参与团队的决策。

86　B

团队成员的培训由谁负责，取决于需要培训的内容。项目管理的知识和技能应该由项目经理负责，业务技术和专业技能应该由他的职能经理负责，公司管理规章制度等应该由人力资源部负责。当然，安排满足项目工作要求的资源是以上所有管理者的共同责任。

87　D

无论是删除这些功能，还是补充资源完成这些功能，都需要评估其对项目的影响，并启用变更控制程序。

88　D

用户满意度往往是项目的绩效指标。团队绩效评估针对的是团队建设的有效性，改进团队绩效可以提升项目绩效。

89 D

语言障碍和文化差异都很难通过短期学习来弥补，把工作分包出去也不能很好地解决这个问题，并且增加了其他风险。项目经理应该做的就是引进专家，因此，选项 D 最合理。

90 D

通过团队的表现，我们可以看出团队进入了震荡阶段，项目经理应该采取的领导风格是影响型，即斡旋和调解，通过自身的影响力帮助团队尽快走出震荡阶段。

91 A

注意题干中给出项目是在商业论证阶段，也就是前期准备阶段，是否做这个项目还不一定，因此，估算不需要太精细。题干中还提示，项目经理能获得的只有以前做过的类似项目的成本估算，很显然，参照以前的项目，用类比估算是最佳选项。

92 C

项目章程对项目经理有明确授权，项目资源的调配和工作的分配是项目经理的权力，发起人无权越俎代庖，直接指挥团队成员。

93 C

团队成员应该做什么工作不能根据自己的兴趣来选择，而是由项目计划决定，所以项目经理必须纠正这个行为，不能造成范围蔓延。

94 A

集中办公（War Room）对于促进团队磨合和提升团队沟通效率是最有效的，其他方式难以替代。

95 D

敏捷开发的原则是文档尽量精简，一切不为用户创造价值的活动都是浪费，所以文档规范不是敏捷开发的原则。

96 B

应急计划、弹回计划、权变措施（除了紧急情况下的已授权的自动权变之外）在实施前都需要经过变更控制程序，并获得批准。

97 A

项目经理组织团队成员分析了疫情的影响并做出了应对计划，并在疫情发生时启用了这个应对计划，这属于应急计划；权变措施的特征是事先没计划，当有情况发生时需要随机应变，临时想办法；弹回计划是放弃项目原目标，尽量减少损失，体面收场，属于撤退计划；选项 D 减轻风险是最容易混淆的选项，虽然"减轻风险"看上去没有错，居家办公的确减轻了被感染的风险，但这道题重点提示的是事先做出了应对计划，所以我们可以判断出题人想考核的是对应急计划的理解。因此，选项 A 更符合题意。

98 D

停止接受新增功能的需求，意味着这类风险来源被阻断，属于风险规避；申请增加预算以引进更多的测试资源，可以减轻测试进度的压力，属于风险减轻。

99 B

进度和成本的权重比为 3 : 1，每个风险都应该用"（对进度的影响 ×3 倍的权重 + 对成本的影响）× 风险概率"这个公式计算评分。经计算，我们可以得出，风险 B 评分最高。

100 A

如图 5-3 所示，通过决策树分析，分别计算每个方案成功的收益和失败的损失。省的钱就是收益，取正值；增加的钱就是损失，取负值。最终选择预期货币价值（EMV）高的方案。

101 C

供应商中途涨价，这对项目而言是一个变更，首先应考虑走变更控制程序。其他可供判断的辅助信息是原材料大幅涨价，这个情况是客观的，供应商无法承担这个压力，宁可选择违约。也就是说，即便换一家供应商，也难以绕开原材料涨价的问题。

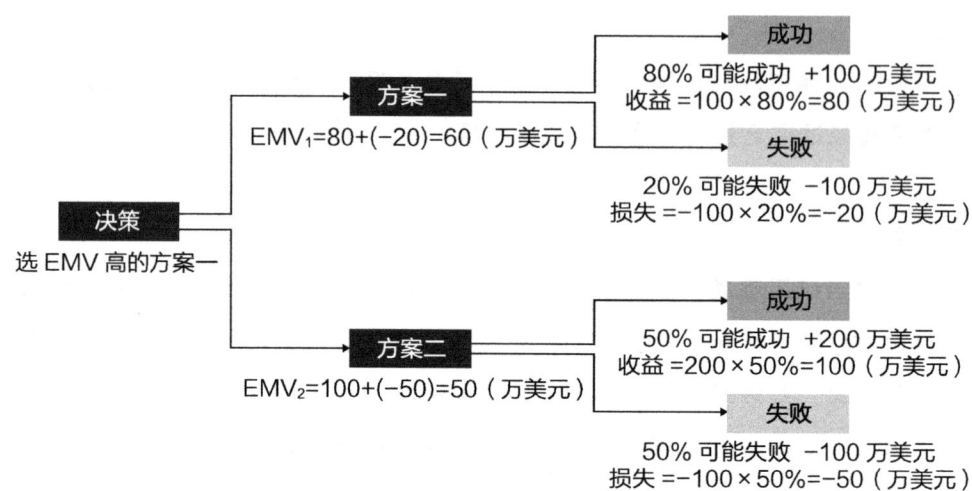

图 5-3　决策树分析

所以项目经理应该客观面对这种情况，主动通过变更化解其对项目的影响。

102　B

对于买方来说，总价类合同比成本补偿类合同风险小，并且总价类合同中固定总价合同风险最小。需要说明的是，风险指的是不确定性，固定总价合同对买方来说几乎没有不确定性。工料合同适合工作内容简单、工作范围明确，但工作量无法事先准确判断的情况。

103　A

当合同双方有分歧时，双方坐下来谈判是最优选择，既不会让冲突升级，又简单、高效，还能保密。

104　B

成本都可以报销的就是成本补偿类合同，买卖双方根据节约的成本按比例分享。根据以上特征，我们可以判断买卖双方签订的是成本加激励费用合同。

105　B

按照成本加激励费用合同的支付规则，合同款 = 实际成本 + 目标费用 −（实际成本 − 预算）× 卖方分担或分享的比例 = 450 + 100 −（450 − 500）× 20% = 560（万美元）。

106　A

　　将原计划自己完成的部分工作改为外包，首先需要走变更控制程序。在签订合同之前，投标人会议和独立估算是开标前的工作，中标后、签订合同前需要进行合同谈判，以明确卖方对合同要求都理解得准确、完整。既然团队已经决定外包，自制外购分析是决定外包之前已完成的工作；采购审计和采购绩效审查是控制采购过程中的工作，不在签订合同之前。因此，选项 A 是正确的。

107　D

　　题干中告知项目经理与分包商签署的是成本加固定费用合同，因此，增加的成本均由项目经理这一方（买方）承担。但是项目经理与客户签署的是总价加激励费用合同，成本超出预算，项目经理这一方（卖方）也要分担超支部分，而且有天花板价格限制，如果合同款超出天花板价格，那么多余的部分都由卖方承担。这意味着变更导致的成本增加会直接影响项目经理这一方的利润。但本题考核的是职业道德，做项目应该本着价值交付的原则，以为客户创造价值为使命，即便这样做会牺牲己方利益。因此，项目经理应该积极接受这个变更，通过变更控制程序，并获得批准。当然，客户如果通情达理，愿意在变更中予以补偿，那更理想。

108　B

　　变更控制委员会（CCB）的决议就是权威结论。如果 CCB 否决了变更，项目经理正确的做法应该是记录并告知相关方。

109　B

　　针对大型项目采取敏捷开发，需要各 Scrum 团队派代表组成 "Scrum of Scrums"，定期召开例会，内容类似 Scrum 团队内部的每日站会，交流各团队工作进展。所以选项 B 团队所剩资源不应是这样的会议上讨论的内容。

110　A

　　相关方分析是对识别出的相关方进行权力、态度、影响阶段等信息的分析。做好相关方分析，并管理相关方参与可有效避免出现题干中的情况。

111　C

最小可行产品（MVP）的原则就是用最快的速度拿出一个可以验证用户需求的产品，甚至是模型。产品肯定需要一步步不断根据用户反馈来完善，所以不可能做到一步到位，一次就确保工作都做对。

112　D

凸显模型就是综合分析相关方权力、紧迫性和合法性，确定相关方需要被关注的优先级，以及管理相关方参与的策略。

113　D

冲刺评审会的目的就是向产品经理展示、验证本轮冲刺完成的可交付成果是否符合要求且确实可用。

114　C

配置管理系统除了产品的功能、组件和版本信息之外，对项目管理的计划、文件也需要定义版本、受控级别、访问权限、修改规则等。

115　D

根据双因素理论，选项 B、C 中提到的都是保健因素，也就是必须提供的条件，若不提供，员工就会不满意；若提供了，员工也不会更满意。选项 A 只是承诺物质激励，并不能满足题干中提到的员工缺乏成就感和被认同的需求。根据马斯洛需求层次理论，被尊重的需求层次高于物质需求；根据题干强调的内容，员工当前主要的需求是获得别人的认同，以及自己获得成就感。只有选项 D 给予更具挑战的机会和适时的鼓励才能有效激励这位团队成员。

116　C

项目管理团队特指帮助项目经理共同完成项目计划、控制等管理活动的成员。大型项目的管理团队成员可能是全职做项目管理的，小型项目的管理团队成员也需要承担项目活动。项目管理团队是项目团队的一部分。

117　C

因为发起人根据市场情报，提出停止某些用户故事的开发，所以项目经理必须重视，与产品负责人（Product Owner）重新确认这些用户故事是否还具有优先级。如果将这些用户故事的优先级调低，那么该团队应该腾出精力开发优先级更高的用户故事。

118　B

制造业产品研发项目一般使用质量功能展开（QFD，一种引导技术）来识别相关方对产品的需求。

119　D

客户有时并不能确定自己到底想要什么。在这种情况下，项目经理应该采用原型法，做出一个形象直观的产品原型，演示给用户看，让用户体验，从而引导用户表达出真实的需求。

120　A

风险的变化对项目最终绩效的影响程度是指因变量（项目最终绩效）对自变量（各种风险）的敏感性。根据敏感性进行从高到低排序就是敏感性分析。

121　A

团队沟通和配合中存在的问题，以及相应的改进方案都应该在回顾会议上讨论。

122　C

敏捷开发中一般不接受在当前冲刺中添加新任务，但是如果遇到特殊情况，如紧急、重要且优先级非常高的任务是可以接受的，这是敏捷的优势。敏捷开发中是否添加新功能不是由敏捷专家（Scrum Master）批准，而是由团队讨论决定，必要时采取投票方式。

123　C

聚焦在能够达成共识的部分，而不是存在分歧的部分，属于冲突解决策略中的缓和/包容。存在分歧的部分不是被双方接受了，只是双方先把注意力集中在没有分歧的部分，所以这种冲突解决的策略不是妥协/调解。

124 B

敏捷开发中新功能是否纳入当前迭代，需要根据新功能的优先级决定。产品待办事项列表（Product Backlog）中的优先级是由产品负责人（Product Owner）维护的，是否纳入本迭代中是由团队讨论决定的。

125 C

当风险发生，导致原冲刺中的工作无法开展时，团队应该及时重新规划本冲刺，置换其他工作。

126 B

团队有新成员加入，将重新经历"震荡—规范—表现"阶段，除非这些新成员和老成员曾经多次合作过。

127 B

用户故事描述应该符合 DEEP 原则，即详略适当的（Detailed Appropriately）、经过估算的（Estimated）、涌现的（Emergent，即在列表中可以增加、删除和动态调整优先级）、按优先级排序（Prioritized）。该原则没有要求颗粒度必须小到一个人独立完成。

128 A

敏捷开发管控进度的工具是燃尽图或燃起图。只要实际上燃尽（起）线没有太偏离参考线，就说明进度正常。

129 D

敏捷团队强调自组织、去中心化。也就是说，团队并不向某一个固定的角色负责，有分歧也不是靠某个固定的角色来决策，而是在团队成员充分讨论的基础上经过民主投票表决。

130 B

敏捷开发的特征之一是关注技术卓越和良好设计。其余选项都正好和敏捷的特征相反。

131　A

自组织团队的特征就是没有"领导"，既不需要组织任命，也不需要团队推举。自组织强调去中心化、团队民主、激发每个人的潜能。在敏捷团队中，成员不需要向敏捷专家（Scrum Master）或者产品负责人（Product Owner）汇报工作，项目方案、团队分歧等也不是由他们进行决策，而是由团队成员民主表决。

132　A

成本效益分析是项目商业论证中的财务评价方法。在商业论证阶段，项目还未正式立项，所以选项 B、C、D 还没有产生。

133　A

题干中提示项目经理是依靠自己的专业能力赢得了团队成员的尊重和信任，所以项目经理使用的是专家权力，属于项目经理自身拥有的，而不是组织授予的权力。

134　D

在领导力的习惯中，并没有要求领导者去替团队成员完成他们无法完成的工作，而是鼓励、引导团队成员挖掘自己的潜力，并提升自己解决问题的能力。

135　D

影响持反对态度的相关方不仅要靠项目经理的沟通能力，还需要动员支持项目的相关方，借助他们的力量去影响和改变持反对意见的相关方，从而使他们转变态度。

136　A

不要把每日站会作为一天的开始，可以让团队成员先处理自己的工作，理清今天的工作目标，找到工作中的障碍。比如，可以将每日站会设置在上午 10 点或 11 点。每日站会要保持每天在同一时间、同一地点召开，需要营造仪式感并体现规范性。除此之外，每日站会要求团队成员都要参加，时长不超过 15 分钟。

137　D

虽然应急计划在事先规划项目的时候就已经完成，但是当风险发生，要启用应急计划时，必须经过整体变更控制程序。

138　A

已经发生的项目事故属于问题，该问题及其处理过程需要被记录。因此，当发现相同特征的类似事故时，项目经理应该查阅问题日志。

139　B

合作/解决的特点是双方都满意，有些冲突可能存在双方都满意的机会，需要双方积极探讨才能挖掘出来。合作/解决是效果最好、最持久，同时也是双赢的冲突解决方法。

140　C

工作绩效报告是项目经理创建的向相关方报告项目绩效状况的文件。

141　A

电机、电池、电控三个项目分属三个团队，这三个团队之间必须密切配合，所以需要有人进行整体协调，这个人就是项目集经理。

142　D

这道题的关键信息是"项目启动会"。项目启动会是讨论并发布项目章程的会议，章程未发布，意味着项目还没启动，更不会有计划和基准。这个阶段有任何新需求都可以提出，因为此时还没有变更管理计划，所以不需要经过变更控制程序。项目启动会由发起人主持，新需求是否纳入项目由发起人组织讨论或由发起人直接进行决策。

143　D

交付成果得到客户的认可和接受，这属于范围确认，应该分期、分批地在日常的工作中完成，不能堆积到最终的验收阶段。

144　B

当项目已经完成收尾，团队也已经解散时，项目无法接受需求变更。在答复客户之前，首席运营官首先要查阅当时的客户验收文件，即对这个可交付成果的验收记录。如果验收过程严谨有效，客户也签署了验收文件，原则上乙方公司就没有责任。即便确有质量缺陷，也应按照合同规定的运营期的质保条款履行质保义务，而履行质保义务并不属于项目变更。

145　D

通过质量检查只能代表结果合格，如果客户不放心，那么还需要确认质量管理过程的合规性，这就需要有质量保证的方法，通过质量审计，保证质量管理过程符合质量管理计划。

146　B

引导式研讨会的特征是由主持人引导来自跨部门、跨专业的参会者，并收集他们的需求。

147　C

"不能及时得到项目的相关信息"不是所有相关方的共性问题，所以不属于沟通管理计划的问题。每个相关方都有其个性化的需求，对项目的参与意愿和参与程度都不同，所以应该根据相关方登记册记录的相关方的特点编制相关方参与计划，以满足不同相关方的个性化需求。

148　B

范围说明书中记录的是要完成的可交付成果及其验收标准。

149　D

不同的相关方参与项目的程度不同，项目经理需要判断每个项目相关方当前的参与程度和期望他参与的程度，并找到差距，做出针对性的努力。这需要用相关方参与程度评估矩阵来管理。

150　B

当可交付成果完成时，应及时"确认范围"，确认范围是为了得到客户对可交付成果的认可。在项目快结束时发现客户认为可交付成果不符合需求，一定是之前"确认范围"出了问题。

151　D

如果相关方参与项目的程度和发表意见的机制没有得到任何规划和限制，往往会导致众口难调、决策效率低下的问题。项目经理应该根据项目的客观需要来编制相关方参与计划，主动管理相关方的期望和参与。比如，严格限制参与计划评审的与会者，并事先规定讨论流程和决策机制。

152　D

活动历时 3～5 天都不影响项目总工期，首先说明这项活动有浮动时间，应该在非关键路径上。而且，2 天的浮动时间不会影响项目总工期，说明这 2 天是总浮动时间；而如果这 2 天是自由浮动时间，那么我们可以得出的是该活动的历时不影响后续工作开始时间的结论。

153　B

成本偏差（CV）＝挣值（EV）－实际成本（AC）＝20（万美元），说明实际成本比挣值少 20 万美元；进度偏差（SV）＝挣值（EV）－计划值（PV）＝-30（万美元），说明计划值比挣值多 30 万美元。由此可以得出，与计划值相比，截至目前实际成本少花了 50 万美元。本题考核的是对计划值、实际成本、挣值的准确理解和对成本偏差、进度偏差的熟悉程度。在实际的挣值分析中，我们并不直接比较计划值和实际成本的差异。

154　D

蒙特卡洛技术是通过模拟各种风险组合以及每种风险发生的概率来估算不同情况下项目需要的成本或工期。

155　A

增加人员施行倒班制可以充分利用设备，实现人换设备不停，但是会增加人员成本（如加班费和夜班补贴等）。所以我们需要做成本效益分析，看节省的租赁费（效益）能否覆盖增加的人员成本。

156　A

因为预算有限，所以选项C增加人手不现实。因为要将项目拉回正轨，所以选项B增加时间不合理。因为没有经过变更控制程序获得CCB的批准，所以选项D随意放弃一部分工作是不可能的。项目经理只有利用资源平滑技术把非关键路径上的资源临时调到关键路径上，才能赶回工期。

157　C

根据当前绩效预测未来的状况属于趋势分析。要想打消发起人的顾虑，项目经理就得用趋势分析，用客观、具体的数字证明现在的偏差是能够在未来被纠正的，而且项目成本不会突破预算。所以，只有选项C最符合题意。

158　C

所有的审计都是面向"过程合规"，质量审计就是确认质量管理过程是否符合质量管理计划。

159　D

进度提前一周，只有四种思路：（1）追加资源赶工；（2）快速跟进活动；（3）抽调非关键路径上的资源，以支援关键路径，属于资源平滑；（4）缩小范围。选项B和C都是思路（1），因为不管加班还是加人，都属于增加资源投入。选项A把冲刺周期由两周改为一周，不但不能提前完成开发工作，还会增加更多的会议时间。题干中明确告知该项目团队是敏捷团队，所以人员规模是固定的，能变的只有项目范围，也就是选项D，把优先级相对低的需求从本冲刺退回到产品待办事项列表中。

160　A

人员遣散计划是由项目经理编制的团队成员完成项目任务后可以离开团队的时间计划，有利于资源经理及时安排资源到其他项目任务上。为什么答案不是选项B资源日历？因为资源日历是团队成员向项目经理提供的，用于查阅该成员已经被占用的时间，据此，项目经理才能根据资源日历评估分配给该成员的任务需要多长时间完成。

161　D

中途变更开发工具是存在风险的，需要评估影响并经过整体变更控制程序。

162　A

缓和 / 包容是迁就对方，为了缓和双方的关系而牺牲自己的诉求来包容对方，合作 / 解决是找到双方都满意的解决方案；妥协 / 调解是双方各让一步，以求达成共识；撤退 / 回避是从冲突中暂时退出，搁置争议。

163　C

对于特殊的相关方，沟通效果最好的方式就是交互式沟通，即有问有答、有来有往，可以及时确认沟通效果和调整沟通尺度；推式沟通和拉式沟通都属于单向沟通，效果差，适合面向有大量受众的沟通场景；选项 D 垂直沟通是指上下级之间的沟通，和前三个选项不可比较。

164　B

因为技术骨干有可能被抽调走，这对项目 A 而言是一个风险，所以，项目 A 的项目经理首先应该更新的是风险登记册。

165　D

帕累托图也称二八原理，可以帮助我们识别并聚焦在少数关键原因上，从而解决大部分的问题。

166　A

虽然谈判是解决争议的最优先的选择，但题干提示双方已多次谈判无效，那么替代争议解决（ADR）就是正确选择。比起诉讼和仲裁，ADR 简便得多，而且诉讼是公开的，不符合题意。

167　D

投标人会议的目的是澄清招标文件中的内容，以确保各家潜在供应商都能准确、完整地把握，而且要体现招标过程的公平、公正、公开，所以召开投标人会议是正确选择。因为还没有到审查建议书和合同谈判的阶段，所以一对一会议不适合。

168 A

凸显模型是通过权力、合法性和紧迫性三个维度对相关方进行分析的，确定哪些相关方应该被优先关注，并避免触发相关方凸显性升级的条件。所以，选项A最符合题意。

169 A

此题的重点信息是"在规划阶段"。在讨论并编制计划时，因为计划还没有确定，所以不需要走变更控制程序，发起人的建议可以经过讨论并直接用于计划的生成。

170 D

经验教训必须及时获取，需要持续在项目全过程中讨论和收集。

171 C

确认需求是非常重要的事，需要逐一反复探讨确认。因此，交互式沟通是非常必要的，如果条件允许的话，面对面的交互式沟通更好。

172 C

分析相关方的权力、态度和需求属于相关方分析。

173 B

变更需求必须按照变更控制程序进行，先评估影响并获得批准。从题干中提示的信息，我们已经可以确定需要变更基准，所以必须由CCB批准。

174 C

分布式的团队无法做到面对面集中办公，所以要利用视频会议等方法及时规范收集信息并更新经验教训登记册。经验教训的收集不是靠专人做，也不是事后做，而是必须及时做，而且由团队成员充分参与。

175 C

遇到意见不一致的相关方，项目经理应该优先选择开诚布公地沟通方式，积极寻找各方都能接受的方案。除此之外，项目经理还要更新沟通管理计划，确定哪些信息可以公开、如何公开，以及哪些信息需要保密。

176　D

因为技术更新会影响项目计划，所以项目经理要遵循变更控制程序先评估影响，提出的应对措施需要事先经过批准。

177　B

当计划被批准，准备执行时开的会叫项目开工会议（Kick-off Meeting），或者叫项目开踢会议。需要注意项目开工会议与项目启动会议的区别，当项目启动阶段结束，准备开始做计划时开的会叫项目启动会议（Initiating Meeting）。

178　C

题干给出的信息显示团队还处于磨合阶段，所以项目经理应该开展团队建设活动，带领团队尽快度过磨合阶段，进入规范阶段和表现阶段。

179　B

发起人询问最终成本，即完工估算（EAC）的值。之前的偏差（成本偏差和进度偏差）是对需求理解错误不得不返工而造成的，现已纠正。这种偏差属于非典型偏差，也就是说，这个偏差不会继续影响之后的绩效，所以我们应该用公式 EAC ＝ AC ＋（BAC － EV）计算。因为这种偏差已经发生并影响成本，所以应如实报告给发起人。

180　D

相关方参与度评估矩阵是记录相关方当前的参与程度和他们被期望的参与程度的表格，可以用来对照检查相关方现在的参与程度是否达到预期。

181　C

沟通风格评估是一种用来比较不同沟通风格的优缺点，并确定最合适的沟通方式的技术。

182　D

团队成员应该充分参与活动历时估算，选择哪种估算方法也应由团队讨论决定。

183　B

当遇到相关方抵制时，项目经理应积极主动地与相关方沟通，邀请相关方积极参与项目，因为只有让相关方充分了解项目，才可能改变他们的态度。

多选题

184　BDF

本题考核的是减轻风险的措施。选项 B 增加安全时间、选项 D 增加关键路径上的资源、选项 F 提高资源质量，都可以在降低进度风险发生的概率和减轻风险影响上发挥作用；选项 A 和 H 属于风险转移；选项 C 属于规避风险；选项 E 虽然可以减轻风险，但这不是项目经理能决定的；选项 G 属于接受风险。

185　BDGH

项目整体变更控制程序中包含的流程见图 5-4。

186　DFH

变更的应对措施主要包含三种：预防措施、纠正措施、缺陷补救。

187　ABDFG

项目经理整合的职责包含选项 A 研究各种备选方法、选项 B 为实现项目目标裁剪过程、选项 D 管理知识领域之间的关系、选项 F 资源分配、选项 G 平衡竞争性需求。其他选项都不是项目经理整合的职责。

188　ABFG

软件配置管理计划包含版本、变更、文档、过程四大类内容。

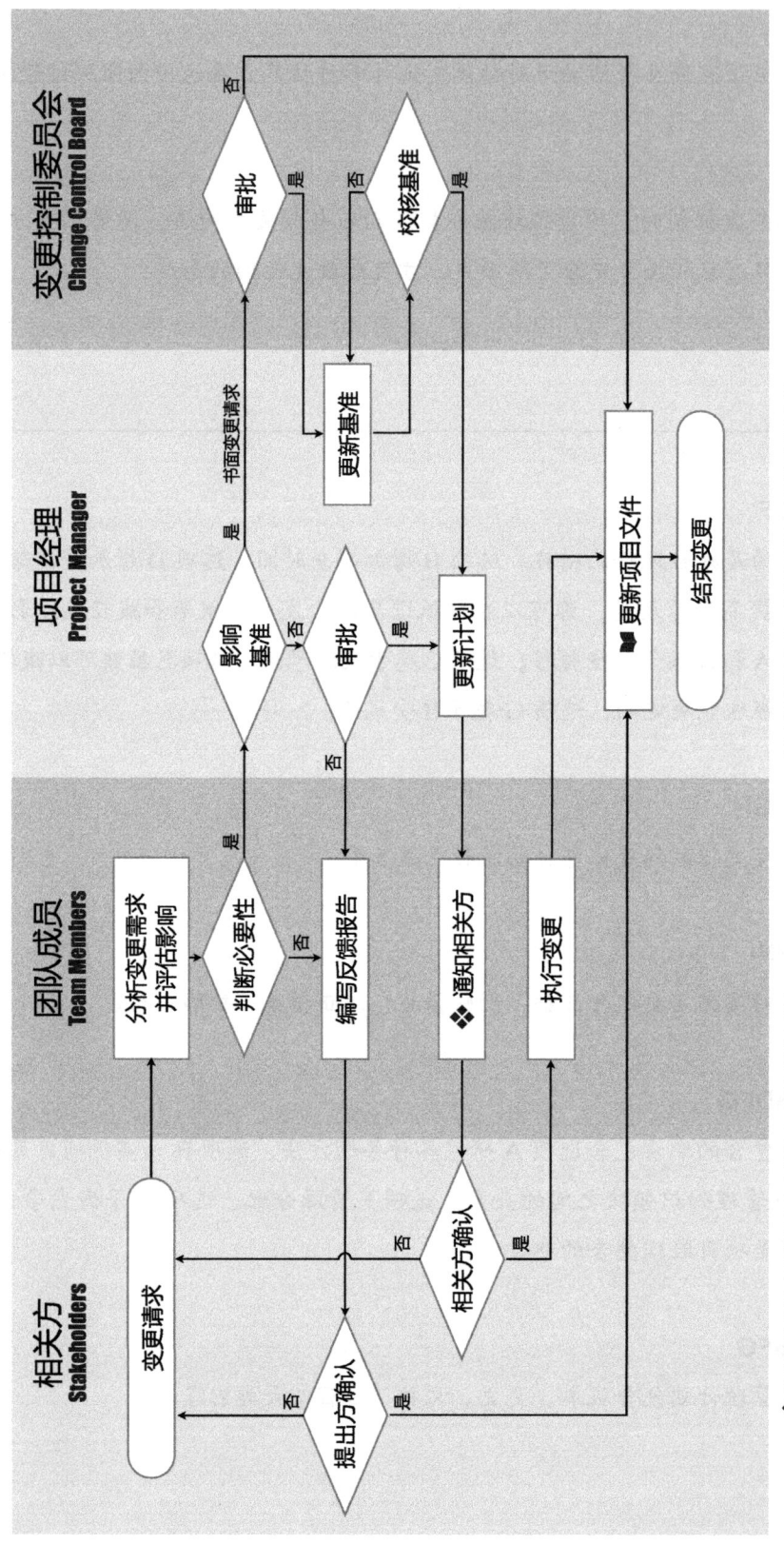

图 5-4 项目整体变更控制程序

◆ 通知可能受此变更影响的所有相关方，包含提出方在内

📖 更新项目文件，包括变更日志和经验教训登记册

189　CDEF

项目在中途取消，项目经理应该专注完成收尾工作。选项 F 关闭采购合同、选项 D 整理并归档经验教训、选项 E 解散团队，都属于选项 C 执行项目收尾的步骤。其他选项都不符合题意。项目收尾流程见图 5-5。

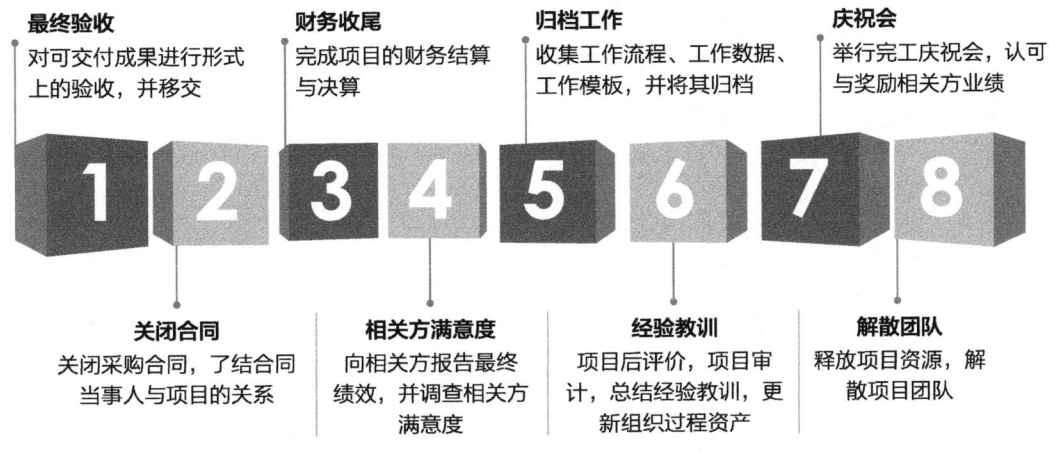

最终验收
对可交付成果进行形式上的验收，并移交

财务收尾
完成项目的财务结算与决算

归档工作
收集工作流程、工作数据、工作模板，并将其归档

庆祝会
举行完工庆祝会，认可与奖励相关方业绩

关闭合同
关闭采购合同，了结合同当事人与项目的关系

相关方满意度
向相关方报告最终绩效，并调查相关方满意度

经验教训
项目后评价，项目审计，总结经验教训，更新组织过程资产

解散团队
释放项目资源，解散项目团队

图 5-5　项目收尾流程

190　BCDGH

开发和验证最小可行产品（MVP）包含很多种方法，其中，选项 B、C、D、G、H 都是开发和验证 MVP 的常用方法，其他选项不符合 MVP 的特征。

191　BCD

从结束时间来看，应该先完成合同收尾，再结束行政收尾。不过行政收尾并不是在项目的最后阶段才开始的，而是贯穿项目全过程，所以选项 B 是正确的。合同收尾是对外，完成本公司与客户以及本公司与分包商、供应商签订的合同中的责任和义务，即验收和支付，用到的方法包括采购审计，确保采购过程符合采购管理计划；行政收尾是对内，把经验教训、文档记录整理完整并交给 PMO，给公司留下组织过程资产。所以选项 C 和 D 是正确的。

匹配题

192

第 1 步　　　　　　经验教训的收集和归档

第 2 步　　　　　　完成项目财务结算与决算

第 3 步　　　　　　可交付成果的最终验收和移交

第 4 步　　　　　　解散团队

第 5 步　　　　　　相关方满意度调查

第 6 步　　　　　　关闭采购合同

第 7 步　　　　　　归档工作流程、数据、模板

第 8 步　　　　　　举行庆祝会

193

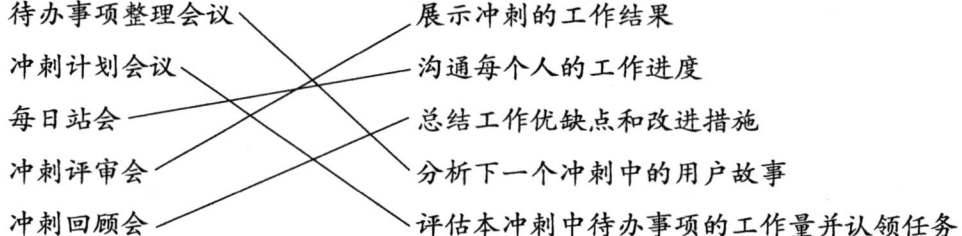

待办事项整理会议　　　　展示冲刺的工作结果

冲刺计划会议　　　　　　沟通每个人的工作进度

每日站会　　　　　　　　总结工作优缺点和改进措施

冲刺评审会　　　　　　　分析下一个冲刺中的用户故事

冲刺回顾会　　　　　　　评估本冲刺中待办事项的工作量并认领任务

194

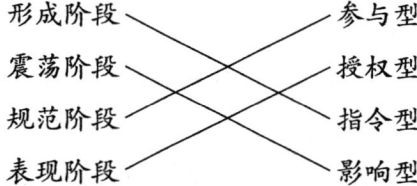

形成阶段　　　　参与型

震荡阶段　　　　授权型

规范阶段　　　　指令型

表现阶段　　　　影响型

195

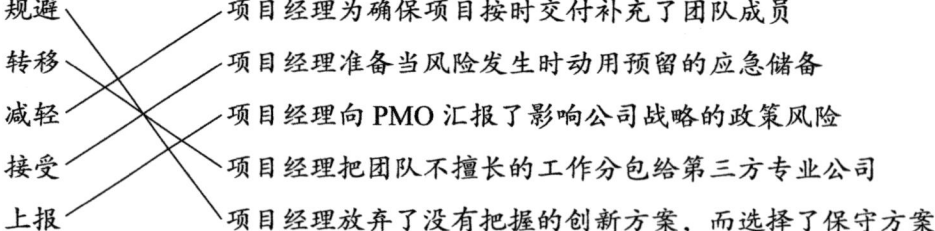

规避　　　　项目经理为确保项目按时交付补充了团队成员

转移　　　　项目经理准备当风险发生时动用预留的应急储备

减轻　　　　项目经理向PMO汇报了影响公司战略的政策风险

接受　　　　项目经理把团队不擅长的工作分包给第三方专业公司

上报　　　　项目经理放弃了没有把握的创新方案，而选择了保守方案

196

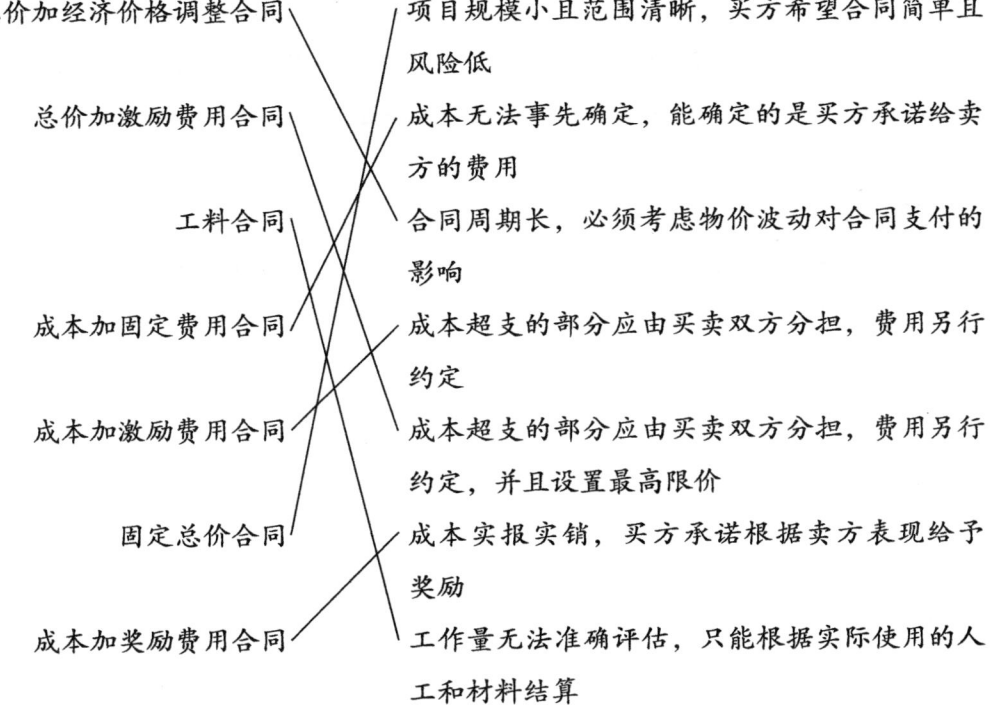

总价加经济价格调整合同 —— 项目规模小且范围清晰，买方希望合同简单且风险低

总价加激励费用合同 —— 成本无法事先确定，能确定的是买方承诺给卖方的费用

工料合同 —— 合同周期长，必须考虑物价波动对合同支付的影响

成本加固定费用合同 —— 成本超支的部分应由买卖双方分担，费用另行约定

成本加激励费用合同 —— 成本超支的部分应由买卖双方分担，费用另行约定，并且设置最高限价

固定总价合同 —— 成本实报实销，买方承诺根据卖方表现给予奖励

成本加奖励费用合同 —— 工作量无法准确评估，只能根据实际使用的人工和材料结算

填空题

197　0.8

项目预算是 100 万美元，时间已经过半，PV = BAC × 50% = 100 × 50% = 50（万美元）；工作完成了 40%，EV = BAC × 40% = 100 × 40% = 40（万美元）。SPI = EV/PV = 40/50 = 0.8

198　10 000

本题考核的是盈亏平衡分析，y 代表金额，x 代表人数。学费收入 y 随学生人数 x 变化，每人 10 美元，y = 10x；课程开发成本属于固定成本（5 万美元），纸质教材含运费属于可变成本（5 元 / 人），y = 50 000 + 5x。通过解二元一次方程组，我们可以得出当 x = 10 000 时，收入刚好等于成本。

199 B

本题考核的是租赁购买分析的计算，测试时间为 20 天。如果选择 A 方案，成本 $C_A = 55\,000 + 500 \times 20 = 65\,000$（美元）；如果选择 B 方案，成本 $C_B = 3\,000 \times 20 = 60\,000$（美元）。显然，B 方案（租赁方案）更合适。

200 C

风险评估分值＝概率 × 影响，风险 C 的评估分值 $= 70\% \times 0.3 = 0.21$，在四个风险中分值最高。

6

PMP 模拟题
第二套

单选题

1. Before preparing the project plan, the project manager needs to interview a subject matter expert (SME) according to the high-level project requirements proposed by the sponsor. Which document does the project manager use?

    A. Project scope statement

    B. Project business demonstration

    C. Project charter

    D. Statement of work

1. 项目经理在编制项目计划之前，需要根据发起人提出的高层级项目需求对一位主题专家（SME）进行访谈。项目经理使用的是哪份文件？

    A. 项目范围说明书

    B. 项目商业论证

    C. 项目章程

    D. 工作说明书

2. The project manager joins a new company that is not in the same business as the project manager. The project manager is inexperienced with the company's projects. Which of the following can help the project manager become competent in project management as soon as possible?

    A. Evaluation of enterprise environmental factors

    B. Review organizational process assets

    C. Consult external experts

    D. Brainstorm with project stakeholders

2. 项目经理加入一家新公司，这家公司的业务和项目经理之前从事的工作不属于同一个领域，项目经理对这家公司的项目缺乏经验。下面哪一项有助于项目经理尽快胜任项目管理工作？

   A. 评估事业环境因素

   B. 审查组织过程资产

   C. 请教外部专家

   D. 与项目相关方进行头脑风暴

3. The CEO asks the project manager to provide the project performance report. What should the project manager highlight in the report?

   A. Complete percentage and residual work

   B. Issue log and lessons learned register

   C. Project KPIs and progress analysis

   D. Project baselines and change log

3. 公司首席执行官要求项目经理提供项目绩效报告，项目经理应该在报告中重点体现什么内容？

   A. 完成百分比和剩余工作

   B. 问题日志和经验教训登记册

   C. 项目关键绩效指标和进展分析

   D. 项目基准和变更日志

4. During the implementation of the project, the project manager found an effective solution to the organization's problems in the project management process and avoided the recurrence of the same problems in the future. What should the project manager do next?

   A. Inform Senior management

   B. Update the risk management plan

   C. Initiate a change request

   D. Update the register of lessons learned

4. 项目经理在实施项目过程中发现了一个有效的方法，解决了组织在项目管理流程中的问题，并且可以避免以后相同问题的重复发生。项目经理下一步应该怎么做？

A. 通知高级管理层

B. 更新风险管理计划

C. 发起变更请求

D. 更新经验教训登记册

5. The project manager has been given a Project Closure Guide. The following information can the project manager obtain from this document, EXCEPT:

A. Validation process and acceptance criteria for deliverables

B. Project plan templates and lessons learned register

C. Final audit requirements for the project

D. Processes and standards for knowledge transfer

5. 项目经理获得了一份《项目收尾指南》，从这份文件中，项目经理可以获得如下信息，除了：

A. 可交付成果的确认流程和验收标准

B. 项目计划模板和经验教训登记册

C. 项目终期审计要求

D. 知识转移的流程和标准

6. The Change Control Board (CCB) has approved a change to the key technology solution. What should the team do before implement the new plan?

A. Update the change log

B. Update the lessons learned register

C. Update the project baselines

D. Inform stakeholders to make corresponding adjustments

6. 变更控制委员会（CCB）已经批准了对关键技术方案的调整。在实施新的计划前，团队应该做什么？

A. 更新变更日志

B. 更新经验教训登记册

C. 更新项目基准

D. 通知相关方做出相应调整

7. Which of the following statement about project life cycles and project phases is true?

A. Similar Application Areas and Organizations have identical project life cycles

B. Project phases within a project life cycle are always sequential

C. Project life cycle does not define the beginning and end of a project

D. Subprojects may have distinct project life cycles

7. 关于项目生命周期和项目阶段，下面说法中正确的是哪一个？

A. 类似的领域和组织有相同的项目生命周期

B. 项目生命周期内的项目阶段总是按次序排列的

C. 项目生命周期并不定义项目的开始和结束

D. 不同的子项目可以有不同的生命周期

8. There is a significant delay in the project schedule and management wants to know all the project milestones that are affected. What should the project manager provide?

A. Deviation analysis report

B. Earned value analysis report

C. Trend analysis report

D. Work performance report

8. 项目进度出现明显的延误，公司管理层希望了解所有受到影响的项目里程碑。项目经理应该提供什么？

A. 偏差分析报告

B. 挣值分析报告

C. 趋势分析报告

D. 工作绩效报告

9. You have just completed the project design phase for a client's product and are about to enter the implementation phase. All the following need to be done, EXCEPT:

A. Lesson learn

B. Quality inspection

C. Scope confirmation

D. Product acceptance

9. 为客户开发产品，你刚刚完成了项目设计阶段的工作，准备进入实施阶段。以下都是此时需要做的工作，除了：

A. 总结经验

B. 质量检查

C. 范围确认

D. 产品验收

10. A project is coming to an end, and the project performance report indicates that there will be a budget surplus. The project sponsor offered to use the remaining budget to develop features that had been removed from the original requirements assessment. What should the project manager do?

A. Refused to sponsor's proposal, and start the project acceptance procedures

B. Adopt the sponsor's proposal and add the deleted functions to the project scope statement

C. Spend the remaining budget before the end of the project and update the project performance report

D. Initiate a change request and assess the impact of the sponsor's proposal on the project

10. 一个项目将要结束，项目绩效报告显示，预算将会有剩余。项目发起人提出，用剩余的预算开发原来需求评估时被删除的功能。项目经理应该怎么做？

A. 拒绝发起人的提议，并启动项目验收程序

B. 采纳发起人的提议，把已删除的功能补充到项目范围说明书中

C. 在项目结束前花完剩余的预算，并更新项目绩效报告

D. 发起变更请求，并评估发起人的提议对项目的影响

11. Which of the following statements is true?

A. The five process groups may appear at each stage of the project

B. Managing any project should include 49 processes

C. Closing process group occurs only in the phase of product delivery

D. The five process groups occur in chronological order

11. 下面说法正确的是哪一项？

A. 五大过程组可能出现在项目的每个阶段

B. 管理任何项目都应该包含 49 个过程

C. 收尾过程组只发生在产品交付阶段

D. 五大过程组是按照时间先后顺序发生的

12. During project closure, which document should the project manager refer to when the Project Management Office asks for updates to the organization's process assets?

A. Issue log

B. Change log

C. Risk register

D. Lessons learned register

12. 在项目收尾期间，项目管理办公室要求项目经理对组织过程资产进行更新，项目经理应该查阅哪一份文件？

A. 问题日志

B. 变更日志

C. 风险登记册

D. 经验教训登记册

13. Company is working to introduce a new automatic production line, the introduction of the early stage of the project need to invest \$8 million at a time. The new production line can create \$2 million profit for the company every year, and the service life of the new production line is 5 years. How much is the ROI and payback period of the project calculated by static evaluation method?

A. ROI 25%, PBP 4 years

B. ROI 20%, PBP 5 years

C. ROI 20%, PBP 4 years

D. ROI 25%, PBP 5 years

13. 公司正在研究引进一条新的全自动生产线，这个引进需要项目前期一次性投入 800 万美元。新的生产线每年可以为公司创造 200 万美元的利润，新的生产线的使用寿命是 5 年。用静态评价法计算，该项目的投资回报率（ROI）和投资回收期（PBP）分别是多少？

A. ROI = 25%，PBP = 4（年）

B. ROI = 20%，PBP = 5（年）

C. ROI = 20%，PBP = 4（年）

D. ROI = 25%，PBP = 5（年）

14. One supplier misread the accuracy standards, resulting in about 10 percent of the parts supplied not meeting quality requirements. The project schedule is tight. What should the project manager do?

A. Review procurement contract with the supplier

B. Retest and use 90% of the parts that meets the quality requirements

C. Reject the parts and start the claim process

D. Assess impacts and initiate the change control procedures

14. 一家项目的供应商因为看错了精度标准，所以，在其提供的零件中，大约有 10% 不符合质量要求。项目工期很紧，项目经理应该怎么办？

A. 和供应商一起审查采购合同

B. 重新检测，使用符合质量要求的余下 90% 的零件

C. 拒绝收货，并启动索赔程序

D. 评估影响，并启动变更控制程序

15. Which project should you recommend to the sponsor according to the comparison data of the following four projects (see Table 6-1)?

Table 6-1　NPV & IRR of The Project

	Project A	Project B	Project C	Project D
NPV	$250,000	$250,000	$300,000	$300,000
IRR	16%	18%	18%	16%

A. Project A

B. Project B

C. Project C

D. Project D

15. 根据表 6-1 四个项目的对比数据，你应该向管理层推荐哪个项目？

表 6-1　项目净现值与内部收益率

	项目 A	项目 B	项目 C	项目 D
净现值（NPV）	25 万美元	25 万美元	30 万美元	30 万美元
内部收益率（IRR）	16%	18%	18%	16%

A. 项目 A

B. 项目 B

C. 项目 C

D. 项目 D

16. Changes lead to more rework, rework leads to more quality defects, quality defects lead to more changes, and the project enters a vicious cycle. What should a project manager do?

A. Reject any change requests until all quality defects have been fixed

B. Suspend the project process until no new changes are proposed

C. Introduce more testing resources to find defects more quickly

D. Review and update the quality management plan to ensure compliance with change management

16. 变更导致返工增加，返工造成更多的质量缺陷，质量缺陷引发更多的变更，项目进入恶性循环。项目经理应该怎么办？

A. 在所有质量缺陷被修正之前，拒绝任何变更请求

B. 暂停项目进程，直至再没有新的变更被提出

C. 引进更多的测试资源，以便更快地发现缺陷

D. 审查并更新质量管理计划，以保证其与变更管理相符

17. A change request submitted by the client has been realized and approved by the client. The project manager found that team had to work overtime to meet this request without affecting the project's schedule baseline. The project manager put the experience into words and record it in the lessons learned register. Which of the following is the project manager updated?

A. Enterprise process assets

B. Business environment factors

C. Project management plan

D. Project documents

17. 客户提出的一项变更需求已经实现，并得到了客户的认可。但项目经理发现，为了满足客户的这个需求，团队不得不加班，这才没有影响项目的进度基准。项目经理把这个经历整理成文字并记在了经验教训登记册中，项目经理更新的是什么？

A. 组织过程资产

B. 事业环境因素

C. 项目管理计划

D. 项目文件

18. One team member suggested using instant messaging instead of email to improve the efficiency of team communication, which was generally accepted by the team members. What should the project manager do before implement this suggestion?

A. Update change management plan

B. Update communication management plan

C. Update the stakeholder engagement plan

D. Update the lessons learned register

18. 一名团队成员建议采用即时通信工具替代电子邮件来提升团队的沟通效率，这项提议得到了团队成员的普遍认同。在实施这项建议前，项目经理应该怎么做？

A. 更新变更管理计划

B. 更新沟通管理计划

C. 更新相关方参与计划

D. 更新经验教训登记册

19. The following are the contents of the organizational governance framework, EXCEPT:

A. The sole responsibility principle

B. Business reporting level

C. Program and portfolio model

D. Emergency response procedures

19. 以下是组织治理框架的内容，除了：

A. 责任人唯一原则

B. 业务汇报层级

C. 项目集和项目组合模式

D. 应急响应程序

20. A risk has been identified during the project planning phase that the market price of a material required by the project will fluctuate frequently. In the execution stage of the project, suppliers are unwilling to deliver the goods on time because of the material price increase, which directly affects the project schedule. What should a project manager do?

A. Send a warning letter to the supplier and suspend payment

B. Make up the difference to the supplier according to the market price

C. Review risk register and implement risk response

D. Initiate change request for changing supplier

20. 在项目计划阶段，一项风险被识别出来，即项目所需的某种材料的市场价格经常波动。在项目执行阶段，供应商因为材料涨价而不愿意按时供货，这将直接影响项目的进度。项目经理该怎么办？

A. 向该供应商发送一封警告信，并暂停付款

B. 根据市场价格，给供应商弥补差价

C. 审查风险登记册，实施风险应对

D. 发起变更请求，更换供应商

21. The following problems can be found in the functional organizational structures in multiple projects environments, EXCEPT:

A. Project performance and department performance are difficult to be integrated

B. Project members are more concerned with their functional specialties than project goals

C. Slower response to client's requirements

D. Lack of security and perception of affiliation to project members

21. 在多项目的环境下采用职能型组织结构时，可能存在以下问题，除了：

A. 项目绩效与部门绩效难以统一

B. 项目成员更在意他们的专业职能，而不是项目目标

C. 对客户需求的反应比较慢

D. 项目成员缺乏安全感和归属感

22. The project manager organizes the team to identify more than 200 project risks. What method or tool should the project manager use to determine the high, middle, and low levels of risk?

A. Sensitivity analysis

B. Probability and influence matrix

C. Decision tree

D. Monte Carlo simulation

22. 项目经理组织团队识别出 200 多个项目风险，项目经理应该使用哪种方法或工具来划分风险的高、中、低等级？

A. 敏感性分析

B. 概率与影响矩阵

C. 决策树

D. 蒙特卡洛模拟

23. Which of the following statements is true compared to functional organization and matrix organization?

A. In functional organizations, project team is more efficient

B. Project managers in matrix organizations are full-time

C. In matrix organizations, team member should report both to functional manager and project manager

D. In functional organizations, project managers have higher authority

23. 对比职能型组织和矩阵型组织，下列哪一项表述是正确的？

A. 在职能型组织中，项目团队的协作效率更高

B. 在矩阵型组织中，项目经理都是全职的

C. 在矩阵型组织中，团队成员通常向职能经理和项目经理同时汇报工作

D. 在职能型组织中，项目经理拥有更高的权限

24. The Marketing Department of the company has announced the specific launch date of the new product, but the development work is still in progress. The company's senior management has repeatedly stressed that the release date cannot be changed. The project manager suggested that a feature with low priority but high development uncertainty be removed from this release. What is the risk response strategy adopted by the project manager?

A. Risk mitigation

B. Risk transfer

C. Risk avoidance

D. Risk report

24. 公司市场部门已经对外公布了新产品发布的具体时间，但开发工作还在紧张地进行中。公司高层一再强调发布时间不可更改。项目经理建议把一项优先级低但开发不确定性很高的功能从这个版本中删除。项目经理采取的风险应对策略是什么？

A. 风险减轻

B. 风险转移

C. 风险规避

D. 风险上报

25. A project team will go to a new country for new projects. PMO may provide the following support, EXCEPT:

A. Provide best practices for projects in this country

B. Provide special training for the laws, culture and local customs of this country

C. Provide templates for the performance report of such projects

D. Provide register of stakeholders in this project

25. 一个项目团队将赶赴一个新的国家开展新项目。PMO 可能提供以下支持，除了：

A. 提供在这个国家开展项目的最佳实践

B. 提供针对这个国家的法律、文化、当地习俗的专项培训

C. 提供这类项目的绩效报告模板

D. 提供这个项目的相关方登记册

26. One of the technicians on the project team has to take a week off. Stakeholders worry about the delay of the project schedule. The project manager is adamant that the project schedule will not be affected. The following are all possible reasons for the project manager to say so, EXCEPT:

    A. The team has redundant resources and the technician's job can be done by someone else

    B. The work of the technician has been ahead of schedule for more than one week

    C. The work that the technician is responsible for is on the non-critical path. The total floating time is greater than one week

    D. The work that the technician is responsible for is on the critical path, but can be shifted to the non-critical path

26. 项目团队中的一位技术人员要请假一周,相关方非常担心项目进度因此而延误。项目经理很坚定地说,项目进度不会受到影响。下面都有可能是项目经理这么说的依据,除了:

    A. 团队资源冗余,这位技术人员的工作可以由其他人分担

    B. 这位技术人员负责的工作已领先计划一周以上

    C. 这位技术人员负责的工作在非关键路径上,且总浮动时间大于一周

    D. 这位技术人员负责的工作在关键路径上,但可以将其改到非关键路径上

27. When the project manager prepares the project plan, he finds that the overall project goals are unrealistic and will not be achieved no matter how hard the team tries. What should a project manager do?

    A. Provide specific training for team members

    B. Accumulate experience in practice and continuously improve the project management process

    C. Timely feedback to the project sponsor and recommend amendments to the project charter

    D. Modify the project benefit management plan according to the actual ability of the team

27. 项目经理在编制项目计划时发现,总的项目目标不切实际,无论团队怎么努力,项目目标都将无法实现。项目经理应该怎么办?

A. 对团队成员提供针对性的培训

B. 在实践中积累经验，持续改进项目管理过程

C. 及时向项目发起人反馈并建议修订项目章程

D. 根据团队的实际能力修改项目效益管理计划

28. A construction project is about to enter the typhoon season, and bad weather can seriously affect the progress of the project. Senior management requires the project manager to take this factor into account when making plans to avoid penalties for schedule delays. What should the project manager do?

A. Transfer the risk to subcontractors by contract

B. Purchase more accurate weather data to mitigate risks

C. Suspend project until end of the typhoon season

D. Perform quantitative risk analysis and reserve sufficient schedule reserves

28. 一个建筑项目所在的地区即将进入台风季节，恶劣的天气会严重影响项目的进度。高层管理者要求项目经理在制订计划时充分考虑这个因素，避免因进度延误而遭受处罚。项目经理应该怎么做？

A. 通过签订合同，将该风险转移给分包商

B. 采购更为精准的天气数据，以减轻风险

C. 暂停项目，直到台风季节结束

D. 实施定量风险分析并预留足够的进度储备

29. The project manager takes over a new delivery project, but the country where the project is located is the company's first cooperation, and has no project delivery experience in that country. What should a project manager do?

A. Review of the lessons learned register of previous projects in this company

B. Analyze the business environment factors of the project

C. Review the company's organizational process assets

D. Organize team members to brainstorm

29. 项目经理接到一个新的交付项目，但是公司是第一次在该项目所在国家进行合作，没有在这个国家的项目交付经验。项目经理应该怎么办？

A. 评审公司以往项目的经验教训登记册

B. 分析项目的事业环境因素

C. 查阅公司的组织过程资产

D. 组织团队成员进行头脑风暴

30. Subcontractors of the project carried out the project as planned due to the lack of timely notification of change and had to rework as a result. This happened many times and involved multiple subcontractors. What should the project manager do?

A. Review the communication management plan to ensure proper communication

B. Review stakeholder participation plan to ensure appropriate participation of subcontractors

C. Review the risk management plan to ensure that related risks are being managed

D. Review the change management plan to ensure that the change process is correct and strictly adhered to

30. 项目的分包商因为没有及时收到变更通知而按原计划实施项目，结果不得不返工。这种情况不止出现一次，而且涉及多家分包商。项目经理应该怎么办？

A. 审查沟通管理计划，确保沟通方式得当

B. 审查相关方参与计划，确保分包商适当的参与

C. 审查风险管理计划，确保相关的风险得到管理

D. 审查变更管理计划，确保变更流程正确且被严格遵守

31. When should experiences and lessons be recorded?

A. At the end of the project

B. At the end of the project phases

C. When a change occurs

D. Throughout the project

31. 经验教训应该在什么时间被记录？

A. 项目结束时

B. 项目阶段结束时

C. 变更发生时

D. 项目全过程

32. Project team members come from five different countries, and they are located in their own countries. Members from different countries have different reporting procedures and working habits, and they show completely different attitudes when faced with differences. This leads to constant team conflict and low morale. Which of the following steps can be taken beforehand to avoid this situation?

A. Develop project charter

B. Develop a risk management plan

C. Develop team charter

D. Develop stakeholder participation plan

32. 项目经理正在领导由五个不同国家的成员组成的项目团队，他们在各自的国家工作。不同国家的成员有不同的汇报流程和工作习惯，在面对分歧时也表现出完全不同的态度。这导致团队冲突不断、士气低落。项目经理应该事先通过以下哪种方法来避免这种状况的发生？

A. 制定项目章程

B. 制订风险管理计划

C. 制定团队章程

D. 制订相关方参与计划

33. Which of the following is a feature of the project management process?

A. Iteratively

B. Independent of each other

C. Indispensable

D. Industry-specific

33. 以下哪个是项目管理过程的特征？

A. 反复迭代的

B. 彼此独立的

C. 缺一不可的

D. 行业专属的

34. A project team member asks for a week's leave, but only if the project delivery time is not delayed. Which of the following tools and techniques might be used by the project manager to make a decision:

A. RACI Matrix, Critical Path Method, Reserve Analysis

B. Gantt Chart, RAM Matrix, Earned Value Analysis

C. Resource Breakdown Structure, Reserve Analysis, Network Diagram

D. Risk Register, WBS, Resource Leveling

34. 一位项目团队成员提出请假离开一周，批准该成员请假的前提是项目交付时间不能延误。项目经理可能会用到以下哪些工具和技术来做出决策？

A. RACI 矩阵、关键路径法、储备分析

B. 横道图、RAM 矩阵、挣值分析

C. 资源分解结构、储备分析、网络图

D. 风险登记册、WBS、资源平衡

35. Which of the following statements about the project management plan is incorrect?

A. The project management plan should be jointly developed by the project manager with the project team

B. Developing project management plan needs to base on the project charter

C. Project management plans usually do not include project execution data

D. The project management plan should not be modified once it is approved

35. 关于项目管理计划，下面哪个表述是不正确的？

A. 项目管理计划应该由项目经理带领项目团队共同开发

B. 制订项目管理计划需要基于项目章程

C. 项目管理计划通常不包含项目执行数据

D. 项目管理计划一经批准就不应该修改

36. The project team has a total of 7 members, and the team has just entered the normal stage. At this time, the company received a new and more important project, and three team members were transferred to be responsible for the new project. The human resources department supplemented the project team with three new members through open recruitment. What will the project team face?

A. New members follow older members from the norming stage to the performing phase

B. The team goes through the forming and storming stages again

C. The team will go back from the norming stage to the storming stage and back to the forming stage

D. The team stays in the norming stage and for a long time

36. 项目团队一共有 7 位成员，团队刚刚进入规范阶段。这时公司接到一个新的更重要的项目，有 3 位团队成员被抽调去负责新项目，人力资源部通过公开招聘的方式为项目团队补充了 3 名新成员。项目团队将面临什么？

A. 新成员会跟随老成员从规范阶段进入表现阶段

B. 团队将重新经历形成和震荡阶段

C. 团队将从规范阶段退回到震荡阶段，再回到形成阶段

D. 团队将停留在规范阶段，并持续较长的时间

37. The project manager has just received a change request from the client. It does not affect the schedule of the project and is easy to implement. What should the project manager do first?

A. Implement the change as soon as possible

B. Contact the project sponsor and get approval

C. Report it to CCB

D. To assess the effect of the changes to other project constraints

37. 项目经理刚刚收到一个来自客户的变更请求，这个变更并不影响项目的进度，也很容易实现。项目经理应该首先做什么？

A. 尽快实施变更

B. 联系项目发起人并获得批准

C. 报告给变更控制委员会

D. 评估这个变更对项目其他制约因素的影响

38. A quality defect was found in the product test. After analysis, there may be many reasons for the defect. Which of the following should be used by the project manager to find the root cause?

A. Scatter diagram

B. Bubble diagram

C. Fishbone diagram

D. Control chart

38. 在产品测试过程中，测试人员发现了一个质量缺陷，经过分析，产生这个缺陷的原因可能有很多。项目经理应该使用以下哪种工具来找到根本原因？

A. 散点图

B. 气泡图

C. 鱼骨图

D. 控制图

39. Replacing the procurement source of a key component has been approved during the project execution. After the product was released, A business manager complained that the component had a negative impact on her work. Which document does the project manager rely on to obtain the acceptance of the business manager?

A. Risk register

B. Lessons learned register

C. Change log

D. Issue log

39. 更换一个关键组件的采购来源在项目执行期间获得批准。在产品发布之后，业务经理抱怨说，这个组件对她的工作产生了负面影响。项目经理依靠哪个文件获得业务经理的验收？

A. 风险登记册

B. 经验教训登记册

C. 变更日志

D. 问题日志

40. Project managers find that testers often skip tests, but the quality of the product doesn't suffer. Testers tell the project manager that it's safe to do so, and that testing doesn't have to be dogmatic and cumbersome. What should a project manager do?

A. Require testers to strictly comply with quality assurance requirements

B. Simplify the testing process to save time and cost

C. Respect the testers' opinions, they are more professional after all

D. Third party testing is added to ensure quality

40. 项目经理发现测试人员总是跳过一些测试环节，不过产品质量并没有因此出现问题。测试人员告诉项目经理之所以这么做是因为自己有把握，测试没必要那么教条和烦琐。项目经理应该怎么做？

A. 要求测试人员严格遵照质量保证要求

B. 简化测试流程，以节省工期和成本

C. 尊重测试人员的意见，毕竟他们更专业

D. 增加第三方检测，以保证质量

41. The client requests to complete an additional function for completion of project, otherwise he do not agree to the acceptance. This function is not within the scope of the project, and the project team has no prior knowledge of it. What should the project manager do to successfully complete the project?

A. Refuse the client's request and insist on submitting the acceptance report

B. Add this function to the project scope and complete it with the team

C. Assess the impact and submit change requests to the CCB

D. Avoid the tedious processes such like modifying project files, and work overtime with the team to meet the client's requirements

41. 客户要求只有完成一项附加功能，项目才算完成，否则不同意验收。这个功能不在项目范围之内，且项目团队事先完全不知道。若要成功完成项目，项目经理应该怎么做？

A. 拒绝客户的要求，坚持提交验收资料

B. 将该功能补充到项目范围中，并和团队完成它

C. 评估影响并向变更控制委员会提出变更请求

D. 避免修改项目文件等烦琐过程，和团队加班完成，以满足客户要求

42. The project manager sets up many evaluation and test steps when creating the quality management plan. Some stakeholders question that these steps increase the cost of the project, while the cost of repair will not be reduced in the future if the product fails. What should a project manager do?

A. Maintain these evaluations, testing and continuous improvement of quality

B. Reduce the budget for repairs to cut project costs

C. Reduce the evaluation and test steps according to the opinions of stakeholders

D. Reduce the budget for evaluation and testing and adjust it to the repair budget

42. 项目经理在创建质量管理计划时设置了很多评估、测试环节。有相关方质疑这些环节增加了项目的成本，然而未来产品如果出现故障，返修的成本并不会减少。项目经理应该怎么做？

A. 保留这些评估、测试环节，并持续改进质量

B. 减少用于返修的预算，以削减项目成本

C. 根据相关方的意见减少评估、测试环节

D. 缩减评估、测试的预算，并将缩减的预算调整到返修预算中

43. Supplier X has won the bid, but he cannot guarantee that a key component can be supplied on time. The project manager identifies another supplier Y in the short list of prequalified suppliers that can offer similar products. What should the project manager do next?

A. Submit a change request to the CCB

B. Terminate procurement from supplier X and sign contract with supplier Y

C. Check the selection criteria of project suppliers and confirm that supplier Y is qualified

D. Request the procurement department to change the supplier

43. 有一家中标的供应商 X 无法保障一个关键部件的按时供货，项目经理注意到通过资格预审的供应商短名单中有另一家供应商 Y 可以提供类似的产品。项目经理下一步应该怎么做？

A. 向变更控制委员会提交一项变更请求

B. 终止向供应商 X 的采购，与供应商 Y 签订供货合同

C. 查阅项目供应商选择标准，确认供应商 Y 符合资格

D. 向采购部门提出变更供应商的请求

44. No sooner had the project manager been appointed than the project sponsor told him that a key stakeholder had disapproved of the project and might boycott it. What should the project manager do next?

A. Require the sponsor to convince the stakeholder to support the project

B. Require senior management to shield from the influence of this stakeholder

C. Update the stakeholder register and stakeholder engagement assessment matrix

D. Provide project business demonstration documents to the stakeholder

44. 项目经理刚刚被任命，项目发起人告诉项目经理，有一位关键的相关方不赞同启动这个项目，而且可能会抵制项目。项目经理接下来应该怎么做？

A. 要求发起人说服该相关方支持项目

B. 要求高级管理层屏蔽该相关方的影响

C. 更新相关方登记册和相关方参与度评估矩阵

D. 给该相关方提供项目商业论证

45. The project manager was informed by the client that due to the force majeure, the contract payment which should be paid according to the project schedule was suspended, and the recovery time was not yet determined. What should the project manager do?

A. Continue project as plan, because it does not affect the project budget approved by project manager's company

B. To avoid financial risk to the company, immediately announce the termination of the project and release the resources

C. Forward the client's notice to all the project subcontractors and suppliers, and to suspend all purchase contract payments based on it

D. Assess the impact of this incident with the team and initiate a change request to CCB

45. 客户通知因遭遇不可抗力，原本按项目进度支付的合同款暂停支付，恢复时间尚无法确定。项目经理应该怎么办？

A. 这并不影响公司已批准的项目预算，继续按计划执行

B. 为了避免给公司带来财务风险，立即宣布停止项目并遣散资源

C. 将客户的通知转发给所有分包商和供应商，并以此为依据暂停支付所有采购合同款

D. 与团队评估这个事件带来的影响，向 CCB 发起变更请求。

46. A change was found in a project audit that was implemented without CCB approval,

which of the following should be reviewed by the project manager?

A. Change log

B. Configuration management plan

C. Change control procedures

D. Requirement traceability matrix

46. 在项目审计过程中发现一项变更被实施却没有经过 CCB 批准的记录，项目经理应该审查下面哪一项？

A. 变更日志

B. 配置管理计划

C. 整体变更控制程序

D. 需求跟踪矩阵

47. The project charter has just been released. The project manager found that a key authorization needed for the project was not in the project charter. What should the project manager do?

A. Prepare the project plan according to the authorized content of project charter already

B. Update project charter and add this necessary authorization

C. Record the lack of authorized information in the risk register

D. Communicate with the sponsor to initiate a change application of charter

47. 项目章程刚刚发布，项目经理发现开展项目所需要的一项关键授权没有体现在章程中。项目经理应该怎么办？

A. 根据章程中已授权的内容编制项目计划

B. 更新章程，将这一必要的授权补充进去

C. 将缺乏授权的信息记录到风险登记册中

D. 与项目发起人沟通，发起章程变更申请

48. The project manager led the team to estimate the project duration as 6 months according to the bottom-up estimating method. The sponsor proposed that the project must be delivered in 4 months and the budget should not be increased. What should a project manager do?

A. Compress the project duration according to the sponsor's requirement

B. Reduce testing to save time

C. Look for new technologies to speed things up

D. Suggest to delete part of the project requirements

48. 项目经理带领团队按照自下而上的估算法估算出项目的工期为 6 个月，但发起人提出必须 4 个月交付项目，而且不能增加预算。项目经理应该怎么做？

A. 按照发起人的要求压缩工期

B. 减少测试环节，以节约工期

C. 寻求新技术，以加快进度

D. 建议删除一部分项目需求

49. When should the scope confirm be done?

A. At the end of the project

B. At the beginning of the project

C. At the end of each phase of the project

D. Once change occur

49. 范围确认应该在什么时候做？

A. 项目结束时

B. 项目开始时

C. 项目每个阶段结束时

D. 变更发生时

50. One of the component suppliers delayed delivery of the component and the quality was not up to standard, which directly resulted in the product not meeting the client's requirements. What should a project manager do first?

A. Cooperate with other suppliers, to ensure qualified components timely supply

B. Request additional resources and let the team develop the components themselves

C. Explain to customer the responsibility shall be borne by the supplier

D. Review the contract with procurement manager and take necessary action

50. 在产品组件供应商中有一家延期交付组件且质量不合格，导致产品无法满足客户要求。如果要解决这个问题，项目经理首先应该怎么做？

A. 与其他供应商合作，保证合格的组件及时供应

B. 申请额外资源，自己开发相应组件

C. 向客户解释，责任应由这家供应商承担

D. 与采购经理一起审查采购协议并采取必要措施

51. In the WBS, the project is decomposed into the work package. Which of the following statements about the work package is incorrect?

A. The resources required to complete the work package can be evaluated

B. The duration and cost of the work package can be estimated

C. Can contain one or more deliverables

D. Logically cannot be broken down any more

51. 在 WBS 中，项目被分解到工作包。下列哪一项关于工作包的表述是不正确的？

A. 工作包所需要的资源可以被评估出来

B. 工作包的工期和成本可以被估算出来

C. 工作包可以包含一个或多个可交付成果

D. 工作包在逻辑上不可以再继续分解

52. The team adopts the agile development method, and the members of the development team feed back to the product owner that the user story with the highest priority in the product backlog cannot be realized in one sprint, which requires at least three sprints. What should such a user story be called?

A. Topic

B. Saga

C. Serial

D. Epic

52. 针对新产品，开发团队采用敏捷开发的方法，团队成员向产品负责人反映，产品待办事项列表中优先级最高的一个用户故事无法在一个冲刺中实现，至少需要经历三个以上的冲刺。这样的用户故事应该叫什么？

A. 主题故事

B. 传奇故事

C. 连载故事

D. 史诗故事

53. In the process of product development, the project sponsor recommends a new material to the project team. The new material is cheaper and has better performance than the existing material. If the new material is used, it will not only improve the product quality, but also significantly reduce the cost. What should the project manager do?

A. Replace existing materials with new ones to reduce costs

B. Continue to use existing materials as the risk of replacing new materials has not been assessed

C. Initiate change requests for material replacement in accordance with the integrated change control procedures

D. The products were divided into two groups and compared with the old and new materials

53. 在产品开发过程中，项目发起人向项目团队推荐了一种新材料，新材料比现有的材料更便宜而且性能更好。如果团队采用新材料，不但有利于提升产品质量，而且可以显著降低成本。项目经理应该怎么办？

A. 采用新材料，替换现有的材料以降低成本

B. 继续使用现有的材料，因为替换新材料的风险尚未评估

C. 按照整体变更控制程序发起替换材料的变更请求

D. 将产品分成两组，分别采用新旧材料进行对比

54. The project manager was leading the team to start implementation of the project plan when he received a notice that the project was cancelled due to lack of funds. What should a project manager do?

A. Complete the project plan according to the project charter

B. Initiate a change request

C. Begin project closing

D. Conduct qualitative and quantitative risk analysis

54. 项目经理带领团队刚刚开始实施项目计划，此时接到通知，因为缺乏资金，项目被取消。项目经理应该做什么？

A. 根据项目章程完成项目计划

B. 发起一个变更请求

C. 启动项目收尾工作

D. 进行风险定性和定量分析

55. Some members of the project X team also undertake the work of project Y at the same time. Which of the following items should be used for estimating activities of project X?

A. The duration of similar activities in other projects in the past

B. Schedule of project Y

C. Resource calendar

D. Comments from the functional managers of the members

55. X 项目团队中的部分团队成员同时还要承担 Y 项目的工作。在估算 X 项目的活动历时时必须用到下面哪一项?

A. 历史中其他项目中类似活动的历时

B. 项目 Y 的进度计划

C. 资源日历

D. 成员所在职能部门经理的意见

56. The project budget has been approved, and the project manager knows that the components to be purchased will be reduced in price during the implementation of the project. What should the project manager do?

A. Purchase components as planned and use the savings for emergency reserves

B. Initiate a change request to obtain approval for the cost change

C. Purchase components as planned, saving funds to cover overruns in other activities

D. Purchase higher grade components to improve product performance

56. 项目预算已获得批准,项目经理在项目实施过程中得知需要采购的部件降价,项目经理应该怎么做?

A. 按采购计划采购既定的部件,节省的资金用作应急储备

B. 发起一项变更请求,以获得对成本变更的批准

C. 按采购计划采购既定的部件,用节省的资金弥补其他活动的超支

D. 采购更高等级的部件,以提升产品的性能

57. The project manager was organizing the team to estimate the duration of the activities. He found that some activities had been repeated on previous projects, but some activities were new and none of the team members had relevant experience. Which estimating method should be used for these two types of activities?

A. Analogous Estimating, Bottom-Up Estimating

B. Analogous Estimating, Expert Judgment

C. Expert Judgment, Parametric Estimating

D. Parametric Estimating, Three-Point Estimating

57. 项目经理正在组织团队进行活动历时估算，他发现有些活动在之前的多个项目中重复做过，但有些活动是全新的，团队成员都没有相关的经验。针对这两类活动，项目经理应该分别采取哪种估算方法？

A. 类比估算，自下而上估算

B. 类比估算，专家判断

C. 专家判断，参数估算

D. 参数估算，三点估算

58. The project team is estimating the duration of the requirements research. The optimistic estimate is 5 days. It is most likely to estimate 8 days. Pessimistic estimate is 17 days, and the beta distribution is adopted to calculate the expected value and standard deviation. Which of the following is true?

A. Expected value 9 days, standard deviation 2 days

B. Expected value 10 days, standard deviation 2 day

C. Expected value 9 days, standard deviation 1 days

D. Expected value 10 days, standard deviation 1 days

58. 项目团队正在进行需求调研工作。乐观估计是 5 天，最可能估计是 8 天，悲观估计是 17 天。采用贝塔（β）分布计算期望值和标准差，以下结果正确的是哪一项？

A. 期望值是 9 天，标准差是 2 天

B. 期望值是 10 天，标准差是 2 天

C. 期望值是 9 天，标准差是 1 天

D. 期望值是 10 天，标准差是 1 天

59. The meaning of Lag is:

A. The total amount of time that activities can be delayed without affecting the overall project duration

B. The total amount of time that activities can be delayed without affecting the earliest starting time of the tight work

C. Waiting time

D. Time parallel to immediately preceding work

59. 滞后量（Lag）的含义是什么？

A. 在不影响项目总工期的前提下，活动可以拖延的总时间

B. 在不影响紧后工作最早开始时间的前提下，活动可以拖延的总时间

C. 等待的时间

D. 与紧前工作并行的时间

60. During the implementation of the project, the client company changed the general manager, and the new general manager put forward new requirements for the project, which would lead to a lot of rework and could not be delivered in time as required by the contract. What should the project manager do?

A. Reject new requirements because the previous scope baseline has been confirmed by the client

B. Accept new requirements and meet delivery time requirements by crashing

C. Accept new requirements and use this opportunity to ask for additional budgets

D. Assess the impact of new requirements and obtain approval from Change Control Board

60. 项目实施期间，客户公司换了总经理，新上任的总经理对项目提出了新的需求，这将导致产品大量返工并且无法按合同要求的时间交付。项目经理应该怎么做？

A. 拒绝新的需求，因为之前的范围基准是客户确认过的

B. 接受新的需求，通过赶工的方式满足对交付时间的需求

C. 接受新的需求，并借此机会向客户追加预算

D. 评估新的需求造成的影响，并获得变更控制委员会的批准

61. The project manager does not allow team members to increase any buffer to the duration estimates of activities. But he himself adds an extra by five weeks to the project schedule which is reported to the sponsor. What do you think about?

A. The project manager is so selfish that he is playing politics

B. The project manager is right, he is fighting for management reserve

C. The project manager is right, he used the critical path method

D. The project manager is right, he used the critical chain method

61. 项目经理不允许团队成员在评估活动历时期间增加安全时间，但他自己在给发起人汇报项目工期时额外多报了 5 周。针对他的这种做法，你怎么看？

A. 项目经理太自私，欺下瞒上

B. 项目经理这么做没错，他争取的是管理储备

C. 项目经理这么做没错，他采用的是关键路径法

D. 项目经理这么做没错，他采用的是关键链法

62. The project was scheduled for 60 days, and the client requested 10 days in advance. What should the project manager do if he finds that activities on the critical path cannot be parallelized?

A. Make change request and implement fast-tracking on non-critical paths

B. Make change request and implement fast-tracking on critical paths

C. Make change request to obtain resources for crashing on critical paths

D. Make change request to obtain resources for crashing on non-critical paths

62. 项目原计划工期是 60 天，客户要求提前 10 天交付。项目经理发现关键路径上的活动无法并行，项目经理应该怎么办？

A. 提出变更申请，在非关键路径上快速跟进

B. 提出变更申请，在关键路径上快速跟进

C. 提出变更申请，以获得在关键路径上赶工的资源

D. 提出变更申请，以获得在非关键路径上赶工的资源

63. The project resources had been overloaded, but the project manager could not get more resources, and there was still a certain amount of surplus in the project duration. What is the best thing for the project manager to do?

A. Change the non-critical path to the critical path

B. Fast-tracking the project

C. Implementation of resource leveling

D. Implementation of resource smoothing

63. 项目资源已过载，但是项目经理无法获取更多的资源，不过项目工期还有一些余量，项目经理最好怎么做？

A. 将非关键路径改为关键路径

B. 快速跟进项目

C. 实施资源平衡

D. 实施资源平滑

64. Project team members come from different departments and are not familiar with each other. The project manager wants team members to be clear about each person's responsibility for each activity on the project. Which of the following tools should be used?

A. Requirement tracking matrix

B. Stakeholder involvement assessment matrix

C. RACI matrix

D. Probability and impact matrix

64. 项目团队成员来自不同部门，互相并不熟悉。项目经理希望团队成员都能明确每个人对项目中每项活动的职责，那么项目经理应该采用下列哪个工具？

A. 需求跟踪矩阵

B. 相关方参与度评估矩阵

C. "执行—负责—咨询—知情" 矩阵

D. 概率和影响矩阵

65. The start time of activity A and B is not limited, and the duration is 2 weeks and 3 weeks respectively. "A" and "B" finish to start "C", "C" takes three weeks; Activity D requires 4 weeks but must begin after B is completed; Both C and D finished, the project can be completed. Activity A is three weeks behind schedule because the resources are not available. This will result in:

A. The project duration is delayed by 3 weeks

B. The project duration is delayed by 2 weeks

C. The project duration is delayed by 1 week

D. The project duration is unchanged, but the floating time of activity C decreases by 1 week

65. 活动 A 和活动 B 的开始时间不受限制，历时分别为 2 周和 3 周；只有完成活动 A 和活动 B，才可以开始活动 C，活动 C 需要 3 周；活动 D 需要 4 周，但必须在活动 B 完成后开始；只要活动 C 和活动 D 都结束了，项目就完成了。活动 A 因为资源不到位，开始时间比计划晚了 3 周，这将导致：

A. 项目总工期延误 3 周

B. 项目总工期延误 2 周

C. 项目总工期延误 1 周

D. 项目总工期不变，但活动 C 的浮动时间减少 1 周

66. The project manager has prepared the procurement statement of work and wants to know how to get approval from stakeholders. What should he do?

A. Review the communication management plan

B. Review the procurement management plan

C. Review the stakeholders' engagement plan

D. Review the risk management plan

66. 项目经理编制了采购工作说明书，想知道如何获得相关方的同意，他应该怎么办？

A. 查阅沟通管理计划

B. 查阅采购管理计划

C. 查阅相关方参与计划

D. 查阅风险管理计划

67. At the project status report, the project manager's CPM graph shows that the total floating time of two activities is negative, and which one of the following conclusions can you draw from the analysis?

A. Both activities are on the critical path

B. The early start time of the two activities is earlier than the late finish time

C. The late finish time of the two activities is earlier than the late start time

D. Because of negative floating time, the project progress is ahead of schedule

67. 在项目进度状态汇报会上，项目经理提供的关键路径法（CPM）图中显示有两项活动的总浮动时间是负的。从该项分析中，我们可以得出下列哪一项结论？

A. 这两项活动都在关键路径上

B. 这两项活动的最早开始时间都早于最晚开始时间

C. 这两项活动的最晚结束时间都早于最晚开始时间

D. 因为活动有负的浮动时间，所以项目进度比计划超前了

68. What should the company management refer to when there is a dispute about the acceptance criteria and procedures for subcontractors' deliverables?

A. Procurement management plan

B. Scope management plan

C. Quality management plan

D. Communication management plan

68. 关于分包商可交付成果的验收标准和验收程序，公司管理层存在争议，此时应该查阅什么？

A. 采购管理计划

B. 范围管理计划

C. 质量管理计划

D. 沟通管理计划

69. Which of the following statements about earned value analysis is correct?

A. EV means earned value, which is the actual profit earned by the project

B. Earned value analysis is used to evaluate project performance when the project is completed

C. Earned value analysis is to evaluate project performance in combination with both schedule and cost

D. Earned value analysis can accurately predict project performance at completion based on performance at any time

69. 以下关于挣值分析的表述正确的是哪一项？

A. 挣值也叫挣得值，是衡量项目实际挣得的利润

B. 挣值分析是用于当项目完成时对项目绩效的评估

C. 挣值分析同时综合考虑进度和成本两个因素来评价项目绩效

D. 挣值分析可以根据项目任何时间点的绩效精准预测项目完工时的绩效

70. The new regulations require that the project be urgently upgraded to more stringent safety verification, because the project schedule is already very tight and the team is very emotional, which of the following should be adopted by the project manager to get the team to accept the task?

A. Power

B. Leadership

C. Interpersonal and team skills

D. Communication skills

70. 新的监管规定要求项目紧急升级更严格的安全验证。因为项目工期本来就非常紧张，团队情绪较大，所以项目经理应该采用以下哪种技能让团队接受这个任务？

A. 权力

B. 领导力

C. 人际关系与团队技能

D. 沟通技能

71. A project of 10 weeks, worth $ 2 million. In the past four weeks, only one third of the work has been completed, and the cost has already been halved. What is the current state of the project?

A. Ahead of schedule and cost overrun

B. Ahead of schedule and cost saving

C. Behind schedule and cost saving

D. Behind schedule and cost overruns

71. 一个工期为10周、价值200万美元的项目，现在已过去4周，团队只完成了三分之一的工作，但已花掉了一半的成本。项目当前处于什么状态？

A. 进度超前，成本超支

B. 进度超前，成本节约

C. 进度落后，成本节约

D. 进度落后，成本超支

72. The project manager is conducting earned value analysis and has calculated the current cost variance and schedule variance. The sponsor wants to know the cost of completing all the work based on the current performance. Which of the following should the project manager provide?

A. Budget at Completion (BAC)

B. Estimate at Completion (EAC)

C. Estimate to Complete (ETC)

D. Variance at Completion (VAC)

72. 项目经理正在进行挣值分析，计算出了当前的成本偏差和进度偏差。发起人想要知道基于当前的绩效水平，完成所有工作所需的成本。项目经理应该提供以下哪一项数据？

A. 完工预算（BAC）

B. 完工估算（EAC）

C. 完工尚需估算（ETC）

D. 完工偏差（VAC）

73. The project stage performance review, the project was originally planned to cost $1 million at this time, the actual cost is $1.1 million, which of the following conclusions can you draw?

A. The CV is -$100,000, and the project cost is overspent

B. The SV is -$100,000, and the project progress is in a backward state

C. The CPI is less than 1, according to the trend of development, the project will exceed the budget

D. Insufficient information to make any conclusions above

73. 项目进入绩效评估阶段，项目原计划在此时花费成本 100 万美元，实际花掉的成本是 110 万美元，你可以得出以下哪个结论？

A. 成本偏差为 -10 万美元，项目成本处于超支状态

B. 进度偏差为 -10 万美元，项目进度处于落后状态

C. 成本绩效指数小于 1，按照此趋势发展，项目在完成时会超出总预算

D. 信息不足，得不出以上任何结论

74. The team is continuing to develop a product according to the agile method, and the operation report shows that the user churn rate has increased significantly due to the poor user experience of a new feature just released. What should the team do?

A. Withdrawing this new feature

B. Solve user experience issues immediately

C. Follow the integrated change control procedures

D. Set the improved user experience as a to-do and evaluate priorities

74. 团队正在按照敏捷方法持续开发产品，运营报告显示，刚刚发布的一项新功能使用户体验不佳，导致用户流失率显著上升。团队应该怎么办？

A. 撤销这项新功能

B. 立刻解决用户体验问题

C. 遵守整体变更控制程序

D. 把改进用户体验设为待办事项并评估优先级

75. You provide a project cost estimate for the project to the project sponsor. He is unhappy with the estimate, because he thinks the price should be lower. He asks you to cut 15% off the project estimate. What should you do?

A. Start the project and constantly look for cost savings

B. Tell all the team members to cut 15% from their estimates

C. Suggest the sponsor that some activities should be cut

D. Don't do anything, because you've reserved more than 15 percent of emergency reserves

75. 你向项目发起人提供了一份项目成本估算。发起人不满意，认为总价应该低一些。他要求你把项目成本估算砍掉 15%。你应该怎么做？

A. 开始运行项目并持续寻找节约成本的办法

B. 告诉你的团队把他们各自的成本估算都砍掉 15%

C. 建议发起人砍掉一些活动

D. 什么都不用做，因为你预留了超过 15% 的应急储备

76. A project manager is sick and asks for leave. You are assigned to the project team to take over the post of project manager. You are deeply impressed by the deep understanding of the team, mutual trust, efficient cooperation and harmonious communication among team members. What stage of Tuckman ladder theory do you judge the team is in?

    A. Forming stage

    B. Storming stage

    C. Norming stage

    D. Performing stage

76. 一位项目经理生病请假，你被派到这个项目团队接替项目经理一职。通过对团队的深入了解，团队成员互相信任、高效协作、沟通融洽给你留下了深刻的印象。你判断这支团队处于塔克曼阶梯理论中的哪个阶段？

    A. 形成阶段

    B. 震荡阶段

    C. 规范阶段

    D. 表现阶段

77. A project with a budget at completion (BAC) of $5 million has already completed 40 percent of the work, and it has already cost $2.5 million. The company stipulates that the ratio of the budget at completion (BAC) and the cost performance index (CPI) is used to predict the estimate at completion (EAC). Which of the following are the correct variance at completion (VAC) and To-complete performance index (TCPI)?

    A. VAC = $1.25 million, TCPI = 0.8

    B. VAC = –$1.25 million, TCPI = 0.8

    C. VAC = $1.25 million, TCPI = 1.2

    D. VAC = –$1.5 million, TCPI = 1.2

77. 一个完工预算为 500 万美元的项目，团队已经完成了 40% 的工作量，此时实际已花费 250 万美元的成本。公司规定用完工预算和成本绩效指数的比值来预测完工估算。请问下面关于完工偏差和完工尚需绩效指数哪个是正确的？

    A. 完工偏差 = 125 万美元，完工尚需绩效指数 = 0.8

    B. 完工偏差 = –125 万美元，完工尚需绩效指数 = 0.8

C. 完工偏差 = 125 万美元，完工尚需绩效指数 = 1.2

D. 完工偏差 = -150 万美元，完工尚需绩效指数 = 1.2

78. A project team is carrying out a fast-iterative project. A key stakeholder directly asks the team members about the project progress. What should the project manager do?

A. Authorize team members to report their concerns to stakeholders

B. Ensure that only PMO provides project information to stakeholders

C. Personally report the project progress to this key stakeholder

D. Provide regular formal updates to stakeholders

78. 一个项目团队正在开展一个快速迭代的项目，一位关键的相关方直接向团队成员询问项目进度。项目经理应该怎么做？

A. 授权团队成员向相关方报告他们关心的内容

B. 确保只有 PMO 向相关方提供项目信息

C. 亲自向这位关键相关方汇报项目进度

D. 向相关方定期提供正式的更新内容

79. Which of the following is a non-consistent cost?

A. Training for team members

B. Raw material inspection

C. Product warranty

D. Equipment maintenance

79. 以下哪个选项属于非一致性成本？

A. 人员培训

B. 原料检验

C. 产品保修

D. 设备检修

80. During project planning, the project team identifies various risks. What should the project manager do to mitigate the impact of these risks on the project?

A. Implement risk avoidance

B. Take contingency measures

C. Executive reserve analysis

D. Implement risk transfer

80. 在项目规划过程中，项目团队识别出多个风险。为了减轻这些风险对项目的影响，项目经理应该怎么做？

A. 实施风险规避

B. 采取权变措施

C. 执行储备分析

D. 实施风险转移

81. The project team has discovered that causes of the product defects can be summarize to five, and each cause has a different number of defects. Which tool can help the project manager to determine the priorities of these causes to deal with?

A. Pareto chart

B. Fishbone diagram

C. Histogram

D. Scatter diagram

81. 项目团队发现造成产品缺陷的原因可以归纳为五种，而且每种原因导致的缺陷的数量是不同的。以下哪个工具有助于项目经理决定这些原因的优先顺序？

A. 帕累托图

B. 鱼骨图

C. 直方图

D. 散点图

82. A telecom operator in a country is facing a 3G network upgrade project. Upgrading to 4G has small investment and small income, and upgrading directly to 5G has large investment and large income. However, whether it is upgraded to 4G or 5G, it is facing the uncertainty of market fluctuations. Which of the following tools can help project manager make sound decisions

A. Monte Carlo analysis

B. Sensitivity analysis

C. Decision tree analysis

D. Hypothesis analysis

82. 某国一家电信运营商正在面临 3G 网络的升级项目，如果升级为 4G，则投入少，收益也少；如果直接升级到 5G，则投入多，收益也多。然而，无论升级为 4G 还是 5G，都面临着市场波动的不确定性。以下哪个工具可以帮助项目经理做出合理的决策？

    A. 蒙特卡洛分析

    B. 敏感性分析

    C. 决策树分析

    D. 假设分析

83. The content of milk powder in each can should be 500g, and the allowable deviation is ± 4g. What is the range of the upper and lower control line in the quality control chart?

    A. 495g ~ 505g

    B. 496g ~ 504g

    C. 497g ~ 503g

    D. 498g ~ 502g

83. 每罐奶粉的含量应该是 500 克，允许的误差是 ±4 克。在质量控制图中，上下控制线的范围是多少克？

    A. 495 克 ~ 505 克

    B. 496 克 ~ 504 克

    C. 497 克 ~ 503 克

    D. 498 克 ~ 502 克

84. Which of the following does not represent the latest quality management concept?

    A. Exceeding user expectations and pursuing the ultimate quality

    B. Defect reduction and cost reduction

    C. Quality comes from prevention, not inspection

    D. Meet the requirements and be suitable for use

84. 以下哪一项不代表最新的质量管理理念？

    A. 超越用户期望，追求极致品质

    B. 缺陷减少，成本降低

C. 质量产生于预防，而非检查

D. 符合要求，适合使用

85. All the following are forms of power derived from the project manager's position, EXCEPT:

A. Formal power

B. Reward power

C. Penalty power

D. Expert power

85. 下面都是项目经理职位所带来的权力，除了：

A. 法定的权力

B. 奖赏的权力

C. 惩罚的权力

D. 专家的权力

86. The project team is trying scrum agile development framework. The operator has collected a new user requirement. Who should she feed back to and communicate with to know when the requirement can be developed?

A. Product Owner

B. Project Manager

C. Scrum Master

D. Development Team

86. 项目团队正在尝试 Scrum 敏捷开发框架，运营人员收集到一项新的用户需求。她应该将这个需求反馈给谁，和谁沟通能知道这个需求什么时候可以被开发？

A. 产品负责人

B. 项目经理

C. 敏捷专家

D. 开发团队

87. Which of the following conflict resolution technologies is not easy to implement, but will always bring the most satisfying results?

A. Forcing

B. Smoothing

C. Compromise

D. Problem solving

87. 下面哪种冲突解决技术虽然不容易做到，但总会带来最满意的效果？

    A. 强制

    B. 缓和

    C. 妥协

    D. 解决

88. The project is about to be delivered for acceptance. A team member thinks it is unnecessary to do the work assigned to him by the project manager, but the project manager is very sure that this work is essential to ensure the smooth acceptance. The project manager has no more time to convince the team member by explaining the background and reasons. What should the project manager do?

    A. The project manager does the work himself

    B. Assign the work to other team members

    C. Respect the opinions of the team member and cancel the work

    D. Require the team member to complete the work

88. 项目即将交付验收，一位团队成员认为项目经理分配给他的工作根本没有必要做，但项目经理非常确定这项工作是保障验收顺利通过必不可少的。项目经理已经没有更多的时间通过解释背景和原因来说服这名团队成员，项目经理应该怎么做？

    A. 项目经理自己完成这项工作

    B. 把这项工作安排给其他团队成员

    C. 尊重这位团队成员的意见取消这项工作

    D. 要求这位团队成员必须完成这项工作

89. Which document should the project manager write about the project team's values, dispute resolution and voting rules?

    A. Project charter

B. Team charter

C. Communication management plan

D. Stakeholder engagement plan

89. 项目经理应该把项目团队共同的价值观、争议解决的方式和表决规则写进哪份文件？

A. 项目章程

B. 团队章程

C. 沟通管理计划

D. 相关方参与计划

90. In a software development project, the development team finds a new tool to improve the development efficiency. It is found that this new tool can shorten the development cycle by 20% and save the development cost by 15%. With the approval of the change control board, the project team began to use the new tool. Which of the risk coping strategies does this belong to?

A. Report

B. Acceptance

C. Mitigation

D. Exploitation

90. 在一个软件开发项目中，开发团队找到一种提高开发效率的新工具。经过分析发现，采用这种新工具可以缩短 20% 的开发周期，并节省 15% 的开发成本。在获得变更控制委员会的批准后，项目团队开始使用这种新工具。这属于风险应对策略中的哪一种？

A. 上报

B. 接受

C. 减轻

D. 开拓

91. At the end of a large project, tensions rise and conflicts between team members become more frequent. The focus of the conflict is because two feuding members are hostile to each other, and the team's attention has been distracted from the project's goals. To restore order, the project manager removed the work of the two members in advance and let others replace them. What kind of conflict resolution strategy does the project manager use?

A. Forcing

B. Avoiding

C. Compromising

D. Solving

91. 在一个大型项目快结束时，团队紧张状态上升，团队成员之间的冲突越来越频繁。冲突的焦点是因为两名有宿怨的成员彼此敌对，团队的注意力已经脱离了项目的目标。为了恢复秩序，项目经理打发掉了这两名团队成员，让其他人代替他们。项目经理使用的是哪种冲突解决策略？

A. 强制

B. 回避

C. 妥协

D. 解决

92. The project manager takes over a customized development software project in the middle of the project. The project manager does not receive the latest information about the project deliverables. What should the project manager do?

A. Refer to project bidding documents

B. Refer to project scope statement

C. Refer to project charter

D. Refer to communication management plan

92. 项目经理中途接手一个为客户定制开发的软件项目，项目经理没有收到关于项目可交付成果的最新信息，项目经理应该怎么做？

A. 查阅项目招标文件

B. 查阅项目范围说明书

C. 查阅项目章程

D. 查阅沟通管理计划

93. A software project is about to enter the testing stage. The project team has 5 members, among which 1 requirement analyst has finished his work and left the team, and 3 test engineers have joined the team. What happens to the team's communication path?

A. Increase to 7

B. Increased by 2

C. Increased by 11

D. Increase to 28

93. 一个软件项目即将进入测试阶段，项目团队原来有 5 名成员，其中 1 名需求分析师完成了自己的工作后离开了团队，有 3 名测试工程师加入团队。团队的沟通路径会发生什么变化？

A. 增加到 7 条

B. 增加了 2 条

C. 增加了 11 条

D. 增加到 28 条

94. The two project teams used to have 5 persons each. Now the two teams are merged into a 10-person team. What's the change of team communication path?

A. Double the number of paths

B. No change

C. Increased by 10

D. Increased by 25

94. 两个项目团队原来各自有 5 人，现在两个团队合并成了一个 10 人的大团队，团队的沟通路径发生了什么变化？

A. 路径数量翻倍

B. 没有变化

C. 增加了 10 条

D. 增加了 25 条

95. In an implementation project, the development phase has been outsourced to an off-shore team. During the execution of the project, the off-shore team states that vital information to proceed in the development is missing. However, the on-shore design team has stated that all design documents have been provided. What could most likely

be the cause of this situation?

A. Failed to create communication management plan correctly

B. Failed to create stakeholders' engagement plan correctly

C. The project manager lacks communication skills

D. Failed to create the risk management plan correctly

95. 在项目实施过程中，开发阶段的工作已经外包给一支海外团队。在项目执行期间，海外团队通知，关于开发的重要信息有遗漏，但国内设计团队说，已经提供了所有的设计文档。造成这种情况最有可能的原因是什么？

A. 未正确创建沟通管理计划

B. 未正确创建相关方参与计划

C. 项目经理缺乏沟通技巧

D. 未正确创建风险管理计划

96. The company plans to develop a new App to seize the potential new market, but the product manager is unable to provide detailed product requirements documents, because no one knows what functions the product should contain in order to truly meet the needs of users. However, it is very important for the product to be launched as soon as possible to gain competitive advantage. Which of the following development methods should the project manager recommend?

A. Waterfall development

B. Incremental development

C. Iterative development

D. Agile development

96. 公司计划开发一款新的 App 来抢占有潜在爆发力的新市场，但产品经理也无法提供详细的产品需求文档，因为没有人知道产品到底应该包含哪些功能才可以真正满足用户的需求，不过产品尽早上市对取得竞争优势非常重要。项目经理应该建议采取以下哪种开发方式？

A. 瀑布开发

B. 增量开发

C. 迭代开发

D. 敏捷开发

97. The project manager is carrying out a project involving technical secrets in a foreign country. The country has had a riot, and the project manager has launched an emergency response mechanism to upgrade security standards, but the militants continue to hit the site. In no time to get approval, project manager ordered the destruction of the confidential data, and organize personnel to evacuate immediately. Which of these is the risk response?

A. Contingency plan

B. Fallback plan

C. Workaround response

D. Risk mitigation

97. 项目经理在海外的某个国家实施一个技术涉密的项目，该国发生了暴乱，尽管项目经理启动了应急响应机制，升级了安保措施，但武装分子不断冲击项目现场。在来不及获得批准的情况下，项目经理下令销毁了项目机密数据，并立即组织人员撤离。这属于哪种风险应对方法？

A. 应急计划

B. 弹回计划

C. 权变措施

D. 风险减轻

98. In the project planning stage, the project manager has found that if team meet a non-essential requirement from the client, they must face the serious decline of system reliability. They cannot solve this problem effectively based on the current resources and time. The project manager puts forward a change request after weighing it over and over again, and proposes to delete this requirement. What kind of risk response strategy does the project manager adopt?

A. Avoid

B. Transfer

C. Mitigation

D. Reception

98. 在项目规划阶段，项目经理发现，如果满足客户提出的一项非必要的需求，就必须面对系统可靠性严重下降的问题，但是基于当前的资源和时间，团队无法有效地解决这个问题。项目经理经过再三权衡，提出了变更请求，建议删除这项需求。项目经理采取的是哪种风险应对策略?

A. 规避

B. 转移

C. 减轻

D. 接受

99. Impact scores: A project team identifies 4 risks and assesses probability of occurrence and potential impact on cost and schedule for each risk. This information is presented in Table 6-2 shown. If the importance of cost objectives is 4 times to project schedule. Which is the most critical risk for the project?

Table 6-2　Risk Probability And Impact

Risk	Probability	Impact on schedule	Impact on cost
A	75%	2	2
B	50%	3	5
C	75%	2	4
D	50%	4	3

A. Risk A

B. Risk B

C. Risk C

D. Risk D

99. 如表 6-2 所示，项目团队识别出了若干风险发生的概率和每个风险对成本、进度的潜在影响。对项目而言，进度和成本的权重比为 4∶1。那么评级最高的风险是哪一个?

表 6-2　风险发生的概率与影响

风险	概率	对进度的影响	对成本的影响
A	75%	2	2
B	50%	3	5
C	75%	2	4
D	50%	4	3

A. 风险 A

B. 风险 B

C. 风险 C

D. 风险 D

100. The project manager is comparing two solutions for the project. The probability of success is 85% for solution 1. If it works, it could save $1 million for the project, but if it doesn't work, it's going to increase the cost of $1 million on the project. Solution 2 has 65% probability of success. If it works, it could save $2 million, but if it doesn't work, it's going to increase the cost of $4 million. Which solution should the project manager recommend? What is the reason?

A. Solution 1, because the EMV of solution1 is $100,000 more than the EMV of solution 2

B. Solution 2, because it can save $1 million more than the solution 1

C. Solution 1, because its probability of success is 20% higher than that of solution 2

D. Solution 1, because If it fails, the cost will be increased by $3 million less than solution 2

100. 项目经理正在分析项目的两个备选方案。方案一成功的概率为 85%，如果成功，可以为项目节省 100 万美元；但是如果失败，就要增加 100 万美元的成本。方案二成功的概率为 65%，如果成功，可以节省 200 万美元；如果失败，就会增加 200 万美元的成本。那么项目经理应该推荐哪个方案？理由是什么？

A. 方案一，因为方案一的预期货币价值（EMV）比方案二多 10 万美元

B. 方案二，因为项目如果成功，方案二可以比方案一多节省 100 万美元

C. 方案一，因为方案一成功的概率比方案二高 20%

D. 方案一，因为如果项目失败，损失比方案二少 100 万美元

101. In the process of project procurement, one of the suppliers offers very low price. But according to internal experts, the price is unrealistic for continued cooperation. What should the project manager do next?

A. Ask the supplier re-quote after re-evaluate the demand and provide detailed cost structure information

B. Update the lessons learned register and let the purchasing department sign the contract immediately

C. Add penalty clauses to the contract to ensure that suppliers perform their obligations

D. Initiate a change request and change the cost baseline accordingly

101. 项目在采购配件的过程中，其中一位供应商给出非常优惠的价格。但是根据内部专家判断，该价格对于持续合作是不现实的。项目经理接下来应该怎么做？

A. 让供应商重新评估需求后重新报价，并提供详细的成本结构信息

B. 更新经验教训登记册，并让采购部门抓紧签订合同

C. 在合同中增加处罚条款，确保供应商履行义务

D. 发起一个变更请求，相应地更改成本基准

102. The project needs to entrust a third party to develop a special new material. The project manager can't evaluate the cost of R & D in advance, but he hopes to save R & D investment as much as possible. Moreover, the sponsor stipulates that the subcontract amount should not exceed 1 million yuan. What kind of contract should the project manager sign with the third party?

A. Cost plus fixed fee contract

B. Firm fixed price contract

C. Fixed price plus incentive fee contract

D. T&M contract

102. 项目需要委托第三方研发一种特殊的新材料，虽然项目经理无法事先评估研发所需的成本，但希望尽可能地节约研发投入，而且发起人规定了分包合同金额不得超过 100 万元。项目经理应该与第三方签署哪种合同？

A. 成本加固定费用合同

B. 固定总价合同

C. 总价加激励费用合同

D. 工料合同

103. A raw material purchase of the project will be signed with the supplier for a 10-year continuous supply contract. The project sponsor provided the project manager with a template of firm fixed price contract. Many suppliers have been slow to respond to concerns about market price volatility beyond their capacity. Which type of contract should the project manager recommend?

A. Cost Plus Incentive Fee Contract (CPIF)

B. Fixed Price with Economic Price Adjustment Contract (FPEPA)

C. Time and Material Contract (T&M)

D. Fixed Price Plus Incentive Fee Contract (FPIF)

103. 项目需要就某项原材料的采购与供应商签订长达 10 年的持续供货合同。项目发起人给项目经理提供了一份固定总价合同模板。许多供应商因为担心市场价格波动超出自己的承受范围而迟迟没有响应。项目经理应该建议签订以下哪种类型的合同？

A. 成本加激励费用合同

B. 总价加经济价格调整合同

C. 工料合同

D. 总价加激励费用合同

104. Which of the following contract types is the main risk borne by the buyer?

A. Firm Fixed Price Contract (FFP)

B. Cost Plus Incentive Fee Contract (CPIF)

C. Cost Plus Fixed Fee Contract (CPFF)

D. Fixed Price Plus Incentive Fee Contract (FPIF)

104. 以下合同类型中，风险主要由买方承担的是哪一个？

A. 固定总价合同

B. 成本加激励费用合同

C. 成本加固定费用合同

D. 总价加激励费用合同

105. The buyer and seller bargain on a fixed price plus incentive fee contract, the aim cost of the contract is $2 million, the aim fee is $500,000. The contract specifies that the ceiling price is $2.8 million, the sharing ratio is 80/20, if the seller accomplished the fact cost is $2.5 million, how much should the buyer pay for the seller totally?

A. $ 2.4 million

B. $ 2.8 million

C. $ 2.9 million

D. $ 3 million

105. 买方和卖方签订了总价加激励费用合同，合同的目标成本是 200 万美元，目标费用是 50 万美元。合同规定了最高价为 280 万美元，分享比率为 80/20。卖方完成工作的实际成本为 250 万美元，那么最终买方要向卖方支付多少合同款？

A. 240 万美元

B. 280 万美元

C. 290 万美元

D. 300 万美元

106. The project manager has completed the procurement statement of work. What should the project manager do in order to ensure that the bidder has no ambiguity about the content of the procurement statement of work?

A. Procurement negotiation with bidders

B. Holding bidders conference

C. Release request for proposal

D. Entrust professional institutions to conduct independent estimation

106. 项目经理已完成采购工作说明书，为了保证投标人对采购工作说明书中的内容理解没有歧义，项目经理应该怎么做？

A. 与投标人进行采购谈判

B. 召开投标人会议

C. 发布建议邀请书

D. 委托专业机构进行独立估算

107. A project manager is developing a project for a client working on a time and material contract. They have performed an earned value analysis and verified that the project can be completed earlier and under the original estimated budget. However, the company that the project manager is working with has a firm fixed price contract with the technical subcontractor. This means that the project manager's company's profits will be reduced and the project manager's bonus will be less than expected. What should the project manager do?

A. Inform the client that they can now add some original requirements have been deleted

B. Tell the technology subcontracting company to slow down so that the project can realize the expected profit

C. Tell the client that the project can be completed in advance and save cost

D. Upgrade test standards and increase test inputs to meet the original project budget

107. 项目经理正在按照工料合同为客户做项目。团队做了挣值分析，确认该项目可以提前完工，而且成本少于最初的预算。不过项目经理所在的公司与技术分包公司签署的是固定总价合同，这意味着项目经理所在公司的利润将会减少，根据项目利润，项目经理的奖金也会比预计的少。项目经理应该怎么办？

A. 通知客户，现在加进来一些原先删除的需求

B. 告诉技术分包公司增加资源并放慢速度，让项目可以实现预计的利润

C. 告诉客户项目可以提前完成并节约成本

D. 提高测试标准、增加测试投入，以符合最初的项目预算

108. The project manager is organizing the team to prepare the project scope statement. The following contents should be included in the project scope statement, EXCEPT:

A. Project deliverables

B. Estimation of project cost and schedule

C. Assumptions and constraints

D. Acceptance criteria and exclusions

108. 项目经理正在组织团队编制项目范围说明书，以下是项目范围说明书中应该包含的内容，除了：

A. 项目可交付成果

B. 项目成本和进度估算

C. 假设条件和制约因素

D. 验收标准和除外责任

109. While creating the project charter, a key stakeholder does not offer any input. The project manager repeatedly asks the stakeholder to provide the necessary input to complete the high-level requirements. Despite the project manager's efforts, the

situation does not improve. What should the project manager do next?

A. Remove the stakeholder from the stakeholder list

B. Assume the requirements of this stakeholder together with project team

C. Add the missing input as a risk to the high-level risk description

D. Escalate the issue to the project sponsor

109. 在制定项目章程时，一位关键的相关方没有提供任何意见。项目经理反复询问并请他提供必要的信息，以便完成高层级的需求。虽然项目经理尽力了，但情况没有得到改善。项目经理接下来应该怎么做？

A. 将该相关方从相关方列表中删除

B. 与项目团队假定相关方需求

C. 将意见缺失作为项目风险，添加到主要风险描述中

D. 将该问题上报给项目发起人

110. Agile coaches repeatedly remind the team to strictly limit the number of WIP in Kanban, otherwise it will bring the following problems, EXCEPT:

A. The longer quality feedback time

B. The longer average cycle time

C. The slower business response

D. The less work in progress

110. 敏捷教练反复提醒团队应该严格限制看板中的在制品数量，否则会带来以下问题，除了：

A. 质量反馈时间变长

B. 平均周期时间变长

C. 业务响应速度变慢

D. 同时开展的工作减少

111. During the project planning phase, the project manager realized that a project stakeholder had a disagreement about the understanding of the deliverables, resulting in a tension between the project manager and the stakeholder. What should the project manager do to solve this problem?

A. Ignore the opinions of this stakeholder and define the project scope according to the understanding of majority

B. Arrange meeting with the stakeholder to get the reason of the understanding differences and actively address them

C. Escalate the issue to the project sponsor so that they can solve the problem

D. Ask other stakeholders with greater power to convince this stakeholder to compromise

111. 在项目规划阶段，项目经理认识到，由于自己与一名项目相关方对项目可交付成果的理解存在分歧，从而造成与该项目相关方的关系紧张。若要解决这个问题，项目经理应该怎么做？

A. 忽略该项目相关方的意见，根据多数相关方的理解确定项目范围

B. 安排与这位相关方进行会谈，了解造成分歧的原因并积极解决分歧

C. 将该问题上报给项目发起人，让他们解决这个问题

D. 让权力更大的其他相关方出面说服这位相关方做出妥协

112. Agile team members need to constantly focus on the gap between the number of remaining to-do items and the plan. What should they use?

A. Burndown chart

B. Value stream map

C. Gantt chart

D. Earned value curve

112. 敏捷团队成员需要经常关注剩余待办事项的数量与计划的差距，他们应该使用以下哪种工具？

A. 燃尽图

B. 价值流图

C. 甘特图

D. 挣值曲线

113. Which of the following should the project manager review for each completed activity during directing and managing a project?

A. Work performance data

B. Risk register

C. Change log

D. Issue logs

113. 在指导和管理项目的过程中，对于已经完成的活动，项目经理应该审查什么？

A. 工作绩效数据

B. 风险登记册

C. 变更日志

D. 问题日志

114. The team is discussing the choice of iteration length in the upcoming agile development. Which of the following is true?

A. The iteration length should be as short as possible, so that it can be more flexible to deal with requirements changes

B. The iteration length should be as long as possible, so that a more valuable iteration plan can be made

C. The iteration length can be adjusted at any time to adapt to the characteristics of different development stages

D. The length of iteration should be appropriate, flexibility and time efficiency are both considered

114. 团队正在讨论在即将开始的敏捷开发中如何选择迭代长度，以下哪一个观点是正确的？

A. 迭代长度尽可能短，这样可以更灵活地应对需求变更

B. 迭代长度尽可能长，这样可以做出更有价值的迭代计划

C. 迭代长度可以随时调整，以适应不同开发阶段的特点

D. 迭代长度适当，兼顾灵活性和时间利用效率

115. Which of the following project lifecycles is the most unfriendly to change?

A. Iterative

B. Agile

C. Waterfall

D. Incremental

115. 以下哪种项目生命周期对变更最不友好？

A. 迭代型

B. 敏捷型

C. 瀑布型

D. 增量型

116. In the process of new product development, the project manager noticed that the company ranking the first in the industry had just released a same type of product. Compared with the competitive product, the technical solutions of the product being developed by the team were outdated and lack of features. Even if it was developed as planned, the product is not competitive at all. What should the project manager do?

A. Lead team to complete product development according to plan

B. Terminate project and demobilize team

C. Update the requirements with reference to the competing product

D. Rediscuss the project business demonstration with the project sponsor

116. 在新产品开发过程中，项目经理关注到行业排名第一的公司刚刚发布同类型的产品。相比竞品，团队正在开发的产品的技术方案过时且功能缺乏特色，即便按计划开发完成也完全没有竞争力。项目经理应该怎么做？

A. 按计划带领团队完成产品的开发

B. 终止项目并遣散团队

C. 参考竞品，更新需求

D. 与项目发起人重新讨论项目商业论证

117. Configuration management may be oriented towards the following objects, EXCEPT:

A. Product versions, functions, components and documents

B. Baselines, plans and files of the project

C. Knowledge, experiences and lessons learned in the project

D. Project manager's leadership and interpersonal skills

117. 配置管理可能面向以下对象，除了：

A. 产品的版本、功能、组件、文档

B. 项目的基准、计划、文件

C. 项目中获得的知识、经验、教训

D. 项目经理的领导力和人际关系技能

118. As the project progresses, the variance analysis shows that actual project performance compared to the performance measurement baseline deteriorates. As a result, estimates for cost, schedule, and scope are no longer valid. The team determines that a high volume of new features, change requests, and defect repairs are the main reason behind the variance. What is the project manager's best course of action to ensure that further estimates for the remainder of the work on the project are made based on real progress?

A. Switch the product development approach to adaptive and measure progress via short iterations

B. Limit the number of new features, change requests, and defect repairs allowed on the project

C. Use a bottom-up estimating technique for cost and schedule, and three-point estimating for scope

D. Measure progress based on the individual baselines instead of the single integrated baseline

118. 随着项目的进展，偏差分析表明，与绩效衡量基准相比，实际项目绩效恶化。因此，对成本、进度和范围的估算不再有效。团队认为，大量的新特性、变更请求和缺陷修复是导致偏差出现的主要原因。为了确保根据实际进展对项目剩余工作做出进一步估计，项目经理的最佳行动方案是什么？

A. 将产品开发方法转换为适应型方法，并通过短的迭代来度量进展

B. 限制项目中新功能的数量，以及更改请求和缺陷修复的数量

C. 对成本和进度采用自下而上的估算方法，对范围采用三点估算法

D. 基于各自的基准而不是一个综合的基准来衡量进展

119. The delivery time is near but the project is behind schedule. Facing with the Christmas holidays, the project manager needs to choose between asking all team members to give up their holidays with overtime compensation and delay the delivery of the project and bear the penalty. Which of the following analytical techniques does he need?

A. Reserve analysis

B. Earned value analysis

C. Alternative analysis

D. Cost-benefit analysis

119. 交付日期临近但项目进度落后，而且圣诞节假期马上就来了。项目经理需要在让所有团队成员放弃假期加班补偿和承担延期交付项目的罚款之间做出选择，他需要用以下哪一种分析技术？

A. 储备分析

B. 挣值分析

C. 备选方案分析

D. 成本效益分析

120. The project manager found that a certain performance of the product did not meet the expected quality standard, but the product was accepted by the client. Which of the following activities does this indicate?

A. Quality audit

B. Change control

C. Scope confirmation

D. Quality Control

120. 项目经理发现产品的某项性能没有达到预期的质量标准，但产品被客户接受了。这表明完成了以下哪项活动？

A. 质量审计

B. 变更控制

C. 范围确认

D. 质量控制

121. At the end of a sprint, a team member told that the new development approach that had been tried in the sprint had not worked, but had led to misunderstandings among members and less efficiency. What should Scrum Master do?

A. Discuss the issue during the sprint retrospective meeting

B. Discuss the issue during the sprint review meeting

C. Discuss the issue during the next sprint planning meeting

D. Discuss the issue in the next daily stand-up meeting

121. 在一个冲刺结束时，一位团队成员告诉大家，在这个冲刺中，新的开发方式并没有起作用，反而造成了团队成员之间的误解，开发效率更低了。敏捷专家应该怎么做？

A. 在冲刺回顾会上讨论该问题

B. 在冲刺评审会上讨论该问题

C. 在下一次冲刺计划会上讨论该问题

D. 在下一次每日站会上讨论该问题

122. The new sprint has just begun, and the product owner has proposed to add a new feature to the sprint, otherwise the product will miss a once in a blue moon market opportunity. What should the development team do?

A. The product owner is required to follow the integrated change control procedures until the approval of CCB is obtained

B. Add the new feature immediately and promise that it will be available at the end of this sprint

C. Discuss with the product owner to add this new feature and replace the low priority tasks in this sprint

D. Tell the product owner that the feature will be developed in the next sprint because the plan for this sprint has already been implemented

122. 新的冲刺刚刚开始，产品负责人提出在这个冲刺中增加一项新功能，否则将错过一次千载难逢的市场机会。开发团队应该怎么做？

A. 要求产品负责人遵循整体变更控制程序，直到获得 CCB 的批准

B. 立即添加新功能，并承诺该功能在这个冲刺结束时可用

C. 与产品负责人讨论增加这项新功能，并置换掉本冲刺中工作量相当但优先级低的任务

D. 告诉产品负责人，该功能将在下一个冲刺中开发，因为本冲刺的计划已经开始实施了

123. The project manager joins a complex project where the requirements are volatile and long lasting. The clients want product to get to market as soon as possible to get a head start, and they want constant feedback from users to validate product requirements and improve features. Which development approach should be recommended for this project?

A. Waterfall

B. Incremental

C. Iterative

D. Agile

123. 项目经理接手一个复杂的项目，该项目的需求不稳定且持续时间长。客户希望产品能更快地进入市场抢占先机，而且希望不断得到用户的反馈来验证产品需求并改进功能。项目经理应该为这个项目推荐哪种开发方式？

A. 瀑布式

B. 增量

C. 迭代

D. 敏捷

124. At the sprint review meeting, the team found that a feature developed did not meet the release requirements. What should they do?

A. Overtime modification ensures that the feature meets the release requirements before the next sprint starts

B. Record the issue in the issue log and reevaluate the release requirements

C. Retrospect improvement ideas, and put the issue in the next sprint to-do list

D. Escalate the issue to senior management and look for alternative releases

124. 在冲刺评审会上，团队发现，开发完成的一项功能没有达到发布的要求，应该怎么办？

A. 加班修改，保证在下一个冲刺开始之前该功能能够满足发布要求

B. 将问题记录在问题日志中，并重新评估发布的要求

C. 回顾改进思路，把问题列入下一个冲刺待办事项列表中

D. 将问题上报给高级管理层，并寻找可替代的发布方案

125. You are the scrum master. You find that a particular stakeholder is proving to be a major distraction to the team. He frequently calls the team to ask for status, get information, provide suggestions and sometimes to request changes. What should you do about this?

A. Escalate the issue and keep the stakeholder off-limits

B. Invite the stakeholder to the appropriate planning or review meetings and request him to bring up his views at those meetings

C. Listen to the stakeholder, but ignore his suggestions

D. Tell the stakeholder directly not to disturb the team during the sprint

125. 你是敏捷专家，你发现有一位相关方是团队的主要干扰人。他频繁地向团队询问项目状态，获取项目信息，提供建议，有时也会变更需求。对此，你应该做什么？

A. 升级问题并限制这位相关方到团队中来

B. 邀请这位相关方参加适当的计划会或评审会，并提供自己的观点

C. 倾听相关方的陈述，但忽略他的建议

D. 直接告诉相关方，不要在冲刺周期中打扰团队

126. Recently, project team members are often transferred to support other projects with higher priority, causing frequent delays in project progress. What should the project manager do?

A. Ask team members to work overtime on days that are not transferred to catch up with the project schedule

B. Omit documentation and simplify testing to ensure project schedule

C. Apply with PMO to increase project priority

D. Start the change control procedures and reassess the schedule baseline

126. 项目团队成员近期常常被抽调去支援优先级更高的其他项目，造成项目进度频频延误，项目经理应该怎么办？

A. 安排团队成员在没被抽调的日子加班，将进度赶上

B. 省略文档工作以及简化测试工作，以保证项目进度

C. 向项目管理办公室申请提高项目的优先级

D. 启动变更控制程序，重新评估进度基准

127. A team that has newly transitioned to Scrum. The product owner wants to know the level of detail he needs to put in to user stories so that the team can work with them. What guidance would you give in this regard?

A. User stories should be as detailed as possible, so that there is no room for ambiguity

B. It can be no more than 1 index card in length and the details given in a separate document

C. The level of detail should be worked out between the team and the product owner

D. User stories can contain less detail, because Agile relies on working software over comprehensive documentation

127. 一个团队刚刚开始使用敏捷方法，产品负责人想知道他需要提供的用户故事的细节程度，以使团队能够理解。你会在这方面给他什么意见？

A. 用户故事应尽可能详细，这样就不会有歧义

B. 用户故事的长度不应该超过一个索引卡片，所有细节应该放在一个单独的文档里

C. 颗粒度应该由团队和产品负责人共同协商得出

D. 用户故事可以包含较少的细节，因为敏捷更注重可工作软件而不是详细的文档

128. Which of the following is the most important in evaluating the success of an agile product?

A. The iteration plan can be completed on schedule

B. All the deliverables passed the review successfully

C. It creates enough value for users

D. The cost does not exceed the budget and resources are not wasted

128. 以下哪一项在评价一个敏捷开发的产品是否成功时是最重要的？

A. 迭代计划能够如期完成

B. 交付成果均能顺利通过评审

C. 为用户创造了足够的价值

D. 成本不超预算，资源没有被浪费

129. An agile team wants to collectively determine the likely size of the user story, what will the team be doing if they use the planning poker technique to accomplish this?

A. Estimating the size of stories by using hours

B. Estimating the size of stories by placing them in buckets

C. Estimating story points by comparing them to similar past features

D. Using story points to estimate the user story size by voting

129. 敏捷团队希望集体决定用户故事可能的规模，如果他们使用计划扑克来完成这项工作，那么团队将会做什么？

A. 通过使用小时数来估算用户故事的规模

B. 通过将用户故事粗略归类来估算它们的规模

C. 通过将用户故事与过去类似功能进行对比来估算故事点

D. 通过投票的方式使用故事点数来估算用户故事的规模

130. What should everyone share at the agile team's daily stand-up meeting, EXCEPT:

A. What did I finish yesterday

B. What will I do today

C. What are the obstacles to achieving my goals

D. What are the suggestions for other team members

130. 在敏捷团队召开的每日站会上，哪项内容是不应该被分享的？

A. 昨天我完成了哪些工作

B. 今天我将完成哪些工作

C. 完成我的目标存在什么障碍

D. 对其他团队成员有哪些建议

131. Who should remove and record obstacles in the current sprint?

A. Project Manager

B. Product Owner

C. Agile Team

D. Scrum Master

131. 谁应该在当前的冲刺中排除并记录出现的障碍？

A. 项目经理

B. 产品负责人

C. 敏捷团队

D. 敏捷专家

132. A project is about to start. A key stakeholder is not optimistic about the project. He

questioned why the project should be implemented. What document can solve the problem?

A. Cost-benefit analysis

B. Project business demonstration

C. Project charter

D. Project baselines

132. 一个项目即将启动，有一位关键的相关方并不看好这个项目，质疑为什么要实施这个项目。以下哪份文件能够消除这位相关方的质疑？

A. 成本效益分析

B. 项目商业论证

C. 项目章程

D. 项目基准

133. The project manager took over a project to develop customized software for client. Due to the constant change from client, the team worked overtime for a long time but still could not satisfy the client. Performance indicators such as schedule and cost of projects are seriously out of baselines. There was a general loss of enthusiasm and motivation among team members, and the former project manager left because of a loss of confidence. What should the project manager do to revitalize the team and deliver the project?

A. Formal change management and use leadership to improve team morale

B. Promise the team a big bonus if they complete the project

C. Bring in new members to replace unmotivated ones

D. Modify the project baselines to relax requirements for performance

133. 项目经理中途接手了一个为客户定制开发软件的项目。因为客户需求不断变更，导致团队长期加班，但仍然无法让客户满意，项目的进度和成本等绩效指标更是与基准严重脱节。团队成员普遍丧失了热情和动力，上一任项目经理因为没有信心而选择了离职。项目经理应该如何让团队重振士气并完成项目交付？

A. 规范变更管理，并使用领导力提升团队士气

B. 向团队承诺，如果完成项目，将获得大笔奖金

C. 引进新成员，替换掉没有动力的成员

D. 修改项目基准，以放宽对绩效的要求

134. The company intends to train a technical expert to become a project manager. The following are the directions he should strive for, EXCEPT:

A. Trust and often encourage team members to help them grow

B. Lead the team to innovate and break through the current situation

C. Continuous learning, strict self-discipline, set an example for others

D. Personally take the initiative to complete the challenging work of team members

134. 公司有意将一位技术专家培养成为项目经理。以下是他应该努力的方向，除了：

A. 信任并常常鼓励团队成员，帮助他们成长

B. 带领团队勇于创新、突破现状

C. 持续学习、严格自律、为他人树立榜样

D. 身先士卒，主动完成团队成员的挑战性工作

135. In agile development, items in the Product Backlog should be the following requirements, EXCEPT:

A. Estimated

B. Can be increased or decreased as needed, and priorities can be adjusted

C. Prioritized

D. Sufficiently specific and detailed

135. 在敏捷开发中，产品待办事项列表（Product Backlog）中的条目应满足以下哪些要求，除了：

A. 经过估算的

B. 随时可根据需要增减和调整优先级的

C. 按优先级排序的

D. 足够具体和充分细化的

136. When a member who has just joined the team is familiar with the project plan, he finds that there is no specific information about the work package he needs in the work breakdown structure, such as the deliverables, allocated resources, duration requirements, etc.Which of the following documents should the project manager suggest him to consult ?

A. Project charter

B. Project scope statement

C. WBS dictionary

D. Requirements traceability matrix

136. 一位刚刚加入团队的成员在熟悉项目工作计划时发现，工作分解结构中没有他需要的关于工作包的具体信息，比如可交付物、匹配资源、工期要求等。项目经理应该建议他查阅以下哪一份文件？

A. 项目章程

B. 项目范围说明书

C. WBS 词典

D. 需求跟踪矩阵

137. A project manager identifies and registers some risks, and then drafts a risk response plan for the project. However, due to funding constraints and the sponsor's unwillingness to create a budget for uncertain activities, the risk response plan is not approved. What should the project manager do?

A. Escalate the issue to senior stakeholders

B. Request approval of a risk response plan that addresses the high-priority risks

C. Review the organizational process assets regarding budget utilization from other projects

D. Accept the sponsor's decision, and continue with project

137. 项目经理识别并登记了多个风险，然后为项目起草了一份风险应对计划。然而，由于资金有限，发起人不愿意为不确定的活动创建预算，所以风险应对计划未获得批准。项目经理应该怎么做？

A. 将该问题升级，上报给高级相关方

B. 请求批准针对高优先级风险的应对计划

C. 审查组织过程资产，参考其他项目的预算使用

D. 接受发起人的决定，并继续执行项目

138. Team members found that the thickness of antirust coating of some products produced recently is not enough, and these products have potential safety hazards. The project manager guided the team to find out that the defect was caused by the aging of the spraying parts, and the team immediately replaced the new spraying parts to solve the quality defect. To be on the safe side, the project manager informed the sales department to recall the defective product and reprocess it. In addition, the regulation of regular inspection and update of spraying parts is added. What measures did the project manager take?

A. Corrective measures, defect remedy and preventive measures

B. Emergency measures, corrective measures and defect remedy

C. Defect remedy, preventive measures and corrective measures

D. Corrective measures, preventive measures and defect remedy

138. 团队成员发现，近期生产的部分产品的防锈涂层厚度不够，这些产品存在潜在的安全隐患。项目经理指导团队找到了产生缺陷的原因，是由于喷涂部件老化造成的，于是团队立即更换了新的喷涂部件，解决了这个质量缺陷。为了稳妥起见，项目经理通知销售部门召回了存在缺陷的产品并重新加工，另外增加了喷涂部件定期检查、更新的规定。项目经理分别采取了什么措施？

A. 纠正措施、缺陷补救、预防措施

B. 应急措施、纠正措施、缺陷补救

C. 缺陷补救、预防措施、纠正措施

D. 纠正措施、预防措施、缺陷补救

139. The project sponsor sees that the latest project performance report shows that the project is behind schedule. The project sponsor asks the project manager whether the project can be delivered on schedule. What should the project manager do before reply to the sponsor?

A. Perform reserve analysis

B. Perform root cause analysis

C. Execution trend analysis

D. Execution process analysis

139. 项目发起人看到最近一期项目绩效报告显示项目进度落后，项目发起人询问项目经理，项目能否按期交付。在回复发起人之前，项目经理应该做什么？

A. 进行储备分析

B. 进行根本原因分析

C. 进行趋势分析

D. 进行过程分析

140. In the project start-up phase, the internal departments of the client company have different understandings of the project objectives and deliverables. What should the project manager do?

A. All departments of the client are required to reach an agreement as soon as possible

B. Confirm that the contract has clear terms for project objectives and deliverables

C. Guide them to communicate fully to form an acceptable solution

D. Clearly define the responsibility of change in the contract

140. 在项目启动阶段，客户公司内部各部门对于项目的目标和可交付成果明显存在不同的理解。项目经理应该怎么办？

A. 要求客户公司内部尽快达成一致

B. 确认合同中对项目目标和可交付成果有明确的条款

C. 引导他们充分沟通，形成一个大家都能接受的方案

D. 在合同中明确界定变更的责任

141. The schedule manager notices that due to a data entry error, the time to complete a task on the critical path has been underestimated. What should the schedule manager do?

A. Promptly discuss the error and potential corrective action with the project manager

B. Promptly report the error to the project sponsor

C. Promptly discuss the error and defect remedy action with the project manager

D. Develop preventive active to ensure that customer does not raise a concern regarding schedule impact

141. 进度计划经理注意到，由于数据录入错误，低估了关键路径上某项任务的完成时间。进度计划经理应该怎么做？

A. 立即与项目经理讨论该错误以及可能的纠正措施

B. 立即将该错误报告给项目发起人

C. 立即与项目经理讨论该错误并采取缺陷补救措施

D. 立即制定预防措施，确保不会引起客户对进度影响的担忧

142. The product development is coming to an end. At the stage review meeting, the marketing director thinks that the product is lack of competitiveness and puts forward suggestions for modification. The project manager realizes that if he follows the advice of the marketing director, it will subvert the whole product design and almost redevelop it. What should the project manager do?

A. Ignore the marketing director's suggestion and deliver the products according to the original plan

B. Modify according to the marketing director's suggestion to make sure the products are competitive

C. Strive for the support of more senior leaders to avoid the spread of project scope

D. Evaluate the impact and implement the integrated change control procedures

142. 产品开发已接近尾声，在阶段评审会上，市场总监认为产品缺乏竞争力，并提出修改建议。项目经理意识到，如果采纳市场总监的建议，那么将需要对整个产品进行颠覆性的设计，几乎要重新开发。项目经理应该怎么办？

A. 忽略市场总监的建议，按原计划交付产品

B. 按照市场总监的建议修改，确保产品有竞争力

C. 争取获得更高级领导的支持，避免项目范围蔓延

D. 评估影响并实施整体变更控制程序

143. During the execution phase of a project, the sponsor decides to terminate the project. What should the project manager do?

A. Discuss the feasibility of terminating the project with the project sponsor

B. Seek advice from the project management office (PMO)

C. Create project closure documents

D. Assess the impact of project termination

143. 在项目执行阶段，项目发起人决定终止项目。项目经理应该怎么做？

A. 与项目发起人讨论终止项目的可行性

B. 征求项目管理办公室（PMO）的意见

C. 创建项目收尾文件

D. 评估终止项目的影响

144. The disruptive technological revolution has created an unprecedented huge market, and companies are racing against the clock to develop new products to occupy this new market. The team received this strategic project, but did not receive the specific requirements. In fact, no one knows what kind of products can really win the market. However, releasing a product in a short time is very important for an enterprise to gain strategic opportunities. What should the team do?

A. Quickly define requirements by benchmarking

B. Speed up R & D progress by fast-tracking

C. Set up a large project team with multiple development groups to develop different parts in parallel

D. Focus on essential functions and release minimal viable products

144. 颠覆性的技术革命创造出了一个前所未有的巨大市场，各家公司都在争分夺秒地开发新产品，以占领这个新市场。团队虽然接到这个战略型项目，但并没有收到具体的需求。事实上，目前也没有人知道什么样的产品能够真正赢得市场。不过，在短时间内发布产品对企业取得战略先机至关重要。团队应该怎么做？

A. 通过标杆对照的方法快速定义需求

B. 通过快速跟进的方法加快研发进度

C. 组建包含多个开发组的大型项目团队，并行开发不同的部分

D. 聚焦必备功能，发布最小可行产品

145. Halfway through the product development project, the client informs the project manager that the project budget has to be cut by 15%. What should a project manager do?

A. Extend project duration and release some resources to save cost

B. Deliver the products as planned and bear the corresponding economic losses

C. Simplify the testing process to reduce costs

D. Apply for scope changes to reduce features have yet to begin development

145. 产品开发项目进展过半，客户通知项目经理不得不削减 15% 的项目预算。项目经理应该怎么做？

A. 延长项目工期、释放部分资源，以节约成本

B. 按原计划交付产品，并承担相应的经济损失

C. 简化测试流程，以降低成本

D. 申请范围变更，以减少尚未开发的功能

146. The quality audit report shows that some quality control processes are seriously non-conforming, and the relevant functional managers propose that the project budget cannot support the implementation of the required quality control standards. What should the project manager do?

A. Revise quality management plan according to budget support standard

B. Ask the sponsor to increase the budget to implement the quality control standard

C. Update quality compliance risk to risk register

D. Review the quality management plan and make budget changes if necessary

146. 质量审计报告显示，某些质量控制过程严重不合规。相关职能经理提出，项目预算无法支持质量控制标准的实施。项目经理应该怎么做？

A. 按照预算支持的标准修改质量管理计划

B. 要求发起人增加预算，以实施质量控制标准

C. 将质量合规风险更新到风险登记册

D. 审查质量管理计划，并在必要时对预算做出变更

147. The project manager discovered that some of the work being done by a subcontractor was not what they should be doing. Which document should the project manager review?

A. Project scope statement

B. Work breakdown structure

C. Procurement statement of work

D. Project charter

147. 项目经理发现一家分包商所做的有些工作并不是他们应该做的。项目经理应该审查哪份文件？

A. 项目范围说明书

B. 工作分解结构

C. 采购工作说明书

D. 项目章程

148. A new manager of the client company is very concerned about the current progress delay of the project and requires the project progress report to be changed from once a week to once a day, which will take up more time for the team to prepare the reports and cause further delay. What should the project manager do?

A. Follow the reporting frequency in the communication management plan

B. Change communication management plan to meet the new manager's requirement

C. Submit a change request to modify the schedule baseline

D. Proactively manage client's expectations and agree on a reasonable reporting frequency

148. 客户公司新入职的一位经理对项目目前的进度延误非常在意，要求项目进度报告从原来的每周一次改为每天一次，而这样做会占用团队更多的时间，进而使进度更加延误。项目经理应该怎么办？

A. 遵循沟通管理计划中的报告频率

B. 变更沟通管理计划，以满足新经理的要求

C. 提交变更请求，以修改进度基准

D. 主动管理客户期望，并就合理的报告频率达成共识

149. The project resources are limited and no more resources can be obtained. The dependence between activities also determines that activities cannot be paralleled. What technology should the project manager use to make full use of existing resources without delaying project completion?

A. Fast-tracking

B. Crashing

C. Resource smoothing

D. Resource leveling

149. 因为项目资源有限，团队无法获得更多资源，而且活动之间的逻辑关系也使活动无法并行，所以项目经理应该使用什么技术来充分利用现有资源，而不会导致项目完成时间延后呢？

A. 快速跟进

B. 赶工

C. 资源平滑

D. 资源平衡

150. In the process of project implementation, a key stakeholder withdraws from the project due to job transfer and is replaced by a new colleague. What should the project manager do first?

A. Update register of stakeholders

B. Update responsibility allocation matrix

C. Update risk register

D. Update stakeholder engagement plan

150. 在项目执行过程中，一位关键相关方因工作调动而退出项目，由一位新入职的同事接替。项目经理首先应该做什么？

A. 更新相关方登记册

B. 更新责任分配矩阵

C. 更新风险登记册

D. 更新相关方参与计划

151. What should the project manager do when he discovers that a team member is developing a feature that is not included in the project scope baseline?

A. Initiate a change to update the scope baseline

B. Encourage the team member to continue developing, and perhaps this feature is valuable

C. Add the new feature to the requirements document

D. Review the scope baseline with team members to avoid scope creep

151. 项目经理发现一名团队成员正在开发的一个功能并不包含在项目范围基准中，项目经理应该怎么做？

A. 发起一项变更，更新范围基准

B. 鼓励团队成员继续开发，或许这项功能很有价值

C. 将这项功能添加到需求文档中

D. 与团队成员审查范围基准，避免范围蔓延

152. When the company finds a project opportunity, the leader asks the project manager who has done similar projects to report a rough cost estimate to decide whether to participate in the project. Which of the following methods should the project manager use?

A. Expert Judgment

B. Analogous Estimating

C. Three-Point Estimating

D. Bottom-Up Estimating

152. 公司了解到一个项目机会，领导让之前做过类似项目的项目经理报一个粗略的成本估算，以决定是否参与该项目。项目经理应该采用以下哪种方法？

A. 专家判断

B. 类比估算

C. 三点估算

D. 自下而上估算

153. The client sends a Request for Proposal (RFP) and hopes to get the feedback as soon as possible. Project Management Office (PMO) Provide documentation of similar projects in the past for the reference of the project manager. Which method should the project manager use in order to estimate project cost and duration?

A. Bottom-Up Estimating

B. Three-Point Estimating

C. Parametric Estimating

D. Analogous Estimating

153. 客户发来建议邀请书并希望越快反馈越好，PMO 提供以往类似项目的文件供项目经理参考。为了估算项目成本和持续时间，项目经理应采用以下哪种估算技术？

A. 自下而上估算

B. 三点估算

C. 参数估算

D. 类比估算

154. In a new drug R & D project, the refrigerated reagent is invalid due to sudden power failure, and the reprocurement needs additional funds. This risk has been identified in the project planning. Which of the following measures should the project manager give priority to?

A. Claim against the power supply company

B. Insurance claim settlement

C. Use contingency reserve

D. Use management reserve

154. 在一个新药的研发项目中，冷藏的试剂因突发停电事故而失效，如果重新采购，需要额外的资金，这个风险在项目规划时已被识别。项目经理应该优先采用下列哪一项措施？

A. 向供电公司索赔

B. 使用保险理赔

C. 使用应急储备

D. 使用管理储备

155. The project manager was in charge of a new energy technology project, and the sponsor heard that the government was going to introduce a new industrial policy, which would directly determine the value of the project and even lead to the suspension of the project. The sponsor asks the project manager to assess the impact of the new policy on the project. Which of the following techniques should the project manager use?

A. What-if scenario analysis

B. Earned value analysis

C. Trend analysis

D. SWOT analysis

155. 项目经理正在负责一个新能源技术项目，发起人听说政府将要出台新的产业政策，新政策如何制定，将直接决定项目的价值，甚至导致项目被迫中止。发起人让项目经理评估新政策对项目的影响，项目经理应该使用下列哪项技术？

A. 假设分析

B. 挣值分析

C. 趋势分析

D. SWOT 分析

156. The project team is estimating the cost of a new project, hoping to refer to similar projects that have been completed before. Which of the following documents is the most accurate and reliable?

A. Business demonstration

B. Project charter

C. Scope statement

D. Closeout report

156. 项目团队正在估算一个新项目的成本，希望参考之前已经完成的类似的项目。以下哪一份文件最为准确和可靠？

A. 商业论证

B. 项目章程

C. 范围说明书

D. 收尾报告

157. The client sent a letter to inform the project manager that they wish to suspend the payment of the phased payment stipulated in the contract due to the temporary fund turnover difficulty, and said that the project delivery time could be postponed. The company's finance department warned that at the current cost rate, the funds would not be available until the next payment from the customer. What should a project manager do?

A. Suspend work and dismiss the team

B. Lowering project quality standards to reduce costs

B. Use cost management reserves to keep the project moving forward

D. Slow down the project and release some resources

157. 客户发函告知，因临时性的资金周转困难，所以希望暂缓支付合同中规定的阶段性付款，并表示可以接受项目交付时间顺延。公司财务部门预警，按现在的成本花费速度，资金无法支撑到客户下一次付款。项目经理应该怎么办？

A. 宣布停工并解散团队

B. 降低项目质量标准，以降低成本

C. 动用成本管理储备，以保持项目进展

D. 放缓项目进度并释放部分资源

158. The sudden increase of requirements leads to team overload, demoralization and conflicts. The project manager has realized that the project cannot be delivered on schedule. If this situation is to be avoided, what should the project manager do in advance?

A. Ensure that the increased requirements are necessary through requirements review

B. Any scope change should strictly follow the integrated change control procedures

C. Ensure that the project has sufficient contingency reserves

D. Ensure that such risks have been identified in advance and response measures have been planned

158. 突然增加的需求导致团队超负荷工作，士气下降，而且冲突不断爆发。项目经理意识到再这样下去，项目将无法按期交付。如果要避免这种局面发生，项目经理事先应该做什么？

A. 通过需求评审，确保增加的需求都是必要的

B. 任何范围变更都应严格遵循整体变更控制程序

C. 确保项目预留了足够的应急储备

D. 确保这类风险已被提前识别并规划了应对措施

159. During a multimillion-dollar project the project team encounters a high failure rate of intermediate deliverables which causes the company's management to be concerned. Which tool should the project manager use to identify the root cause of this issue?

A. Fishbone diagram

B. Histogram

C. Scatter diagram

D. Flow chart

159. 在执行一个价值数百万美元的项目期间，项目团队遭遇到中间可交付成果的高故障率，导致公司管理层十分担忧。项目经理应该利用下列哪一项工具来识别这个

问题的根本原因？

A. 鱼骨图

B. 直方图

C. 散点图

D. 流程图

160. What should the project manager do when a supplier proposes to upgrade the equipment to a new model with better performance for free?

A. Refuse the supplier's kindness and ask the supplier supply the old model stipulated in the contract

B. Accept the supplier's suggestion and update the acceptance criteria of the equipment

C. Perform cost-benefit analysis and evaluate the benefits of new models

D. Initiate a change and follow the integrated change control procedures

160. 一家供应商提出，可以将设备免费升级为性能更好的新型号，项目经理应该怎么做？

A. 拒绝供应商的好意，请供应商按合同规定的老型号供货

B. 接受供应商的建议，并更新设备的验收标准

C. 执行成本效益分析，评估新型号给项目带来的效益

D. 发起一项变更，并遵循整体变更控制程序

161. The project manager is implementing the delivery project for a local client in another country. The government requires project teams to hire 50 percent of their human resources locally. But the project manager find that most candidates do not have the necessary skills. What should the project manager do to solve this problem?

A. The domestic team can make up for the shortage of local personnel through remote support

B. Subcontract major tasks to local teams to transfer risk

C. Hire local human resources and provide training for the required skills

D. Let another 50% of own members do most of the work

161. 项目经理在国外为当地客户实施交付项目。该国政府要求项目团队 50% 的人力资源必须从当地雇佣。但项目经理发现，大部分候选人不具备必要技能。若要解

决这个问题，项目经理应该怎么做？

A. 通过国内团队的远程支持来弥补当地人员能力的不足

B. 将主要任务分包给当地团队，以转移风险

C. 雇佣当地人力资源，并提供必要的技能培训

D. 让团队中其余 50% 的成员承担大部分工作

162. In order to adapt to the rapid changes in the market, the company decided to change from the traditional waterfall development to agile development. However, it is difficult for the team to adapt to and begin to resist this change. They feel that the development efficiency does not increase, but decreases, and conflicts and frustrations increase. In order to promote agile transformation, the following should be done, EXCEPT:

A. Eliminate team members who are not suitable for agile and recruit members with agile experience

B. Organize agile training to help the team master agile tools and methods

C. Employ agile coach to guide team agile practice

D. Create appropriate rules, processes, environments and cultures for agile

162. 为了适应市场的快速变化，公司决定从传统的瀑布式开发转为敏捷开发。但是，团队成员很难适应，并且开始抵制这个变化，开发效率不增反降，冲突和挫折增多。为了促进敏捷转型，以下是应该做的，除了：

A. 淘汰不适应敏捷的团队成员，招聘有敏捷经验的人员

B. 组织敏捷培训，帮助团队掌握敏捷的工具和方法

C. 雇佣敏捷教练，指导团队敏捷实践

D. 创造适合敏捷的制度、流程、环境和文化

163. When the project manager found that the project plan was updated, the new version of the plan was officially released, and some subcontractors were still working with the old project plan. This happened more than once. What should the project manager do?

A. Review the communications management plan

B. Conduct a project performance review on these subcontractors

C. Review the integrated change control procedures

D. Review stakeholder engagement plan

163. 项目经理发现，项目计划更新后，新版本的计划也已正式发布，其中一些分包商仍然在参照旧的项目计划工作。这种情况已经不止一次出现，项目经理应该怎么做？

    A. 审查沟通管理计划

    B. 对这些分包商进行项目绩效审查

    C. 审查整体变更控制程序

    D. 审查相关方参与计划

164. A project team has delivered 3 important projects successively. The team members trust each other, appreciate each other, and cooperate tacit together. They have received a similar new project. Which stage is the most likely for the team to enter?

    A. Forming stage

    B. Storming stage

    C. Norming stage

    D. Performing stage

164. 一个项目团队连续成功交付了 3 个重要项目，团队成员之间相互信任、彼此欣赏，而且配合默契。他们又接到一个类似的新项目，团队最有可能进入以下哪个阶段？

    A. 形成阶段

    B. 震荡阶段

    C. 规范阶段

    D. 表现阶段

165. The project manager leads the team members to score the probability of each risk and its impact, multiply the probability score and impact score together, and rearrange the order of risks according to the product size. Which of the following activities do they do?

    A. Sensitivity analysis

    B. Quantitative risk analysis

    C. Qualitative risk analysis

    D. Monte Carlo analysis

165. 项目经理带领团队成员为每一个风险发生的概率和潜在的影响打分，并把概率分数和影响分数相乘，根据乘积大小，重新排列风险的顺序。他们做的是以下哪项活动？

A. 敏感性分析

B. 风险定量分析

C. 风险定性分析

D. 蒙特卡洛分析

166. A purchase is over budget, but the supplier's work is not yet complete. The contract signed with the supplier is cost plus fixed fee contract, how should the project manager deal with it?

A. Conducting procurement performance review

B. Change the supplier contract to a firm fixed price contract

C. Suspend payment until the contracted results are completed

D. Implement a strict change control procedures

166. 一项采购已经超出预算，但供应商的工作还未完成。公司与供应商签署的是成本加固定费用合同，项目经理应该怎么处理？

A. 开展采购绩效审查

B. 将供应商合同变更为固定总价合同

C. 暂停支付，直至完成合同约定的可交付成果为止

D. 实施严格的变更控制程序

167. At the start of the project, it is agreed that the person in charge of each related department should attend the weekly meeting of the project. Although the project went well, the project manager found that fewer and fewer department heads attended weekly meetings. To encourage active participation, what should a project manager look up?

A. Stakeholder register

B. Communication management plan

C. Human resource management plan

D. Stakeholder engagement plan

167. 项目在启动时约定，各相关部门的负责人应参加项目的每周例会。但是项目经理发现，虽然项目进展顺利，但每周参加例会的部门负责人越来越少。若要鼓励各相关方积极参与，项目经理应该查阅什么？

A. 相关方登记册

B. 沟通管理计划

C. 人力资源管理计划

D. 相关方参与计划

168. The sponsor approved a budget for major events and stressed that this budget was the ceiling. What kind of contract should the project manager sign with the stage construction supplier in order to control the risk of over budget?

A. Firm fixed price contract

B. Fixed price plus incentive fee contract

C. Cost plus fixed fee contract

D. Time and material contract

168. 发起人批准了举办大型活动的预算，并强调这个预算就是上限。项目经理为了控制预算超支的风险，应该和舞台搭建供应商签署哪种合同？

A. 固定总价合同

B. 总价加激励费用合同

C. 成本加固定费用合同

D. 工料合同

169. The project manager joins a project that is in the implementation phase and has experienced significant schedule delays and cost overruns due to scope creep. What should the project manager do at the upcoming CCB meeting to get the project back on track?

A. Propose new project baselines through trend analysis and obtain approval from the CCB

B. Propose new project budget through cost-benefit analysis and obtain approval from CCB

C. Propose new delivery times through PERT and obtain approval from CCB

D. Eliminate work that has not been started through needs analysis to meet performance goals

169. 项目经理接手一个项目，该项目正处于实施阶段，因范围蔓延已出现严重的进度延误和成本超支。在即将举行的变更控制委员会（CCB）的会议上，项目经理应该怎么做，可以让项目回到正常状态？

A. 通过趋势分析提出新的项目基准，并获得变更控制委员会的批准

B. 通过成本效益分析提出新的项目预算，并获得变更控制委员会的批准

C. 通过计划评审技术提出新的交付时间，并获得变更控制委员会的批准

D. 通过需求分析删减尚未开始的工作，以满足绩效目标

170. When the project is delivered, which of the following should the project manager complete before applying to the client for the last payment?

A. Confirmation of the lessons learned register by the project management office

B. Archive project assumption logs, problem logs, and change logs

C. Quality inspection of project deliverables

D. The project acceptance report is signed by the client

170. 项目交付完成，项目经理向客户申请最后一次支付前先要完成下列哪一项工作？

A. 项目管理办公室（PMO）对项目经验教训登记册的确认

B. 项目假设日志、问题日志、变更日志的归档

C. 项目可交付成果的质量检查

D. 获得有客户签字的项目验收报告

171. The company's new product will be released within two months, with 90 percent of the features developed. At this point, management notifies the project manager to terminate the product release and cancel the project for policy reasons. What should the project manager do next?

A. Finish the project deliverables as planned

B. Disband resources and record project status

C. Testing and acceptance of the developed features

D. Close the project and update the lessons learned register

171. 公司的新产品将在两个月内发布，90% 的功能已开发完成。这时管理层通知项目

经理，因为政策原因终止产品发布并撤销项目。项目经理下一步应该怎么做？

A. 按原计划完成项目可交付成果

B. 释放资源并记录项目状态

C. 测试和验收已开发的功能

D. 对项目进行收尾，并更新经验教训登记册

172. The project manager has received a project to develop a new product. The goal of this new product is to develop new business areas with great potential. Competitors are also developing the similar products. Whoever gets the user's acceptance first will get a huge competitive advantage. What should the project manager do?

A. Plan for a minimum viable product (MVP)

B. Ask the company for more resources to join the team

C. Mobilize the team to work 12 hours a day, 7 days a week before release

D. Eliminate reviews and reduce testing

172. 项目经理接到一个开发新产品的项目，这个新产品的目标是开拓极具潜力的新业务领域。竞争对手也在开发同类产品，谁先获得用户认可，谁就会获得巨大的竞争优势。项目经理应该怎么做？

A. 规划一个最小可行产品

B. 向公司申请更多的资源加入团队

C. 动员团队在新产品发布前，每周工作 7 天，每天工作 12 小时

D. 取消评审环节，并减少测试

173. Midway through a project, the project manager is replaced, the new project manager noticed project cost overruns, behind schedule and team morale is low, the new project manager should do?

A. Apply to the project sponsor to increase the budget and postpone the delivery time

B. Get approval from the project sponsor to reassemble the team

C. Reduce project scope to meet original budget and schedule

D. Work with the team to find out the cause of the problem and discuss the improvement plan

173. 项目中途，项目经理被替换，新上任的项目经理注意到，项目成本超支、进度落

后，而且团队士气低落。新上任的项目经理应该怎么做？

A. 向项目发起人申请增加预算并顺延交付时间

B. 获得项目发起人的批准，重新组建团队

C. 缩减项目范围，以满足原始预算和工期

D. 和团队一起找到问题产生的原因并讨论改进方案

174. After a requirement change was approved and implemented, the project manager found that the materials provided by a supplier could not meet the new requirement. Which of the following is the most likely cause of this?

A. There is an error in the description of material requirements in the procurement statement of work

B. The supplier misunderstands the requirements of the contract

C. The supplier lacks the necessary quality control before the material leaves the factory

D. The approved change was not notified to stakeholders before implementation

174. 一项需求变更被批准并实施后，项目经理发现，一家供应商提供的材料无法满足新的需求。以下哪一项最可能是出现这种情况的原因？

A. 采购工作说明书中对材料的要求描述有误

B. 供应商对合同的要求理解有误

C. 供应商在材料出厂前缺乏必要的质检

D. 批准的变更在实施前没有通知相关方

175. As the project delivery date nears, the team is in the most intense critical phase. At this time, project manager found that a work package in the work breakdown structure was missing, but there were no resources available within the company. In order for the project to be delivered on time, the project manager finds an external team that can take on the work package. What should the project manager do next?

A. Prepare the procurement statement of work

B. Update the risk register

C. Start the change control procedures

D. Update the responsibility assignment matrix

175. 项目交付日期临近，团队正处于最紧张的冲刺阶段。这时项目经理发现，工作分解结构中的一个工作包被遗漏，但是公司内部已经没有可以分配的资源。为了使项目如期交付，项目经理找到了一支可以负责这个工作包的外部团队。项目经理下一步应该做什么？

A. 编制采购工作说明书

B. 更新风险登记册

C. 启动变更控制程序

D. 更新责任分配矩阵

176. The project manager was in charge of a new car development project and team members raised the risk that the front suspension might break in cold weather. If that risk were real, it would affect not only this new model, but all cars with the same suspension. What should a project manager do?

A. Report the risk to senior management in accordance with integrated risk management principles

B. Suspension quality is not within the scope of new car development projects, do not worry

C. Make qualitative and quantitative analysis of this risk

D. Suspend project implementation and replace suspension supplier

176. 项目经理正在负责一个型号的新车开发项目。团队成员提出，前悬架在寒冷天气下可能出现断裂的风险。如果这个风险真的存在，不仅会影响这个型号的新车，同时也会影响采用相同悬架的所有车型。项目经理应该怎么办？

A. 按照整合式风险管理原则，将该风险上报给高级管理层

B. 悬架质量不属于新车开发项目的范围，不用担心

C. 对这个风险进行定性和定量分析

D. 暂停项目实施，并更换悬架供应商

177. After the client accepts the project deliverables, project manager begins to organize and archive project files. At this time the project manager is appointed to manage a new and more important project, what should the project manager do?

A. Delegate other members to close the previous project

B. Close the previous project as planned

C. Drop the remaining closing on the previous project and start the new one

D. Simplify the closing of the previous project and take time to finish it during the new project

177. 客户验收完项目可交付成果后，项目经理开始对项目文件进行整理并存档。这时项目经理被任命管理一个新的更重要的项目，项目经理应该怎么做？

A. 委托别人完成前一个项目的收尾工作

B. 按照计划完成前一个项目的收尾工作

C. 放弃前一个项目余下的收尾工作，开始新的项目

D. 简化前一个项目的收尾工作，在新项目工作期间抽时间完成

178. A new technology development project, during the research and development process, the team found that the technology is already out, even if it is developed according to the plan, there is little market value, what should the project manager do?

A. Continue to complete the project as planned and update the lessons learned register

B. Obtain approval from the sponsor to terminate the project early and complete the closure activities

C. Update the project charter and continue to develop according to the latest technical goals

D. Update the event to the risk register and conduct quantitative risk analysis

178. 有一个新技术开发项目，在研发过程中，团队发现这项技术其实已经落后，即便按计划开发出来也没有什么市场价值。项目经理应该怎么办？

A. 按计划继续完成项目，并更新经验教训登记册

B. 获得发起人批准提前终止项目，并完成收尾活动

C. 更新项目章程，按最新的技术目标继续研发

D. 将该事件更新到风险登记册并进行定量风险分析

179. A product development effort is coming to end and is about to enter the full test and integration phase. After earned value analysis, the current project cost performance index (CPI) = 1.2, schedule performance index (SPI) = 0.8. The VP of marketing was concerned that the product would not be released on time, and asked for a shorter testing schedule, because the launch date was already public and the company had invested huge amounts of money and resources in the new product launch. What should the project manager do?

A. Submit a change request to CCB for an additional budget to supplement testing resources

B. Submit a change request to CCB for an extension of the release date

C. Simplify testing as required by VP of marketing to ensure release on schedule

D. Increase testing resources to shorten schedule and continuously monitor project performance

179. 一个产品开发工作接近尾声，即将进入全面测试和集成阶段。经过挣值分析，目前项目成本绩效指数（CPI）= 1.2，进度绩效指数（SPI）= 0.8。因为产品发布时间早已公布于众，而且公司已经为新产品发布投入了巨额资金和资源，所以，市场副总裁非常担心产品不能如期发布，要求缩短测试时间。项目经理应该怎么办？

A. 向 CCB 提交一项变更请求，申请追加预算以补充测试资源

B. 向 CCB 提交一项变更请求，申请将产品发布时间延后

C. 按照市场副总裁的要求简化测试，以保证产品如期发布

D. 通过增加测试资源投入来压缩工期，并持续监控项目绩效

180. The project manager found that a contractor always had fewer workers on the project site than they reported. What was the most likely contract the project manager signed with the contractor?

A. Fixed price incentive fee contract (FPIF)

B. Firm fixed price contract (FFP)

C. Cost plus fixed fee contract (CPFF)

D. Cost plus incentive fee contract (CPIF)

180. 项目经理发现，一家承包商在项目现场的工人数量总是没有他们上报的多。项目经理与承包商最有可能签署的是哪一种合同？

A. 总价加激励费用合同

B. 固定总价合同

C. 成本加固定费用合同

D. 成本加激励费用合同

181. The latest quality report for a deliverable show major non-compliance issues with quality standards. During a review meeting, a functional manager points out that the budget will not support implementation of these standards, and claims that they are unimportant at this stage of the project. What should the project manager do?

A. Accept the expert judgement of the functional manager, and revise the quality management

B. Ask the project sponsor for a budget increase to important the quality standards

C. Update the project management plan to include a new risk associated with quality compliance

D. Review the quality management plan, and apply appropriate corrective actions regarding the budget

181. 可交付产品的最新质量报告显示了可交付成果与质量标准不一致的主要问题。在一次评审会议上，一位职能经理指出，预算将不支持这些标准的实现，并声称，在项目的这个阶段，这些标准并不重要。项目经理应该做什么？

A. 接受职能经理的专家判断并修改质量管理计划

B. 要求项目发起人增加预算，以提升质量标准的重要性

C. 更新项目管理计划，包括与质量合规相关的新风险

D. 审查质量管理计划，并就预算采取适当的纠正措施

182. The project manager finds that many team members' time is always assigned to other projects by their functional managers. This project is obviously behind schedule. What should the project manager do to get the project back on track?

A. Require team members to guarantee the work of this project first

B. Negotiate with the functional managers one by one for their supports

C. Meet with the PMO to request a higher priority for this project

D. Request to change the schedule baseline and get CCB's approval

182. 项目经理发现，很多团队成员的时间总是被他们的职能经理分配到别的项目上，项目已明显落后于进度计划。项目经理想把项目拉回正轨，应该怎么办？

A. 要求团队成员优先保障本项目的工作

B. 与职能经理进行逐一谈判，争取他们的支持

C. 与 PMO 开会，申请提升该项目的优先级

D. 请求变更进度基准并获得 CCB 的批准

多选题

183. Which of the following is the work before signing the contract with the supplier in the procurement process? (Choose 5)

A. Preparation of the procurement statement of work

B. Updating the lessons learned register

C. Independent estimation

D. Supplier selection analysis

E. Claim management

F. Procurement negotiation

G. Final account of project profit

H. Meeting of bidders

183. 以下哪些是采购流程中在与供应商签订合同之前应该完成的工作？（选 5 项）

A. 准备采购工作说明书

B. 更新经验教训登记册

C. 独立估算

D. 供方选择分析

E. 索赔管理

F. 采购谈判

G. 项目利润决算

H. 召开投标人会议

184. The agile expert is coaching the development team to hold a daily scrum meeting. What should be included in the daily scrum meeting? (Choose 3)

A. Reading agenda and discipline by the scrum master

B. Summarizing yesterday's team work by the scrum master

C. Sharing work done yesterday by team members

D. Assigning today's work to the team members by the scrum master

E. Sharing what they are going to do today by team members

F. Sharing experiences by team members

G. Sharing suggestions to improve teamwork by team members

H. Sharing what are the obstacles to achieving your goals by team members

184. 敏捷专家在辅导团队召开每日站会。以下哪些是每日站会中应该包含的内容？

（选 3 项）

A. 敏捷专家宣读会议议程和纪律

B. 敏捷专家对昨天的团队工作进行总结

C. 团队成员分享自己昨天已完成的工作

D. 敏捷专家为团队成员布置今天的工作

E. 团队成员分享自己今天将要开展的工作

F. 团队成员分享自己取得的经验

G. 团队成员分享改进团队协作的建议

H. 团队成员分享完成目标存在的障碍

185. In addition to the daily scrum meeting, what meetings do agile teams have in each sprint cycle? (Choose 3)

A. Sprint retrospect meeting

B. Version planning meeting

C. Product planning meeting

D. Sprint review meeting

E. Sprint audit meeting

F. Proposal review meeting

G. Sprint planning meeting

H. Performance review meeting

185. 敏捷团队除了召开例行的每日站会，在每个冲刺周期中，还会召开哪些会议？

（选 3 项）

A. 冲刺回顾会

B. 版本规划会

C. 产品规划会

D. 冲刺评审会

E. 冲刺审计会

F. 方案评审会

G. 冲刺计划会

H. 绩效评审会

186. The project manager is preparing the configuration management plan. What objects should the configuration management plan target? (Choose 3)

A. Product features, components and documentations

B. Knowledge, experience and lessons learned from the project

C. List of stakeholders

D. List of team members

E. List of identified risks

F. Project baselines, plans and documentations

G. List of project suppliers

H. List of competitive products

186. 项目经理正在编制配置管理计划，配置管理计划应该面向哪些对象？（选 3 项）

A. 产品的功能、组件和文档

B. 从项目中获得的知识、经验和教训

C. 项目相关方名单

D. 团队成员的名单

E. 被识别出来的风险清单

F. 项目的基准、计划和文件

G. 项目供应商名单

H. 竞品列表

187. What are the roles of an agile team adopting scrum development framework? (Choose 3)

A. Sponsor

B. Product Owner

C. Change Control Board

D. Project Manager

E. Scrum Master

F. Development Team

G. Project Steering Committee

H. Project Management Office

187. 采用 Scrum 开发框架的敏捷团队有哪几种角色？（选 3 项）

A. 项目发起人

B. 产品负责人

C. 变更控制委员会

D. 项目经理

E. 敏捷专家

F. 开发团队

G. 项目指导委员会

H. 项目管理办公室

188. Project team members consult the project manager, which of the following does not need to follow the integrated change control procedures? (Choose 3)

A. Change suppliers halfway

B. Scope change due to technical reasons

C. Update change log

D. Update schedule

E. Change project budget

F. Update the lessons learned register

G. Update issues log

H. Enable contingency planning

188. 项目团队成员请教项目经理，以下哪些不需要经过整体变更控制程序？（选 3 项）

A. 中途更换供应商

B. 技术原因导致范围变化

C. 更新变更日志

D. 更新进度计划

E. 改变项目预算

F. 更新经验教训登记册

G. 更新问题日志

H. 启用应急计划

189. The project team and the project sponsor agree that the agile method will be adopted to develop the software. What principles should the team adhere to? (Choose 5)

A. Embrace change

B. Distributed team

C. Working software

D. Inspire and trust

E. Self-organizing team

F. Regular retrospect

G. Unified leadership

H. Cycle flexibility

189. 项目团队与项目发起人达成一致意见，将采用敏捷方法开发软件，那么团队应该坚持哪些原则？（选 5 项）

A. 拥抱变化

B. 分布式团队

C. 可工作软件

D. 激发和信任

E. 自组织团队

F. 定期回顾

G. 统一领导

H. 周期灵活

190. The agile development team should discuss the items in the product backlog with the product owner before each sprint. Which of the following characteristics should the product manager make the items in the backlog have? (Choose 4)

A. Estimated

B. Validated

C. Emergent

D. Detailed Appropriately

E. With person in charge

F. Prioritized

G. Redundant

H. Constant

190. 敏捷团队在每个冲刺前都要和产品负责人讨论产品待办事项列表中的事项，产品经理应该使产品待办事项列表具备以下哪些特征？（选 4 项）

A. 经过估算的

B. 经过验证的

C. 涌现的

D. 有描述的属性

E. 有责任人的

F. 有优先级的

G. 有冗余的

H. 稳定不变的

191. The team is working on a very complex and challenging project. The project manager invites senior experts from the industry to share with the team. Which of the following is tacit knowledge of experts? (Choose 3)

A. Statistical data

B. Parameter model

C. Insight

D. Practical experience

E. Analysis report

F. Design drawings

G. Intuition

H. Flow chart

191. 团队正在做一个非常复杂且极具挑战的项目，项目经理邀请行业资深专家来给团队做分享。以下哪些属于专家的隐性知识？（选 3 项）

A. 统计数据

B. 参数模型

C. 洞察力

D. 实践经验

E. 分析报告

F. 设计图纸

G. 直觉

H. 流程图

匹配题

192. Each role in the agile team needs to work together, please match their correct responsibilities.

Product Owner	Realize user stories in the sprint
Scrum Master	Maintain and prioritize product to-do lists
Development Team	Guide, support and service the agile team

192. 敏捷团队中的各个角色需要分工合作，请为他们匹配正确的职责。

产品负责人	实现冲刺中的用户故事
敏捷专家	维护产品待办事项列表并排出优先级
开发团队	指导、支持和服务团队顺利开展敏捷

193. According to the Tuckman ladder theory, a project team usually goes through five stages. Please match the stages and team characteristics.

Forming stage	Members begin to accept each other and change themselves to fit each other
Storming stage	Members have returned to their departments to accept new tasks
Norming stage	Frequent conflicts and low morale among members
Performing stage	Members from different departments form a new team
Disbanding stage	The members have a good cooperation, excellent performance and high morale

193. 根据塔克曼阶梯理论，项目团队通常会经历五个阶段，请将项目阶段和团队特征进行匹配。

形成阶段	成员开始彼此接受并改变自己，以适应对方
震荡阶段	成员已回归到自己的部门接受新的任务
规范阶段	成员之间矛盾冲突频发且士气低落
表现阶段	从不同部门来的成员形成一个新的团队
遣散阶段	成员配合默契、绩效优秀，且士气高涨

194. In the project, conflict is difficult to avoid. How should the project manager match the appropriate conflict resolution method?

Force/direct	To protect the morale of team members, the project manager agreed to a risky plan
Withdraw/avoid	The project manager suggested that the urgent work should be finished first, and the difference should be discussed later
Smooth/accommodate	The project manager no longer explains the reason and asks team members to perform the task
Compromise/reconcile	Two team members discussed a solution that both sides were satisfied with
Collaborate/problem-solve	The project manager accepted two new requirements while persuading the client to withdraw three

194. 在项目中，冲突很难避免。项目经理应该怎么匹配合适的冲突解决方法？

强迫 / 命令	为了保护团队成员的士气，项目经理同意了具有一定风险性的方案
撤退 / 回避	项目经理建议先完成紧急的工作，对于分歧部分，以后再议
缓和 / 包容	项目经理不再解释原因，而是要求团队成员执行任务
妥协 / 调解	两名团队成员商量出双方都满意的解决方案
合作 / 解决	项目经理接受了两项新需求，同时说服客户收回三项需求

195. Project and risk are always met by chance. What are the measures taken by the project manager?

Contingency plan	When the test engineer suddenly fell ill, the project manager asked her boyfriend to help with the test temporarily

| Fallback plan | When demonstrating the scheme, the computer went down, and the project manager completed the demonstration with the iPad prepared in advance |
| Workarounds | Due to the epidemic, the project manager was forced to give up the grand delivery ceremony and completed the delivery online minimalist |

195. 项目风险总是不期而遇，项目经理采取的措施分别属于哪种应对方法？

应急计划	测试工程师突发疾病，项目经理让其男朋友临时帮忙测试
弹回计划	在演示方案时电脑宕机，项目经理用事先准备好的 iPad 完成了演示
权变措施	因为疫情，项目经理被迫放弃了隆重的交付仪式，在线以极简风格完成了交付

196. Project manager and team make quality management plan. Which scenario should the following quality management tools match?

Fishbone diagram	Discover abnormal data in time and give early warning
Check list	Looking for the relationship between quality indicators and various variables
Pareto graph	Quality analysis based on "man machine material method environment"
Histogram	Find out the main factors that cause most of the defects
Scatter plot	Distribution of display quality data
Control chart	Find the root cause of quality defects
Stratification method	Count the number of different defects

196. 项目经理在和团队编制质量管理计划，以下质量管理工具应该分别匹配哪种场景？

鱼骨图	及时发现异常数据并预警
检查表	寻找质量指标与各种变量之间的关系
帕累托图	根据"人机料法环"做质量解析
直方图	找出产生大部分缺陷的主要因素
散点图	显示质量数据的分布规律

控制图　　　　　找到产生质量缺陷的根本原因
层别法　　　　　统计各种不同缺陷的数量

填空题

197. The project manager led 4 team members to do a project with changeable requirements. Because of the great pressure of schedule, 2 new members joined the team, and _____ communication paths were added to the team.

197. 项目经理带领 4 位团队成员做一个需求多变的项目，因为进度压力大，有 2 位新成员加入团队，团队的沟通路径增加了 _____ 条。

198. The investment of the project is $4 million, the annual income is $1.2 million, the annual operating cost is $0.8 million. If the interest is not considered, the payback period of the project investment is _____ years.

198. 项目投资金额为 400 万美元，每年收入为 120 万美元，每年运营成本为 80 万美元。如果不考虑利息，项目投资回收期为 _____ 年。

199. The project manager obtained three new project opportunities. After analysis, he found that the net present value and internal rate of return of the three project opportunities are respectively as shown in Table 6-3. The project investment all depends on bank loans, and the bank loan interest rate is 6%. The project manager should choose project _____ .

Table 6-3　NPV & IRR of The Project

Project	A	B	C
NPV（million US$）	100	100	-100
IRR	7%	9%	5%

199. 项目经理获得了 3 个新的项目机会，他经过分析发现，3 个项目机会的净现值和内部收益率分别如表 6-3 所示。项目投资全部需要依靠银行贷款，银行贷款利率为 6%。项目经理应该选择 _____ 项目。

表 6-3　项目净现值与内部收益率

项目	A	B	C
净现值（NPV）	100 万美元	100 万美元	−100 万美元
内部收益率（IRR）	7%	9%	5%

200. The project consists of 7 activities from A to G, their duration estimation and antecedent activities are shown in Table 6-4. There are _____ critical paths for this project.

Table 6-4　List of Activities

Activities	Duration（Days）	Antecedent activities
A	1	——
B	2	A
C	3	A
D	5	B
E	3	B, C
F	4	C
G	2	D, E, F

200. 项目共包含 A~G 7 项活动，它们的历时估算和前序活动如表 6-4 所示。这个项目有 _____ 条关键路径。

表 6-4　活动列表

活动	历时（天）	前序活动
A	1	——
B	2	A
C	3	A
D	5	B
E	3	B、C
F	4	C
G	2	D、E、F

7

PMP 模拟题
第二套答案及解析

单选题

1　C

题干中提示了两点关键信息：一是编制计划前，二是高层级需求。编制计划最主要的输入就是章程，章程中表述了项目高层级的需求。高层级是指概括性的总体需求，不够具体和细致。访谈主题专家的目的就是对章程中的高层级需求进行确认，以便在编制计划时能够将其细化。

2　B

组织过程资产中包含这家组织的历史项目管理的知识、经验、模板等。通过组织过程资产，项目经理可以快速了解这个行业及这家企业的业务特点。

3　C

这道题考核的是对项目绩效报告的掌握。项目绩效报告中最核心的内容应该是项目关键绩效指标（比如进度、成本、质量等）和项目进展分析（如进度完成情况及预算使用情况）。选项 C 相比其他选项更为准确。

4　D

题干中提示项目经理发现了有效的方法，而且可以复用，这属于经验，应该将其更新到项目经验教训登记册中。如果这条经验被 PMO 评估为对公司有普遍的价值，就可以将其升级成为组织过程资产。

5　B

这道题的考点是项目收尾过程应包含的工作，其中，可交付成果的确认流程和验收标准（选项A）、项目终期审计要求（选项C）、知识转移的流程和标准（选项D）都是收尾过程的内容。但项目计划模板和经验教训登记册（选项B）属于组织过程资产，是历史上的其他项目留下来的。

6　D

这道题考核的是对整体变更控制程序的掌握。当变更被批准后，在新计划实施前，团队务必要通知所有可能受这个变更影响的相关方，并获得他们的确认。

7　D

不同的子项目可能性质不同，比如，产品硬件部分适合瀑布型开发，但软件部分适合敏捷型开发。生命周期主要取决于项目的特征，同一个组织很可能有不止一个类型的项目，所以选项A不对；项目阶段可能出现循环迭代，比如敏捷模式，因此，选项B不对；项目生命周期就是定义项目的开始和结束，所以不能选C。

8　D

给公司管理层提供决策支持的是工作绩效报告。在工作绩效报告中，不仅有问题陈述，还有原因分析，以及改进方案。

9　D

在设计阶段结束进入实施阶段时，产品还没有开发出来，因此，阶段关口不应该包括产品验收（选项D）。其余选项都是需要做的。

10　D

在进行需求评估时，被删除的功能已经不属于项目的范围，即便预算有剩余，也不能直接用于开发这些范围之外的功能。对于发起人提出的这个要求，和新增加的功能的处理方法一样，都必须走变更控制程序。

11　A

项目的每个阶段都包含一批工作，可以将其当作一个子项目去管理，并且应该按照五大过程组来规范执行管理过程。

12　D

项目管理过程中记录的经验教训是组织过程资产的主要来源，因此，经验教训登记册比其他文件对更新组织过程资产更加直接、有效。

13　A

投资回报率（ROI）＝年均净现金流（流入－流出）／投资＝200／800＝25%。如果每年净现金流不变，那么投资回收期（PBP）＝1/ROI＝1/25%＝4（年）。

14　D

当供应商提供的零件质量不合格，对项目计划产生影响时，项目经理应评估影响并拿出应对措施，走变更控制程序并获得批准，所以选项 D 非常合适。选项 A 是混淆选项，题干中的信息表明质量不合格的原因是清楚的，不存在分歧，因此，项目经理不需要和供应商一起审查采购合同。

15　C

净现值（NPV）是在偿还银行贷款本金和利息之后项目的净结余，应优先选择数额高的。当 NPV 相同时，选内部收益率（IRR）高的，IRR 高代表项目的抗风险能力强。

16　D

进入恶性循环的原因不是变更，变更只是触发了这个循环，真正的原因是质量管理的方法、工具、标准等可能存在不合理之处，项目经理应该审查并优化质量管理计划，摆脱这个恶性循环。

17　D

在项目中出现的经验教训应该及时被记录在经验教训登记册中，这个登记册属于项目文件，所以这个动作属于更新项目文件。经验教训不一定都会成为组织过程资产，通常经验教训登记册由 PMO 定期评估，并将共性的和再次发生的可能性较大的裁剪到组织过程资产库中，以此来维护组织过程资产的有效性。如果答案中没有项目文件，那么选择组织过程资产就是正确的了。

18　B

沟通工具和沟通方式是在沟通管理计划中被定义的，因此，若要改变沟通工具和沟通方式，项目经理应更新沟通管理计划。

19　A

选项A，责任人唯一原则属于管理要素，其他选项都属于组织治理框架的内容。

20　C

材料价格波动的风险应该事先已被识别出，且做过风险应对计划。当该风险发生时，按计划应对是最佳选择。

21　D

项目成员缺乏安全感和归属感是项目型组织的缺点。

22　B

划分风险的高、中、低等级属于风险定性分析，选项中只有概率和影响矩阵属于风险定性分析中使用的工具，其余三项都是在风险定量分析中使用的工具。

23　C

矩阵型组织最重要的特征就是团队成员有两个汇报对象：职能经理和项目经理。

24　C

把优先级低但不确定性高的功能删除，即通过主动改变计划来避免遭遇风险，这属于风险规避策略。

25　D

项目的相关方登记册必须是由项目经理根据项目的独特性逐一识别的。在开展新项目之前，PMO只能提供通用的、共性的参考资料或历史数据。像相关方登记册这样的项目文件必须由项目经理负责带领团队共同编制和维护。

26　D

虽然技术人员请假一周，但不影响项目的整体进度，选项A、B、C都是合理的理由。选项D，哪些工作在关键路径上是由工作本身的时间特点决定的，不是可以被随便修改的。另外，若要将关键路径上的工作变到非关键路径上，只有压缩关键路径上的工作，或者延长非关键路径上的工作，使关键路径与非关键路径发生交换才能实现，但这不是合理的方案。

27　C

总的项目目标不切实际，说明项目章程本身不合理。因为项目章程的负责人是项目发起人，所以项目章程的修改需要征得发起人同意。因此，最合理的做法是把客观情况及时反馈给项目发起人。

28　D

恶劣天气（如台风）属于已知—未知风险，应通过应急储备来解决。为了让应急储备更可靠，应该对台风这个风险进行更为精确的定量分析。暂停项目过于保守，转移给分包商并不能完全转移进度延误的风险，精准的天气数据是有利的，但是需要转化成有效的应对方案。

29　B

这道题考核的是事业环境因素和组织过程资产的区别。题干中提示公司以前没有在这个国家合作过，所以没有相关经验，更没有在这个国家交付项目的组织过程资产。所以，项目经理只能从头开始分析在这个国家交付项目的事业环境因素。选项D组织团队成员进行头脑风暴不合适，因为团队成员没有相关经验，所以头脑风暴的价值很有限。

30　D

分包商没有收到变更通知，项目经理需要审查的是变更管理计划，而不是沟通管理计划，因为在整体变更控制程序中有明确的通知相关方的步骤，需要检查整体变更控制程序是否被严格执行。当个别分包商因为参与度不够或参与过度而产生问题时，项目经理需要审查相关方参与计划。对于因沟通方式和频率而产生的沟通问题，项目经理应该审查沟通管理计划。根据题干描述，风险已不止发生一次，风险的发生不代表风险管理计划有问题，所以不能选 C。已经发生的是问题，所以审查风险管理计划没有道理。

31 D

在整个项目期间，团队获取到的经验和教训应该及时更新到经验教训登记册中。

32 C

项目团队内部的沟通规则、冲突解决原则、团队纪律等都要靠团队章程来统一。

33 A

项目管理过程是在项目的每个阶段反复进行的，迭代就是项目管理过程的特征。过程之间存在大量输入、输出的数据流，彼此不是独立的，所以不能选 B；项目管理过程也需要根据项目的具体需求做合理的裁剪，不一定都需要，所以，选项 C 是不对的；项目管理过程作为一套通用的体系面向所有行业，并没有行业局限性，所以，选项 D 也不对。

34 A

判断团队成员的暂时性离开是否影响项目工期，需要先通过 RACI 矩阵确定团队成员的职责，分析他所负责的工作是否在关键路径上。如果在非关键路径上，则总浮动时间需要大于一周；如果在关键路径上，则需要通过储备分析判断应急储备是否足够弥补团队成员请假造成的影响。选项 A 非常合理，选项 B、C、D 中都包含没有必要的工具和技术。

35 D

项目管理计划在项目管理过程中也会根据需要而不断更新。比较容易选错的是选项 C，项目管理计划是一套规则文件，比如成本管理计划是规定货币种类、精确度、控制标准等，而不是预算，预算是独立的项目文件，所以选项 C 的表述是正确的。

36 B

当项目团队人员发生变动时，团队要重新经历形成、震荡阶段，然后再进入规范和表现阶段，除非新来的成员曾经与其他成员合作过。

37　D

根据整体变更控制程序，需要先评估变更的影响。题干指出，变更不影响进度，但不代表不会影响成本、质量等其他制约因素。

38　C

找出缺陷的根本原因需要使用鱼骨图，鱼骨图也称因果图或石川图。

39　C

变更日志记录了变更请求处理的经过和批准的决议。受到影响的相关方一般都有机会在变更控制过程中发表意见。

40　A

质量保证的目的就是确保质量控制的过程合规，也就是符合质量管理计划的要求。不管结果是否合格，测试人员都必须重视过程的合规。

41　C

这属于范围变更的典型例子，只要是变更，都必须按照整体变更控制程序执行。

42　A

评估、测试环节确实不一定能减少出现故障后的返修成本，但是可以有效减少出现故障的概率。评估、测试成本是产品开发过程中的预防性成本，属于一致性成本，应该保留。返修成本是非一致性成本，与一致性成本不可互相取代。

43　A

变更供应商也是变更，需按照整体变更控制程序执行。

44　C

当有相关方不赞同时，项目经理应该把相关方的情况及时更新到相关方登记册中，同时更新相关方参与度评估矩阵，使相关方按照团队希望的参与程度去努力。

45 D

这是一道标准的变更题。只要和计划出现不一致的情况，不管是谁的原因造成的，都需要按变更控制程序执行。

46 A

变更的所有过程都应被记录在变更日志中。没有经过 CCB 批准的记录，就必须审查变更日志，以便确认没有批准纪录的原因是没有遵守变更控制程序，还是变更没有影响基准，所以不需要 CCB 的批准。

47 D

虽然章程很少被修改，但章程是可以修改的。因为章程是发起人发布的，所以修改章程也必须经过发起人的批准。

48 D

当工期被缩短且不能增加预算时，只能利用项目范围、进度、成本之间相互影响和制约的关系，取得工期和范围之间的平衡。删除一部分需求也就是适当缩小范围，从而缩短工期。

49 C

范围确认是让主要相关方（如客户）正式确认本阶段完成的可交付成果符合要求。范围确认是在项目每个阶段结束时都要做的。

50 D

供应商供货达不到要求，属于采购管理的问题。因为采购过程是采购经理参与和主导的，采购协议不是项目经理直接与供应商签署的，因此，项目经理有必要先在内部和采购经理一起审查采购协议，分析问题产生的原因，并协商解决措施。

51 D

工作包只是 WBS 元素中的最低层级，也就是项目经理管理分解到的最低层级。工作包交给执行团队还需要被进一步分解为活动，活动还可以被分解为个人的任务。因此，工作包在逻辑上还可以再分解。

52　D

对于大型的用户故事，团队往往无法在一个冲刺之内实现，我们通常把这类用户故事叫作史诗故事，或者干脆就叫史诗。团队一般在进入冲刺之前，把史诗进一步分解为多个用户故事。在 Scrum 开发框架中确实有选项 A 主题故事，它指的是同一主题的多个用户故事，比如围绕"用户撤销订单"的若干个用户故事。但主题故事不符合题干所描述的特征，所以不能选 A。 在 Scrum 开发框架中并没有传奇故事和连载故事这样的说法，所以选项 B 和 C 属于混淆选项。

53　C

不管新材料是谁推荐的，更换材料属于典型的变更场景，必须按照变更控制程序先评估影响，再一步一步地进行变更决策。

54　C

项目不管什么原因被中止，项目经理最重要的工作都是妥善完成收尾。

55　C

资源日历是项目团队成员（资源）的工作日历。项目经理只有通过了解资源日历，才能够知道每个资源可用的时间，从而避开与其他项目工作的冲突。

56　B

采购的部件降价会使成本降低，项目经理应该及时修改预算，但是必须经过变更控制程序。

57　B

类比估算适合基于历史数据的估算，既高效又经济。题干中提示之前团队在多个项目中都做过这些活动，因此，有丰富的历史数据可以参照，类比估算比较合适。对于新的从未做过的活动，无论类比估算、三点估算还是参数估算都缺乏依据，最合适的方式就是请教这个领域有经验的专家。自下而上估算是指将活动向上汇总到工作包、子项目、项目，而本题问的是活动历时估算，所以自下而上估算不合适。

58　A

β分布的期望值 T_e＝（O＋4M＋P）/6＝（5＋4×8＋17）/6＝9，标准差 σ＝（P－O）/6＝（17－5）/6＝2。

59　C

滞后量（Lag）的含义是在前一项工作完成后增加等待的时间，而不是让后序工作马上开始。

60　D

项目应该遵照被批准的计划，不能因为客户换领导而随意改变，如果要改变，就必须经过变更控制程序。

61　D

关键链法是高德拉特在制约理论基础上提出的分析技术，强调储备（缓冲）集中管理，避免储备事先被分配到活动上，但风险未发生，从而造成浪费。

62　C

压缩工期只有两种方法可以选择：快速跟进和赶工。题干中已经说明关键路径上的活动无法并行，所以快速跟进被排除，只剩下赶工一个选择，赶工需要为关键路径上的活动增加资源。需要注意的是，获取更多的资源需要先经过变更控制程序。

63　C

资源过载是指资源供给无法满足某一时间段的资源需求。项目经理应该首先考虑资源平衡，通过错开这个时间段同时进行的活动，或延长某些活动的历时，以匹配有限的资源。虽然资源平衡可能造成总工期延长，但题干中告知工期还有余量，所以可以接受一定程度的工期延长。因此，选项C是正确的。

64　C

团队成员对每项活动的职责可以用RACI矩阵来表示。如果要了解颗粒度更大的工作包与团队中不同角色的关系，那么我们可以使用RAM责任分配矩阵。

65 C

如图 7-1 所示，B—D 是关键路径，A—C 路径总共有 2 周的浮动时间（活动 A 和活动 C 之间 1 周，活动 C 之后 1 周）。

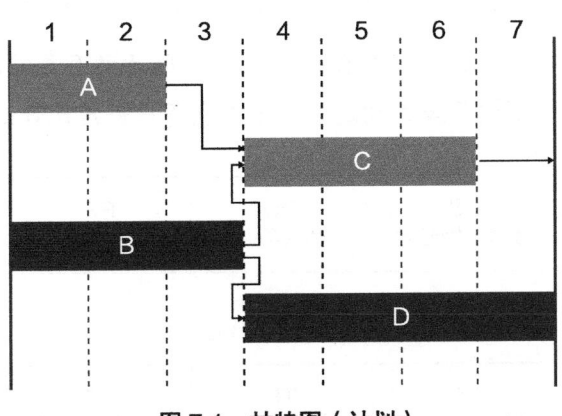

图 7-1 甘特图（计划）

如图 7-2 所示，活动 A 晚 3 周开始，消耗掉 2 周的浮动时间之后，A—C 变成了关键路径，还使总工期延长了 1 周。

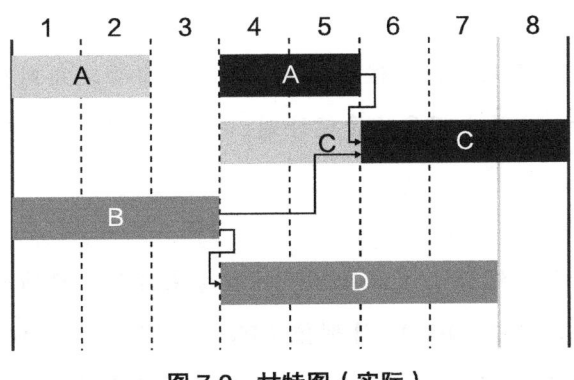

图 7-2 甘特图（实际）

66 B

采购管理计划中定义了采购的流程、决策的机制、应遵循的标准、采购的方法和工具等。采购工作说明书（SOW）应遵循采购管理计划，并在获得相关方的同意后便于实施，所以选项 B 最合适。选项 A 沟通管理计划是针对沟通的机制、规则、方法等，无法聚焦在具体的采购问题上。选项 C 相关方参与计划是针对每个相关方参与程度而设计的，也不适用于采购决策中。选项 D 风险管理计划与本题不搭边。

67 A

浮动时间≤0 的活动一定在关键路径上，所以选项 A 正确。选项 B 最早开始时间（ES）早于最晚开始时间（LS），说明 LS-ES>0，浮动时间为正，与题干不符。

如图 7-3 所示，选项 C 最晚结束时间（LF）早于最晚开始时间（LS），这两个值之间的差是活动历时（DU），不是浮动时间。选项 D 活动有负的浮动时间，如果不能压缩该活动工期的话，必然导致工期延误，不可能得出进度比计划超前的结论。

图 7-3 活动参数

68 A

采购管理计划定义了采购的流程、验收标准等。当管理层对交付成果的验收标准和验收程序有争议时，应该查阅采购管理计划。

69 C

挣值分析的核心就是综合了成本和进度的数据来评估项目绩效和预测项目未来进展，所以选项 C 正确。挣值（EV）、计划值（PV）、实际成本（AC）都是成本的范畴，不涉及利润，所以选项 A 不正确。挣值分析是项目过程中的绩效评估，主要不是用于项目完成时的评估，所以选项 B 不正确。选项 D 错在"任何时间点"和"精准预测"，挣值分析的预测都是粗略的，不可能太精确，而且"任何时间"太绝对，对于项目刚开始的数据，挣值分析无法做到精准预测。

70 C

本题选项 A、B、D 均有道理，但是都不全面。选项 C 人际关系与团队技能是综合应用权力、领导力和沟通技能，可以缓和团队抵触情绪，并影响团队使其接受任务。

71 D

10 周计划已过去 4 周, 假设团队匀速完成工作, 那么按计划应该完成 200 万美元的 40%, 也就是 80 万美元 (PV)。然而, 团队实际只完成了 1/3 的工作, EV = 200 × (1/3) = 66.7 (万美元); 成本花掉一半, AC = 200 × 50% = 100 (万美元)。CV = EV − AC = 66.7 − 100 = −33.3 (万美元), 说明成本超支; SV = EV − PV = 66.7 − 80 = −13.3 (万美元), 说明进度落后。

72 B

本题考核的是对完工估算的理解, 完工估算 (EAC) 是指根据当前绩效估算完工需要的成本。

73 D

计划此时花掉 100 万美元 (PV), 实际花掉 110 万美元 (AC)。在挣值分析中, 这两个值并不互相比较, 而且, 因为没有 EV 的值, 所以得不出选项 A、B、C 的结论。

74 D

在敏捷开发中, 团队对用户反馈应做出快速响应。因为新功能让用户体验不佳, 所以团队应把提升用户体验作为一个待办事项, 并评估优先级, 根据优先级来确定是否马上解决, 还是在下一个冲刺中解决。

75 C

你给发起人提供的成本估算应该是基于客观、严谨和诚信的前提, 发起人要求砍掉 15% 的成本估算, 那么只有缩小项目范围才是直接、有效的措施。让团队成员都砍掉 15% 的成本估算, 说明估算水分太大, 所以选项 B 不对。在这种情况下开始运行项目风险太大, 所以选项 A 不对。应急储备是用来应对识别出来的已知—未知风险, 这些风险如果没发生, 不能启用应急储备; 当风险发生的可能性没有完全消除之前, 不能减少或取消应急储备, 而且选项 D 的意思是通过减少应急储备来减少估算, 所以选项 D 不对。

76 D

通过团队的表现, 我们可以看出, 这支团队已经到达了塔克曼阶梯理论中的表现阶段。

77 B

完工偏差（VAC）= 完工预算（BAC）- 完工估算（EAC），已知 BAC = 500（万美元），完成了 40% 工作量，则挣值（EV）= 500×40% = 200（万美元）。实际成本（AC）= 250（万美元），则成本绩效指数（CPI）= EV/AC=200/250 = 0.8，EAC = BAC/CPI = 500/0.8 = 625（万美元），VAC = BAC - EAC = 500 - 625 = -125（万美元），完工尚需绩效指数（TCPI）=（BAC - EV）/（EAC - AC）=（500 - 200）/（625 - 250）= 0.8。按照 TCPI 的初始公式计算，$TCPI_0$=（BAC - EV）/（BAC - AC）=（500 - 200）/（500 - 250）= 300/250 = 1.2，因为 $TCPI_0$ >1，所以通常不可行。因此，唯一正确的选项就是 B。

78 D

何时、以什么方式、提供哪些信息给相关方，属于沟通管理计划中事先定义好的内容，相关方获得项目进展信息是合理需求，项目经理应遵照沟通管理计划定期提供正式的报告，不宜破坏规则。

79 C

选项 C 产品保修成本是产品出厂后出现质量问题，为了解决问题而发生的成本，属于非一致性成本。其余三个选项都是为了避免产品质量有缺陷而事先付出的预防成本，属于一致性成本。

80 C

注意题干中强调在项目规划过程中，也就是说，项目计划还没完成，项目还没开始实施。选项 A、B、D 都是项目实施过程中采取的措施，只有选项 C 可以被用在项目规划过程中，此时，项目经理可以通过储备分析预留合理的储备来应对风险。

81 A

帕累托图的原理就是将缺陷按原因归类后排序（缺陷从多到少），然后画出缺陷累计曲线。少数原因造成的缺陷已占到总缺陷数量的大部分，所以只要帮助项目经理集中精力找出少数原因，就能解决大部分缺陷。

82　C

在选择方案时把未来市场的变动风险考虑进去，就是决策树分析。每种方案的预期货币价值（EMV）= 市场好的收益 × 市场好的概率 – 市场差的损失 × 市场差的概率。通过决策树分析，选择预期货币价值高的方案。

83　C

规格线应该是距离期望值上下各 4 倍标准差的位置。题干中提示允许的误差是 ±4 克，由此可以判断标准差是 1 克。控制线应该是距离期望值上下各 3 倍标准差的位置。因此，控制线的范围是 497 克～503 克。

84　A

最新的质量管理理念不是追求完美、追求极致，而是符合用户的使用需求。其实，所谓完美并不美。

85　D

专家 / 权威的权力是项目经理自身的权力，而非职位带来的权力。

86　A

在敏捷开发中，产品负责人（Product Owner）是专门负责收集、整理需求，维护待办事项列表，以及主导待办事项优先级讨论的人员。

87　D

合作 / 解决是效果最好的冲突解决技术，能够达到双赢，而且副作用最小、效果最彻底、影响最持久。

88　D

本题考核的是冲突解决方法。题干给出的信息是团队成员和项目经理就工作有没有必要做而产生冲突，项目经理有把握这些工作必须做而且没时间去解释，所以只能采取强迫 / 命令的方法，让团队成员服从指挥。

89   B

团队章程是为团队创建团队价值观、共识和工作指南的文件。

90   D

新工具可以提升效率、降低成本，这对于项目而言是一种机会，积极主动地拥抱机会就是应对策略中的开拓。

91   A

被强制的一方虽然体验很差，但在情况紧急时，为了顾全大局，强制也是一种必要的、有效的正确选择。

92   B

项目范围说明书中有对项目应该包含的可交付成果及其验收标准的描述，而且是随着项目的变化持续更新的，因此，项目经理中途接手项目，从项目范围说明书中能够获取可交付成果的最新信息。

93   C

团队原来有 5 名成员，走了 1 名，来了 3 名，变成了 7 名，沟通路径 $C_7^2 = N \times (N-1)/2 = (7 \times 6)/2 = 21$（条）；原来团队有 5 名成员时，沟通路径 $C_5^2 = N \times (N-1)/2 = (5 \times 4)/2 = 10$（条）。所以，沟通路径新增：$C_7^2 - C_5^2 = 21 - 10 = 11$（条）。

94   D

两个 5 人的团队合并成了一个 10 人的团队，虽然总人数没有变，但是沟通路径增加了。沟通路径的计算公式是 $C_n^2 = n \times (n-1)/2$，5 人团队的沟通路径 $C_5^2 = 5 \times 4/2 = 10$（条），两个团队就是 20 条；10 人团队的沟通路径 $C_{10}^2 = 10 \times 9/2 = 45$（条）。因此，团队合并后，沟通路径增加了 25 条。

95   A

沟通管理计划应明确定义团队之间沟通的方式和频率、确认的方式和时限等，以确保沟通的及时性和有效性。

96　D

当需求不明确时，需要快速交付，尽早得到用户的反馈。这些信息告诉我们，敏捷开发是最合适的方式。

97　C

项目章程中通常都有默认授权，当关乎团队成员和相关方人身安全的风险发生时，项目经理可以直接实施自动权变措施，不必等待批准。

98　A

事先删除这个需求，就能躲开非常难以处置的风险，这属于风险规避策略。

99　D

进度和成本的权重比为4∶1，这说明要采用加权的风险影响与概率矩阵，通过公式"（对进度的影响分数 × 进度权重80% + 对成本的影响分数 × 成本权重20%）× 风险概率"计算评分，看哪个评分（风险评级）最高，如表7-1所示。

表7-1　风险发生的概率和影响

风险	概率	对进度的影响	对成本的影响	风险评级
A	75%	2	2	1.5
B	50%	3	5	1.7
C	75%	2	4	1.8
D	50%	4	3	1.9

100　A

本题考核的是决策树的应用，预期货币价值（EMV）=成功的收益 × 成功的概率 - 失败的损失 × 失败的概率。方案一，EMV = 100 × 85% - 100 × 15% = 70（万美元）；方案二，EMV = 200 × 65% - 200 × 35% = 60（万美元）。方案一的预期货币价值比方案二高10万美元，因此，选项A正确。

101　A

采购过程中供应商给出低于常理的报价往往是因为供应商对采购需求的理解不完整或不准确，应该让供应商重新评估和确认需求。

102 C

题干中有两个重要信息：一是分包合同金额不得超过 100 万元，说明有上限；二是项目经理希望尽量节约研发投入。若要节约研发投入，就需要和分包商形成利益共同体，如此，分包商才有动力节约成本。激励条款（分担/分享比率）就是能达到这个目的的有效措施。分包合同金额不能超过 100 万元，那么在合同中加上这个天花板价格就可以。所以，项目经理应该与第三方签署总价加激励费用合同（FPIF）。

103 B

总价加经济价格调整合同（FPEPA）就是在总价的基础上，增加因市场变化、材料价格波动等不确定因素而调整合同价格的条款，买卖双方共担风险，有利于其建立长期的合作关系。

104 C

成本加固定费用合同约定，成本实报实销，都由买方承担，另外给卖方的费用是固定的，对于卖方来说没有任何的不确定性，无论成本是多少，最终得到的都是固定的费用。风险是指不确定性，都由买方承担。

105 B

针对总价加激励费用合同，合同款 = 实际成本 + 目标费用 - （实际成本 - 目标成本）× 卖方分担比例 = 250 + 50 - （250 - 200）× 20% = 290（万美元），因为该数值大于最高限价 280 万美元，所以，买方只需支付 280 万美元。

106 B

投标人会议面向所有合格的投标人，目的就是澄清采购文件中的内容。

107 C

这道题考的是项目经理的职业道德。项目能够提前完工并且节约成本，即便影响公司利润和自己的奖金，也应如实告知客户，维护客户的权益。

108 B

项目范围说明书主要定义的是项目范围，也就是项目都包含哪些可交付成果及其验收标准，并不包含成本和进度信息。成本和进度应在专门的预算和进度计划中被定义。

109 C

关键相关方意见缺失是一个重要的风险，应体现在章程的风险描述部分，可以提醒主要相关方在评审章程时注意。

110 D

如果不限制在制品数量，就会导致同时开展的工作（在制品）增多，进而出现选项 A、B、C 描述的后果。所以，只能选 D。

111 B

当遇到分歧时，应首先考虑"合作/解决问题"的冲突解决策略，积极主动地正面沟通永远是第一选择。

112 A

燃尽图就是对比实际剩余工作量和计划剩余工作量的曲线图，在敏捷开发中非常常用，可以用来展示和评估项目进展。因此，选项 A 最符合题意。

113 A

工作绩效数据是在执行项目活动的过程中，从每个正在执行的活动中收集到的原始的观察结果和测量值。工作绩效数据包括已完成的工作、关键绩效指标、技术绩效测量结果、进度活动的开始日期和结束日期、变更请求的数量、缺陷的数量、实际成本和实际持续时间等。

114 D

在敏捷开发中，迭代（冲刺）的长度不宜太长，因为如果长度太长，就丧失了对变化的适应性，丢掉了敏捷的初衷；长度也不宜太短，因为如果长度太短，每个冲刺的计划会、评审会、回顾会所用的时间占比就会过大，而实际投入开发的工作时间就会太少。因此，合适的长度是很重要的，多数敏捷团队会选择 2 周作为迭代的长度。

115　C

瀑布开发模型属于预测型生命周期，强调事先编制完善的计划，尽量少变更，最好不变更。

116　D

新产品开发需要关注竞品、市场、技术的变化，如果出现对项目产生重大影响的外部变化，应该及时和项目发起人重新讨论项目商业论证，保证产品具有足够的商业价值。

117　D

项目经理的领导力和人际关系技能属于项目经理个人不断积累和培养的软技能，不属于配置管理的对象。

118　A

根据题干的信息，造成绩效恶化的原因不是原来对成本和进度估算不准，而是需求变化太频繁，所以，项目经理应该重新考虑项目开发方式是否恰当。只有从瀑布开发转为迭代甚至敏捷开发，才能更好地适应这种需求多变的场景。

119　C

让团队成员加班和延期交付项目都是当前的备选方案，项目经理需要综合分析得失利弊后做出选择，这种分析技术是备选方案分析。

120　C

产品被客户接受了，说明产品符合客户的需求。某项性能没有达到预期的质量标准，只能说明质量控制不合格，可能是客户疏忽了，也可能是一个潜在的质量隐患，客户还没发现。

121　A

冲刺中的方法、协作、沟通和团队问题都应在回顾会议中讨论。产品增量是否满足要求是评审会上要解决的问题。本次迭代要开发哪些产品增量是规划会的内容。每天个人已完成的工作、将要完成的工作及遇到的障碍是在每日站会上分享的内容。

122　C

冲刺已经开始，意味着本冲刺规划的工作内容已经过确认、工作量已经过评估。通常我们不鼓励在冲刺内增加新工作，除非特别必要。只要增加新工作，就要重新评估优先级，用优先级更高的新工作替换掉原来优先级相对低的工作，以保证冲刺计划的合理性。

123　D

敏捷开发的优势是适应易变的需求、快速交付和持续反馈。选项 D 敏捷是四个选项中与题干场景最吻合的。瀑布对变更不友好，所以最不合适。迭代和增量并不同时具备更快的频率和更早的交付能力。

124　C

冲刺中没有达到发布要求的功能，可以被列入下一个冲刺的待办事项列表中继续改进。

125　D

敏捷专家（Scrum Master）的职责之一就是保护团队在冲刺过程中不受干扰。

126　D

因为该项目优先级低，资源常常被更高优先级的项目抽调走而导致进度延误，这说明当初做项目计划时没有充分考虑这个因素的影响。项目经理应该更保守地估计资源的可用情况，重新评估进度计划，设定更为客观可行的进度基准。

127　C

用户故事是为了让团队能够准确理解需求，细节的颗粒度应该由团队和产品负责人协商，在确保理解无误的基础上尽量精简。

128　C

敏捷开发的原则就是为用户创造价值，选项 A、B、D 都不是评价敏捷是否成功的指标。

129　D

敏捷估算扑克是让团队成员各自估算故事点数，然后选择对应的扑克出牌（相当于投票），以此方式来估算用户故事的规模。

130　D

团队在每日站会上只分享每个人的工作进展，对别人的建议不评价，也不展开讨论。

131　D

敏捷专家（Scrum Master）在敏捷开发中的职责之一就是移除当前冲刺（Sprint）中的障碍。

132　B

项目商业论证中包含项目启动的意义、商业价值、可行性研究等，可以用来打消相关方对为什么实施这个项目的顾虑。

133　A

针对题干中描述的场景，选项 A 是最合适的。通过规范变更管理，比如重新审定变更控制程序并严格执行，可以减少频繁变更对项目的影响。通过使用领导力技能，可以激发团队的热情并提升团队士气。

134　D

培养自己的领导力，重点在于激发别人，帮助团队成员成长，让他们取得进步并获得成就感，而不是替团队成员完成本该由他们自己完成的工作。就算你可以比他们干得更好，也不能这么做，你要给别人成长的机会。

135　D

产品待办事项列表中的条目应符合 DEEP 原则，即详略适当的（Detailed appropriately）、经过估算的（Estimated）、涌现的（Emergent）、按优先级排序的（Prioritized）。

136 C

工作分解结构（WBS）本身包含的信息非常有限，主要是呈现项目工作的结构。工作包的具体信息都被记录在 WBS 词典中。

137 B

风险应对计划需获得批准。因为资金有限，不能覆盖所有被识别出来的风险，所以项目经理需要做出相应的预算调整，保留适当的风险敞口，但针对高优先级的风险应对计划应被批准。

138 A

更换老化了的喷涂部件属于纠正措施。召回存在缺陷的产品并重新加工属于缺陷补救。增加对喷涂部件定期检查、更新的规定，是为了避免再次发生类似的问题，属于预防措施。本题考核的是对三种变更应对措施的理解。

139 C

根据现在的项目绩效来预测未来的发展趋势属于趋势分析。

140 C

目前是项目启动阶段，相关方对项目目标和可交付成果存在不同的理解属于正常现象。项目经理需要通过引导来促进他们沟通，以形成共识，最终确定项目的目标和范围。

141 A

这道题考核的是"预防措施""纠正措施""缺陷补救"的区别。当团队发现了计划中的错误时，应该采取纠正措施；对于尚未发生但可能发生的风险，应该采取预防措施；对于已经产生的质量缺陷，要采取缺陷补救措施；但是对于监控中出现的偏差，团队首先应该内部讨论，而不是直接报告给发起人。

142 D

不管谁提出修改建议，也不管建议多么具有颠覆性，都应该认真履行整体变更控制程序。只有如此，才能规范地处理好这类事件。

143　C

这道题的考点是"项目收尾文件"。项目被提前终止，项目经理首先需要创建项目收尾文件，按规范一步步完成收尾活动。选项 A、B、D 可能都是项目经理需要做的，不过都属于收尾活动的组成部分。

144　D

对于市场的真实需求尚未明确，又需要尽早上市的产品，采取最小可行产品来验证用户需求是最佳选择。

145　D

题干中提示，项目中途要削减 15% 的预算，这已经超出了项目经理管理能力的范围，应该考虑减少一部分尚未开始的工作，使项目重新回到控制之中，所以，选项 D 是正确的。选项 A，延长工期、释放资源首先需要通过变更控制程序，效果不一定能得到保证；选项 B，一味由乙方承担损失是不对的；选项 C，降低产品质量是最不能让人接受的选项。

146　D

质量管理过程合规是项目团队必须满足的要求，优先级比控制预算高，所以必须保证过程合规，如果有必要的话，可以通过变更修改预算。

147　C

采购工作说明书（SOW）定义了需要分包商负责的工作范围。项目范围说明书是项目经理负责整个项目的范围，而采购工作说明书中的范围只是整个项目范围中需要分包出去的部分。

148　D

客户的期望也不一定都合理，不能一味地满足，应该从其客观需求出发，合理满足，所以要主动管理客户的期望，以求达成共识。

149　C

因为题干中强调活动之间的逻辑关系使活动无法并行，所以选项 A 快速跟进被排除。题干中提示该项目无法获得更多资源，这意味着选项 B 赶工被排除。压缩工期只有快速跟进和赶工两种办法。资源平滑（Resource Smoothing）是指利用非关键路径上的浮动时间，向前或向后挪动工作，以实现资源数量随时间的波动幅度减少。我们也常常利用这个原理，通过调动非关键路径上的活动资源来支援关键路径上的活动，以保证项目工期。所以，选项 C 正确。资源平衡（Resource Leveling）是指错开资源冲突的活动，减少或消除资源过载的现象，但常常会导致项目工期延长。

150　A

当相关方人员变动时，项目经理应该及时更新相关方登记册。人员变动并不代表职责会变，所以责任分配矩阵、相关方参与计划都不需要变，也不一定会出现新的风险，只有相关方登记册是必须立刻更新的。

151　D

针对这类题，我们首先应根据题干的信息判断是传统场景还是敏捷场景。如果是传统场景，范围之外的任何工作都应避免，即便增加工作，也必须先经过整体变更控制程序。在敏捷场景中，对于团队讨论并表决的工作，应尊重团队意见。题干中提到了范围基准，靠基准控制项目范围是传统项目场景的特征，所以，选项 D 是正确的。

152　B

在项目早期，只要有一个大致的、粗略的成本估算就可以，要求估算速度快，不要求非常精确。题干提示，让之前做过类似项目的项目经理提交报告，所以我们已经有充足的依据可以判断采取类比估算法是最合适的。

153　D

题干提供了两个关键信息："越快越好"和"PMO 提供以往类似项目的文件"，提示应采取类比估算。类比估算的特点是利用历史数据进行类比，省时省力。

154　C

题干中提示，这个风险在规划时已被识别，但对于突发的停电事故，我们无法预测其发生的概率和对项目的影响，说明它属于已知—未知风险，对应的储备就是"应急储备"。如果公司提前买了保险，虽然保险金额可以涵盖停电损失，保险公司可以理赔，但需要先抓紧使用应急储备，重新采购试剂，避免影响研发进度。

155 A

假设分析是逐个逐级确认或排除各种假设情形，并评估其对项目的影响。

156 D

参考之前完成的类似的项目，参考价值最大的应该是最晚形成的收尾报告。文件形成时间越晚，意味着经历了实际项目过程中的不断变更和调整，越能反映项目的真实成本。相反，越早期的文件越粗略，也越不准确，对当时的项目也只是一个大概的估算。

157 D

这道题的考点是"资金限制平衡"，如果项目所需资金无法按承诺时间和额度提供，就可以选择调整进度计划，放缓项目进度并释放部分资源，以减少资金压力。

158 B

需求增加，导致范围变化，进而导致进度和成本失控。项目经理要从根源入手，严格遵循整体变更控制程序，而且把住需求增加的入口，防止范围蔓延。

159 A

鱼骨图也叫因果图或石川图，用于识别问题的根本原因。

160 D

虽然是供应商主动提出免费升级设备，但只要有变化，就可能带来风险，所以必须评估其对项目的影响，并且严格遵循整体变更控制程序。

161 C

在海外项目中，这种情况很常见。项目经理不但要遵守当地的劳务政策，而且要完成项目工作，所以必须给当地雇员提供必要的技能培训。虽然在现实中也可选择A、B、D三个选项的做法，但只有选项C才是最优选择。

162　A

敏捷转型是一个系统工程，从人员的意识、知识、方法、工具到管理流程、制度、文化，都需要全方位的转变。团队应该有耐心和较为长远的规划，选项 B、C、D 都是合理的，只有选项 A 是不应该做的，即不应该简单粗暴地对现有人员进行大换血。

163　A

沟通管理计划中定义了项目信息存储及传递的方式、频率、载体等。如果团队成员不能及时获得必要信息，就要审查沟通管理计划是否有问题，以及执行计划是否有问题。容易选错的选项是 C 审查整体变更控制程序，虽然变更控制程序中有升级计划后通知相关方这个环节，但其他相关方都收到了通知，说明不是这个程序有问题，而是与这部分相关方的沟通方式有问题或执行有误。

164　D

团队经历了多个项目，已经完成了塔克曼阶梯理论中的形成、磨合、规范阶段，当再接新项目时，可以直接进入表现阶段。

165　C

打分、计算乘积、排序都是为了确定风险的优先级，属于风险定性分析。

166　A

开展采购绩效审查可以找到超出预算的原因。B、C、D 都不是最合适的选项。

167　D

若相关方参与度下降，项目经理应审查相关方参与计划及其执行情况。

168　A

固定总价合同（FFP）对甲方风险（不确定性）最小，所有项目风险都由乙方承担。在四个选项中，只有选项 A 固定总价合同肯定不会超过预算。

169　A

因范围蔓延导致的严重的进度和成本偏差，很难通过计划的优化来消除，只能实事求是地根据趋势分析制定新的项目基准，并获得 CCB 的批准。

170　D

本题考点是收尾流程，项目经理需先获得有客户签字的验收报告，再申请支付。

171　D

对于提前终止的项目，项目经理最重要的工作就是做好收尾工作，而释放资源是在完成项目收尾的其他步骤之后才能做的。

172　A

最小可行产品（MVP）开发周期短、成本低，可以尽早验证用户需求。

173　D

项目中途，新上任的项目经理接手老项目，需要和团队一起分析原因并找到改进方案。首先，项目经理需要加速和团队成员的磨合；其次，项目经理要通过开诚布公的讨论提升团队的士气；最后，因为团队更了解项目的真实情况，所以项目经理要发动团队的力量找到改进方案。

174　D

变更被批准后，在实施前必须通知与变更有关系的所有相关方，只有在得到相关方的确认后，才可以实施变更。

175　C

项目范围内的工作由自制转为外包前，必须经过变更控制程序，获得批准后方可执行。

176　A

如果风险不仅会影响单个项目，而且会影响项目集或项目组合甚至公司战略，就应该将该风险及时上报，让更有能力、更有资源的高层管理者去统一处理。这道题的考点是整合式风险管理。

177　B

项目必须得到善始善终，因为前一个项目的收尾，其优先级高于后一个项目的开始，所以项目经理需要按计划完成前一个项目的收尾工作后，再开始新的项目。

178　B

不能创造商业价值的项目是没有意义的，应该及时终止，但要妥善完成收尾活动。

179　D

CPI = 1.2，说明成本比较节约；SPI = 0.8，说明进度落后。项目经理可以通过增加资源投入来压缩工期。

180　C

这道题考核的是哪种合同类型最容易让承包商虚报用工人数。成本加固定费用合同中规定，成本实报实销。也就是说，乙方上报的多，甲方支付的就多，乙方通过虚报用工人数可以获取不正当的收益。在成本加固定费用合同中，费用是固定的，没有激励作用，承包商更可能会采取不正当的手段获益，所以甲方应加强管控并严格审计。

181　D

关于可交付成果与质量标准不一致的问题，项目经理首先要审查质量管理计划，判断是标准不适当，还是执行有偏差，找到原因后经过变更控制程序，并采取适当的纠正措施。

182　C

项目的优先级决定了项目资源保障的力度，而项目的优先级往往是由 PMO 确定的。

多选题

183　ACDFH

选项 A、C、D、F、H 都是采购流程中在与供应商签订合同之前应该完成的工作，而选项 B、E、G 是在与供应商签订合同之后才可能做的工作。采购一般流程如图 7-4 所示。

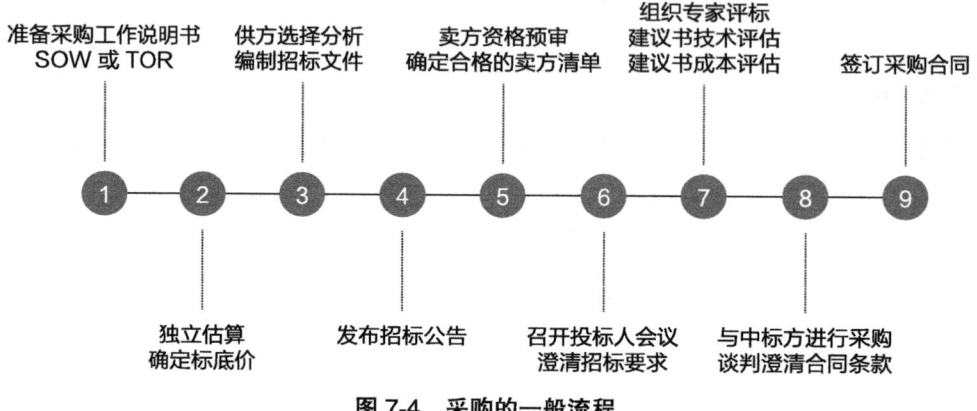

图 7-4　采购的一般流程

184　CEH

团队在每日站会中分享的内容如下:(1)昨天已完成的工作;(2)今天将要开展的工作;(3)完成目标存在的障碍。对应选项 CEH 是正确的。其他选项的内容都不应该在每日站会中讨论,这样才能保证每日站会在 15 分钟之内完成。

185　ADG

在每个冲刺周期中,必须召开的会议包括冲刺计划会、冲刺评审会、冲刺回顾会。其他选项都不是冲刺周期内必须召开的会议。

186　ABF

配置管理计划面向三个方面的内容:选项 A,产品的功能、组件和文档;选项 B,从项目中获得的知识、经验和教训;选项 F,项目的基准、计划和文件。其他选项的内容都有专门针对性的文件记录。

187　BEF

Scrum 敏捷框架中敏捷团队只包含三种角色:产品负责人(Product Owner)、敏捷专家(Scrum Master)、开发团队(Development Team)。

188 CFG

日志类文件的更新不需要经过整体变更控制程序，谁经手这类文件谁更新，并且可以随时随地更新。变更日志、经验教训登记册、问题日志都属于日志类的项目文件。

189 ACDEF

敏捷开发有 12 条原则，如图 7-5 所示。选项 A、C、D、E、F 都属于敏捷开发的 12 条原则的内容，其他选项不是敏捷开发的原则。

1 客户满意	我们最重要的目标是通过持续不断地及早交付有价值的软件，使客户满意		7 可工作软件	可工作的软件是进度的首要度量标准
2 拥抱变化	欣然面对需求变化，即使在开发后期也一样。为了使客户获得竞争优势，善于掌控变化		8 可持续开发	敏捷倡导长期、稳定的可持续开发
3 短周期	经常地交付可工作的软件，相隔几星期或一两个月，倾向于采取较短的周期		9 技术卓越	对技术精益求精，对设计不断完善，将提高敏捷能力
4 相互合作	业务人员和开发人员必须相互合作，项目中的每一天都不例外		10 简洁	以简洁为本，极力减少不必要的工作量
5 激发和信任	激发个体的斗志，以他们为核心搭建项目。提供环境和支援，信任他们可以达成目标		11 自组织	最好的架构、需求和设计出自自组织团队
6 面对面	不论团队内外，传递信息效果最好、效率最高的方式是面对面的交谈		12 回顾总结	团队定期地反思如何能够提高成效，并依次调整团队的行为

图 7-5　敏捷开发的 12 条原则

190 ACDF

产品待办事项列表应该符合 DEEP 原则，即详略适当的（Detailed appropriately）、经过估算的（Estimated）、涌现的（Emergent，可以随时在列表中增加、删除和动态调整优先级）、按优先级排序的（Prioritized）。

191 CDG

隐性知识属于难以描述、难以表达的知识，比如洞察力、直觉、经验、诀窍等。

其他选项都是可以用文字、图表、模型等表达出来的显性知识。

匹配题

192

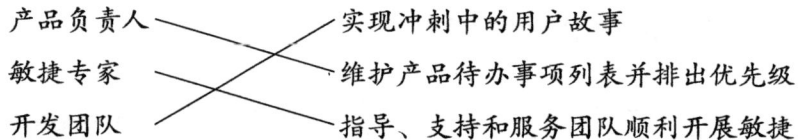

产品负责人 —————— 实现冲刺中的用户故事

敏捷专家 —————— 维护产品待办事项列表并排出优先级

开发团队 —————— 指导、支持和服务团队顺利开展敏捷

193

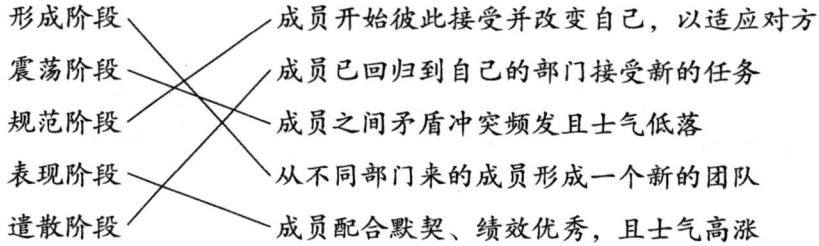

形成阶段 —————— 成员开始彼此接受并改变自己，以适应对方

震荡阶段 —————— 成员已回归到自己的部门接受新的任务

规范阶段 —————— 成员之间矛盾冲突频发且士气低落

表现阶段 —————— 从不同部门来的成员形成一个新的团队

遣散阶段 —————— 成员配合默契、绩效优秀，且士气高涨

194

强迫 / 命令 —————— 为了保护团队成员的士气，项目经理同意了具有一定风险性的方案

撤退 / 回避 —————— 项目经理建议先完成紧急的工作，对于分歧部分，以后再议

缓和 / 包容 —————— 项目经理不再解释原因，而是要求团队成员执行任务

妥协 / 调解 —————— 两名团队成员商量出双方都很满意的解决方案

合作 / 解决 —————— 项目经理接受了两项新需求，同时说服客户收回三项需求

195

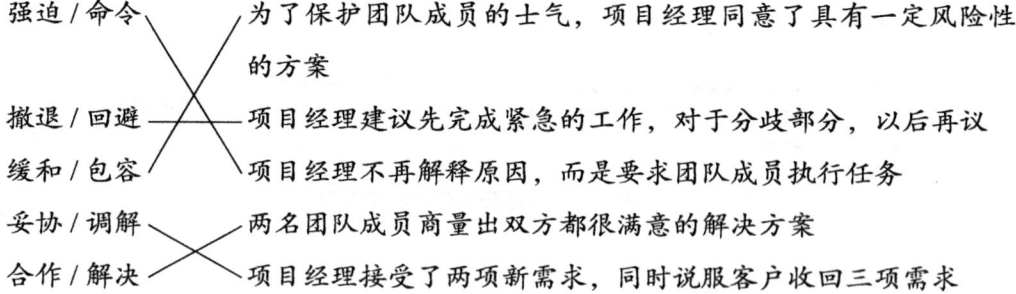

应急计划 —————— 测试工程师突发疾病，项目经理让男友临时帮忙测试

弹回计划 —————— 演示方案时电脑宕机，项目经理用事先准备好的 iPad 完成了演示

权变措施 —————— 因为疫情，项目经理被迫放弃了隆重的交付仪式，在线以极简风格完成了交付

196

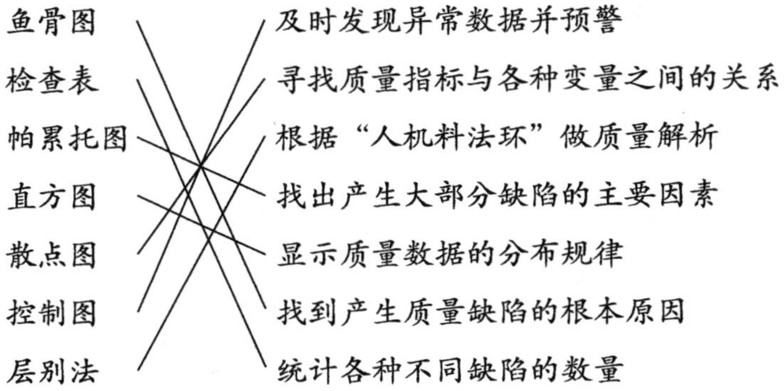

鱼骨图　　　　　　及时发现异常数据并预警

检查表　　　　　　寻找质量指标与各种变量之间的关系

帕累托图　　　　　根据"人机料法环"做质量解析

直方图　　　　　　找出产生大部分缺陷的主要因素

散点图　　　　　　显示质量数据的分布规律

控制图　　　　　　找到产生质量缺陷的根本原因

层别法　　　　　　统计各种不同缺陷的数量

填空题

197　11

根据沟通路径的数量的计算公式 $C_n^2 = n \times (n-1)/2$，原来项目经理带领4人，加上自己，团队一共5人，那么 $C_5^2 = 5 \times (5-1)/2 = 10$（条）；后来增加了2人，团队由5人变成7人，那么 $C_7^2 = 7 \times (7-1)/2 = 21$（条）。所以，沟通路径增加了11条。

198　10

本题考核的是静态投资回收期的计算。每年收入为120万美元，支出为80万美元，每年净现金流 = 120 - 80 = 40（万美元）；项目投资金额为400万美元，投资回报率（ROI）= 40/400 = 10%。静态投资回收期（PBP）= 1/ROI = 1/10% = 10（年）。

199　B

本题考核的是投资项目的多方案比选。项目C净现值（NPV）< 0，可以直接排除。因为项目A和B的净现值相同，所以我们只需比较内部收益率（IRR）即可。内部收益率越高，说明项目的抗风险能力越强，融资渠道越丰富，所以，我们应该选择项目B。

200　2

本题考核的是对关键路径的识别。我们先根据题干提供的信息画一幅单代号网络图（如图7-6所示），理清活动之间的逻辑关系。我们可以看出，本项目由4条路径构成，分别把每条路径上的活动历时加在一起，可以得到路径 A—B—D—G 和路径 A—C—F—G 的活动历时都是 10 天，比其他 2 条路径的活动历时更长，所以这 2 条路径是关键路径。

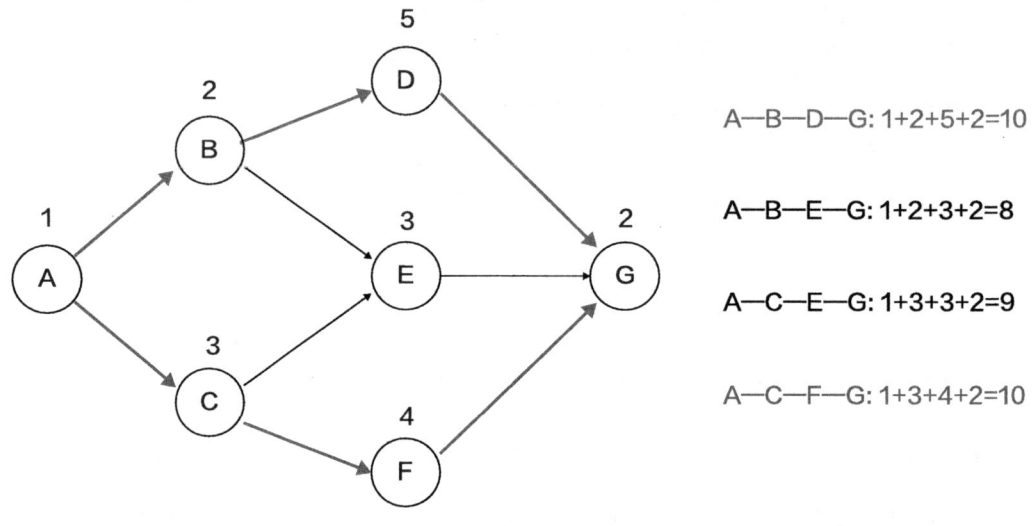

A—B—D—G: 1+2+5+2=10

A—B—E—G: 1+2+3+2=8

A—C—E—G: 1+3+3+2=9

A—C—F—G: 1+3+4+2=10

图 7-6　单代号网络图